SEMEIA 25

Julius Wellhausen and His
Prolegomena to the History of Israel

Guest Editor of This Issue:
Douglas A. Knight

© 1983

by the Society of Biblical Literature

SEMEIA 25

Copyright © 1982 by the Society of Biblical Literature

All rights reserved. No part of this work may be reproduced or transmitted in any form or by any means, electronic or mechanical, including photocopying and recording, or by means of any information storage or retrieval system, except as may be expressly permitted by the 1976 Copyright Act or in writing from the publisher. Requests for permission should be addressed in writing to the Rights and Permissions Office, Society of Biblical Literature, 825 Houston Mill Road, Atlanta, GA 30329, USA.

ISSN 0095-571X
ISBN 1-58983-142-X

Printed in the United States of America
on acid-free paper

Julius Wellhausen. Greifswald, ca. 1878.

Julius Wellhausen. Göttingen, ca. 1900.

CONTENTS

Contributors to This Issue vi

Abbreviations vii

Preface ix

Chapter 1: Julius Wellhausen and His
Prolegomena to the History of Israel
      Rudolf Smend 1

Chapter 2: Wellhausen and the Interpretation of Israel's Literature
      Douglas A. Knight 21

Chapter 3: Wellhausen as a Historian of Israel
      John H. Hayes 37

Chapter 4: Wellhausen and the History of Israel's Religion
      Patrick D. Miller, Jr. 61

Chapter 5: Wellhausen and Judaism
      Lou H. Silberman 75

Chapter 6: Wellhausen in English
      Brevard S. Childs 83

Chapter 7: Wellhausen on the New Testament
      Nils A. Dahl 89

Chapter 8: Wellhausen as an Arabist
      Kurt Rudolph 111

CONTRIBUTORS TO THIS ISSUE

Brevard S. Childs
Yale University Divinity School
409 Prospect Street
New Haven, Connecticut 06510

Nils A. Dahl
Rektorhaugen 17
Oslo 8
Norway

John H. Hayes
Candler School of Theology
Emory University
Atlanta, Georgia 30322

Douglas A. Knight
Vanderbilt University Divinity School
Nashville, Tennessee 37240

Patrick D. Miller, Jr.
Union Theological Seminary in Virginia
3401 Brook Road
Richmond, Virginia 23227

Kurt Rudolph
Karl-Marx-Universität
701 Leipzig
German Democratic Republic

Lou H. Silberman
5282 Paseo del Arenal
Tucson, Arizona 85715

Rudolf Smend
Georg-August-Universität
Nikolausberger Weg 5b
3400 Göttingen
Federal Republic of Germany

ABBREVIATIONS

AGWG	Abhandlungen der Kgl. Gesellschaft der Wissenschaften zu Göttingen
ARW	*Archiv für Religionswissenschaft*
AnBib	Analecta Biblica
BA	*Biblical Archaeologist*
Bib	*Biblica*
BJS	Brown Judaic Studies
BO	*Bibliotheca orientalis*
BWANT	Beiträge zur Wissenschaft vom Alten und Neuen Testament
BZAW	Beihefte zur *Zeitschrift für die alttestamentliche Wissenschaft*
CBQ	*Catholic Biblical Quarterly*
DBSup	*Dictionnaire de la Bible, Supplément*
DLZ	*Deutsche Literaturzeitung*
EB	*The Encyclopædia Britannica*, 9th edition
GGA	*Göttingische gelehrte Anzeigen*
HTR	*Harvard Theological Review*
ICC	International Critical Commentary
JBL	*Journal of Biblical Literature*
JBR	*Journal of Bible and Religion*
JDT	*Jahrbuch für deutsche Theologie*
JR	*Journal of Religion*
JSOT	*Journal for the Study of the Old Testament*
MGWJ	*Monatsschrift für Geschichte und Wissenschaft des Judentums*
NGWG	Nachrichten von der Kgl. Gesellschaft der Wissenschaften zu Göttingen
PR	*The Presbyterian Review*
RB	*Revue biblique*
RGG	*Religion in Geschichte und Gegenwart*
RHR	*Revue de l'histoire des religions*
SBLDS	Society of Biblical Literature Dissertation Series
TBü	Theologische Bücherei
TLZ	*Theologische Literaturzeitung*
TS	Theologische Studien
TTijd	*Theologisch Tijdschrift*
TZ	*Theologische Zeitschrift*
VTSup	Vetus Testamentum, Supplements
WMANT	Wissenschaftliche Monographien zum Alten und Neuen Testament
ZDMG	*Zeitschrift der deutschen morgenländischen Gesellschaft*

PREFACE

In 1878 Julius Wellhausen published the first edition of the *Geschichte Israels*, which in all subsequent editions beginning with the second in 1883 appeared under the title *Prolegomena zur Geschichte Israels*. At its annual meeting in New Orleans on 20 November 1978, the Society of Biblical Literature marked the hundredth anniversary of this landmark study with a special series of six papers and discussion. Those essays on the significance of the *Prolegomena* are here presented in revised form. So that the picture of Wellhausen's diversified scholarship would be complete, the participants of the conference agreed that chapters on his New Testament and Arabic studies should be added. We are grateful to Nils A. Dahl and Kurt Rudolph for accepting the invitation to contribute these articles. In the latter's absence during the publication stage, William A. Graham of Harvard University very kindly agreed to proofread the last chapter on Wellhausen's Arabic scholarship. Also, a word of appreciation is due to Richard McLean, graduate student at Vanderbilt University, for assistance at various points in the preparation of the volume. The editor gratefully acknowledges the support of a Fulbright Award and a Vanderbilt University Fellowship for the sabbatical leave in Jerusalem in 1981–82, during a portion of which time the work on this volume was completed. Finally, we wish to thank Rudolf Smend for providing the two photographs of Wellhausen—one taken ca. 1878 at age 34, the year in which his *Prolegomena* first appeared, and the other taken around 1900.

D.A.K.

JULIUS WELLHAUSEN
AND HIS *PROLEGOMENA*
*TO THE HISTORY OF ISRAEL**

Rudolf Smend

Georg-August-Universität Göttingen

ABSTRACT

Wellhausen, of whom we still lack a full biography, combined in his person a compelling spirit, congeniality, and naturalness. As a student he was attracted early to the study of the Old Testament and Semitics He held professorships in Greifswald, Halle, Marburg, and Gottingen In 1882 he effectively moved from Old Testament to Arabic studies, and again in 1902 to New Testament research His *Prolegomena*, with its bold hypotheses and cogent argumentation, marked a momentous advance in the understanding of ancient Israel

On 2 August 1881, William Robertson Nicoll, at the time a minister of the Free Church of Scotland and later to wield "decisive power" in British politics as editor of *The British Weekly* (Taylor: 262), came to the small German university town of Greifswald in Pomerania to visit the thirty-seven-year-old Professor of Old Testament in the Faculty of Theology, Julius Wellhausen. Wellhausen had recently become famous. Three years previously he had written the book whose jubilee we observe in this year 1978, the "History of Israel," first volume, later called *Prolegomena to the History of Israel*. To a Scot he was then doubly interesting because of his connection with Professor William Robertson Smith who had just, on 26 May 1881, been removed for heresy by the General Assembly of the Free Church of Scotland, from his chair in its college in Aberdeen (Black and Chrystal: 404–51; Anderson). It was not only their personal friendship that linked the two scholars, but also a similar fate as Professors of Theology: Wellhausen was then on the point of voluntarily resigning from his theological teaching post, no longer seeing himself in a position to train servants of the existing Protestant Church.

Nicoll went to see him on that second of August together with a German friend. Next day he wrote to his wife:

[Dr. Wellhausen] lives in a flat, the third story of a large house. We were most cordially received, and enjoyed him immensely. He immediately produced cigars and wine (I have smoked a great deal here) and we sat talking for about an hour in his library. It is a large plain room with very few books, and those mainly texts of the Bible, in Hebrew, Syriac, etc. The only English books I saw were Colenso on the Pentateuch, Palgrave's *Arabia*, and Wright on Zechariah. When we rose to go, he said he had plenty of time, and would like to spend the evening with us. He would have asked us to stay with him for the night, but his wife had been ill; they have no children. Accordingly we went out with him and had a delightful evening in the open air.

He is a stout man, rather little, with a round face, a darkish moustache and beard, and a frank bold manner. He speaks English tolerably, and what with his English and my German we got along very comfortably. We walked out to a ruined monastery by the sea, sat down and drank some beer, and were so engrossed in talk that we lost the steamer back and walked home, which did not matter much. It was very pleasant, and I shall not forget that bright August night sitting by the sea, looking over to the beautiful island of Rügen.

They spoke about Robertson Smith, about German and Dutch Hebraists, about exegetical questions, about Wellhausen's plans, about religion in Scotland and Germany, about Gibbon and Carlyle (Darlow: 40–43). After some decades, on the occasion of Wellhausen's seventieth birthday, Nicoll summed up his impression in the sentence: "A man more frank, friendly, cordial and hospitable I never hope to see." While in Greifswald he enquired about Wellhausen from his completely different colleague, the conservative New Testament and Systematics scholar Hermann Cremer, friend of Kähler and Schlatter. Cremer confirmed their theological difference, adding: "But he is one of the greatest geniuses in the world, and a most noble, simple, openhearted man"/1/.

Apparently Nicoll had made such use after his return of Wellhausen's frank remarks about Robertson Smith that the latter must have considered him actually a Free Church spy/2/. The consequence had to be borne by the next Scottish Reverend to visit Wellhausen, in August 1882. "He was rather lame, and was called Smith, and was due to preach to the Scottish herring fishermen who bring their wares to Stettin"/3/. He wrote for a fundamentalist church paper in London, in which this sentence had just appeared in January 1882: "Ye cannot serve God and Mammon. Ye cannot believe the Bible and Wellhausen" (Bigger: 1). Accordingly, Smith may well have expected a bad encounter as he knocked on Wellhausen's door at eight o'clock in the morning, with an apology on his lips for the early hour. To his surprise he found him "already busy at his desk, with his coat off, and standing in his shirt-sleeves deep in the study of Arabic"—it was usual then among German professors to work standing at a reading-desk. In other ways too Wellhausen disappointed his expectations. He had obviously "pictured a sharp-faced, pallid, carping critic with diabolic features"/4/, and so, as he reported later to the readers of that paper, was "a little surprised . . . , to find a strong, thick, burly, farmer-looking man of thirty-eight, with a frank, open countenance, on which good-humour seemed to sit, and from which, as I soon found, humour also was not wholly absent. Entirely destitute of all stuck *upness*, and extremely genial and pleasant in his manner, he turned out to be in many aspects a very different sort of man from what I had expected to meet." This time Wellhausen was extremely reserved over opinions about others and manifestly made himself out as understanding and speaking even less English than was in fact the case. He mentioned only Friedrich Delitzsch's book, *Wo lag das Paradies?*, that was lying on the table, saying "that it was rather a thick book for so thin a subject," and then he spoke with his visitor about many other things, climbed with him despite his lameness the tower of the church of St. Nicholas, and showed him the university buildings. Very impressed personally, but materially only imperfectly satisfied, this Reverend also went on to two scholars of the opposition, Theodor Zöckler in Greifswald and Franz Delitzsch in Leipzig, in order to get their picture of the future of the Wellhausen heresy. He learned that "several able pens" were on the point of refuting Wellhausen. Here too, prophesied Zöckler, the law of church history would hold "that after a brief space of glittering notoriety the error died, and the truth was more firmly established than before." Greater anxiety was expressed by Delitzsch. "Certainly," he said, "if his (Wellhausen's) conclusions be true, the Old Testament cannot in any distinctive sense be the Word of God." What was happening here was a danger for the church, "troubling the Church of God." "Again and again he repeated, in his deep guttural tones, the phrase 'Troubling the Church of God.'" With these words in his ear, Smith returned to Scotland.

There is yet a third British visitor to have reported his experiences with Wellhausen. He was not a Scot but a Welshman, a Baptist and a professor of Old Testament and Semitic languages, T. Witton Davies of Bangor. He studied with Wellhausen in Göttingen in the summer of 1898. He writes:

> Wellhausen, for one who figures so largely in modern theological literature, is in the prime of life, and as healthy and vigorous a man as I have seen. He is but fifty-eight years of age, of medium size, though of more than average stoutness. He is full-faced, looks the picture of a man that enjoys life. He is getting grey, but he has in him, judging from looks, a vast amount of work yet. . . What struck me most of all in his personal intercourse, and in his lectures, was his encyclopaedic knowledge. . . To him, according to the old saw, nothing human is without interest. He was to me the soul of kindness and good fellowship, and however wrong he may be in some of his teachings, he is one of the kindest, most genial, and even devout, of men. . . A cheerier, happier home than that of the Wellhausens is not to be found. Neither friend nor foe doubts the transcendent genius of Wellhausen as an investigator and also as a writer, for his style is wholly un-German, and ranks with the best. I was not prepared to find him so free and friendly.

The honorable invitation you have extended to me is a sign that on the British side of the Channel and on the American side of the Atlantic Ocean the interest in Wellhausen has not dimmed since the days of Nicoll,

Smith, and Witton Davies. In the United States the hundredth anniversary of his birth was observed thirty-four years ago/5/, and so now too the hundred-year jubilee of the *Prolegomena to the History of Israel*. In Germany, as far as I know, that idea has occurred to no one/6/. Among you there is a sounder relation to tradition—and to the tradition of a discipline—than in Germany, where it is common to say Yes or No to one's own parents, grandparents, and great-grandparents in a very foolish way, and, in the case of No, to forget them or, more accurately, to displace them—something that is usually brought down on the head of the next or following generation.

That Wellhausen could be forgotten or displaced even to a certain extent is connected with the fact that no biography of him exists. The best account is still the fine and competent memorial address delivered in 1918 by Eduard Schwartz in the Göttingen Academy of Sciences. Enno Littmann, his successor in the Göttingen chair for Oriental Languages, wanted to write a biography but sadly did not achieve it. Today, sixty years after Wellhausen's death and twenty years after Littmann's, the task is different and more difficult, above all because the biographer can no longer have enjoyed a personal impression. In addition, there is much less written material than in other cases. Wellhausen died childless, and his widow destroyed all letters and manuscripts. There have been preserved here and there only a few books that he possessed and furnished with marginal notes, much worth reading. Nevertheless there are quite a lot of letters from his hand scattered in public and private possession. So far about 700 have been found, from which quite a good picture of the man can be won. I hope to be able to arrange a printed edition of these in the near future and would be very grateful to learn of any further material unknown to me. Apart from the letters preserved, mediated acquaintance was still possible a few decades ago through varied personal connections. Here and there a minister or professor was still alive who knew Wellhausen by sight or had even been close to him, and whoever was in this position counted it among the greatest and happiest experiences of his life. I had the benefit that my grandfather was Wellhausen's closest friend, although certainly not his most important. Accordingly my father and his brother and sister grew up under Wellhausen's eyes, and naturally I have had them tell me much. Still alive today in Göttingen is my 88-year-old uncle Leopold Smend, a lawyer, with whom Wellhausen liked to go swimming 70–80 years ago in a pool on the Leine, the "Mississippi of Göttingen." Even with a world reputation Wellhausen was frequently to be seen in the water. Of course my uncle denies the rumor, still heard today, that Wellhausen's preference was to swim on Sunday morning and so to arrange matters that, bathing dress over his shoulder, he met on his return the pious people of Göttingen on their way to church. However, this rumor still shows how Wellhausen's relationship to the church was thought of and how also to a fair extent it was.

That brings us now to his biographical details. Following this overview of his life I shall offer a short characterization of Wellhausen's contributions to scholarship, and finally we will pay closer attention to the *Prolegomena*. In all this I can do no more than offer you some few comments. It would be impudence in one short paper to attempt to give a complete picture of the person and work of so rich, manysided and lively a spirit. Such an overall view, I must concede, I myself still do not have. Yet I hope one day to have it and then to pass it on. With this in mind, I ask you to understand that what I provide below is a quite preliminary sketch.

Wellhausen had learned to swim in a river broader than Göttingen's Leine, in the Weser. There, in the small town of Hamelin, he was born on 17 May 1844. Yet this town's fame has derived not from him but for centuries, rather, from the Pied Piper who, the story goes, freed it in 1284 from a mighty plague of rats, then took revenge on the thankless towns-people by leading their children out of the town—with the same pipe that had enticed the rats to destruction—and into a mountain where they disappeared for ever. It is easily understood that orthodox polemic against Wellhausen did not fail to compare him with the Pied Piper.

But that was in a much later period. He had a happy childhood in Hamelin despite the heavy shadows cast on it by the constant illness of his father and the early death of his brothers. Julius Wellhausen was the only one of the children to outlive the parents. He too was aware throughout his life what illness is. His latter years were a martyrdom. At sixty he was virtually deaf, and soon thereafter agonizing arterial sclerosis set in and made all work impossible for him. Despite this he represented a living argument against psychosomatic medicine, at least its general validity. At heart he was a person unusually sound, serene, and composed in all circumstances. He had been a happy child, raised in an environment which was rural rather than urban. It is no accident that Rev. Smith describes the grown man as "farmer-looking." Many others had a similar impression. Throughout his life he felt better among country people than among intellectuals, lived with the seasons and observed plant growth on many hikes, and even had an antipathy to large cities, especially Berlin. "What characterized his nature was straightforwardness" (Schwartz: 29 [359]). On this straightforwardness depended a good part of the genius that almost everyone dealing with him perceived. We have to be very careful not to confuse this with simplicity or lack of discrimination; he had a sharp eye for the most subtle things.

His father was a Lutheran minister with strong liturgical interests, supporter of a confessional high-church movement which was opposing the theological liberalism then pressing strongly ahead. The son did not follow the father in these matters—rather, the opposite. Yet it was in his father's footsteps that he began the study of theology in Göttingen in 1862. He loved the narratives of the Old Testament and many hymns of the church, and also several examples of the piety of the Middle Ages. Yet as early as his first semester he noted that that did not suffice for a study of theology. As a student he was gripped by a book that chanced to fall into his hands in the

Easter holidays of 1863, the *History of the People of Israel*, by the Göttingen Professor Heinrich Ewald. It captivated him so much that he learned Hebrew properly—poor teaching at school had left him still sick of it—and threw himself completely into the study of the Old Testament. With Ewald he studied not just biblical exegesis but also Arabic and Syriac, in a manner that was rather brutal and barely didactic by today's ideas, yet effective. Quite as important for him as the merciless philological schooling was that Ewald was then second to none in understanding how to read the Bible historically.

Yet it was just at this point that the pupil detached himself from the teacher. His own acquaintance with the Old Testament led him to a conception of the history of early Israel, especially the law's position in it, which Ewald, a singular and not very tolerant man, found evil heresy. There was also a political conflict. Ewald was faithfully devoted to the royal house that ruled in Hannover until 1866. After Hannover's incorporation into Prussia he declined to take the oath to the King of Prussia and thereby eventually lost even his university chair. He demanded of his favorite pupil, who had Prussian sympathies although his family was loyal to the royal house of Hannover, that he should declare the King of Prussia an evildoer and scoundrel. Wellhausen declined and was never forgiven by Ewald/7/.

So the pupil had to begin his academic career without the support of his teacher. In 1868 he gained the post of a "Repetent" in the Göttingen Theology Faculty, and in 1870 he graduated there to the licentiate and became a "Privatdozent." In 1872 the more senior Ewald-pupil August Dillmann recommended him for an established professorship in Greifswald. It was there he worked from 1872 to 1882, there he wrote the works which revolutionized Old Testament studies, and there he married Marie Limpricht, daughter of a colleague in the Arts Faculty, a sensitive woman with ambitions as a pianist and later a pupil of Max Reger/8/.

The end of his Greifswald period coincided with the end of his activity as professor of theology. On 5 April 1882 he informed the Prussian Minister of Culture in Berlin of his decision to resign from his post and to become qualified as a "Privatdozent" in Semitic Philology. By way of explanation he wrote: "I became a theologian because the scientific treatment of the Bible interested me; only gradually did I come to understand that a professor of theology also has the practical task of preparing the students for service in the Protestant Church, and that I am not adequate to this practical task, but that instead despite all caution on my own part I make my hearers unfit for their office. Since then my theological professorship has been weighing heavily on my conscience"/9/. Wellhausen had presented this case to the Ministry of Culture several times since early 1879 and had prepared for the change of department by familiarizing himself with ancient Arabic literature. In order to study and copy manuscripts he made rather protracted stays in Leiden, Paris, and London, one after the other in

1880. London appeared to him then in sharp contrast to Berlin. "Instead of the idle freedom and play in London parks, you can see only scoured nannies and military walkers in the Thiergarten (in Berlin)—I like London a thousand times better. It is the antithesis between art and nature, or perhaps between artificiality and naturalness"/10/. Of the rest of England he saw nothing then; Scotland he came to know in the summer of 1883 when Robertson Smith invited him to share a holiday on the coast. These journeys gave him pleasure, and his observations on them were keen and interested. In general he remained in his own country as did most German professors then. He never seems to have thought seriously of a visit to the United States, or to Palestine although that must have suggested itself to the Old Testament scholar. It was only metaphorically that Abraham Kuenen in Leiden could use these words to comment on Wellhausen's transfer to Arabic studies: "To my sorrow I see Wellhausen setting his face to Mecca and Medina. He will find a surfeit of work and will do great things there too, but we still have much need of him in Jerusalem!"/11/.

The transfer was completed quite gently in its external aspects, too. Wellhausen did not have to begin again as a "Privatdozent" but was appointed "Ausserordentlicher Professor" in Semitic Languages in the Arts Faculty of the University of Halle. He was there from 1882 until 1885, unwillingly. All the more pleasant was his move to Marburg as professor in 1885. The time there until 1892 was auspicious. He liked the area and the people. Out of consideration for the Old Testament scholar in the Theology Faculty, W. Graf Baudissin, he had to undertake not to lecture on the Old Testament, but this did not disturb him, at least not at first. Later what he called his "muzzle" was slackened and removed. The fine Marburg period came to an end with the death in 1891 of Ewald's successor in Göttingen, Paul de Lagarde, who was active in many fields. In his scholarship he was respected by Wellhausen, in his character despised. Wellhausen wanted at first to remain in Marburg but then finally let himself be persuaded. As I was told by Walter Bauer, author of the New Testament Greek lexicon, an article in a Hannover Church newspaper is supposed to have settled the matter. According to it, if Professor Wellhausen came to Göttingen the saying would come true: "a wild sow in the master's vineyard." At that Wellhausen immediately accepted the call.

In Göttingen life was not as free and natural as in Marburg, but more pretentious, aloof, unconcerned—corresponding to the contrast between Hannoverians and Hessians. Wellhausen expressed the relationship as follows: "In Marburg everyone can say to his colleague: you are a blockhead. In Göttingen everyone carries around with him a big secret." In spite of this he was soon quite at home again in the university where he had started. In the two decades that remained to him he produced much, in several fields. Advancing ill health forced on him ever severer curbs to his academic activity, until he sought retirement at 69. He took his departure in the summer semester of 1913, his sufferings intense, with a lecture on the book of Job.

His active career, begun with doctoral graduation in 1870, spanned almost precisely the period of the German state founded by Bismarck; he died on 7 January 1918, the year in which that state foundered. Johann Gustav Droysen and Theodor Mommsen, Friedrich Nietzsche and Paul de Lagarde, William Gladstone and Lord Acton, were his readers. German scholars of his own generation who were close to him personally and shared his concerns were Theodor Nöldeke, Ulrich v. Wilamowitz-Möllendorff, and Adolf Harnack. Wellhausen had lived in complete awareness of his period, which was one of the great intellectual heydays, and his wits were alert as he followed what happened round about him. Yet in contrast to those just mentioned he was scarcely ever a public figure. He was not concerned with exerting a wide influence, nor even with popularizing his own academic discoveries. He shunned congresses and conferences, went on no lecture tours, and hardly ever participated in the normal sociability of colleagues. He saw no point in forming a school; of those who are generally considered "Wellhausianer," none had traversed with him the academic path of undergraduate and graduate studies. He could mercilessly mock colleagues who followed him blindly; we can read how he deals with W. Nowack in the third edition of his exposition of the Minor Prophets (1898:89n., 215n.). But he was a faithful and reliable friend to his friends, who "experienced his greatness only as a blessing, never as a burden" (Schwartz: 30 [360f.]). How he treated strangers is attested by the British visitors mentioned above.

As far as work was concerned, his preference was "sibi cantare et musis," with no furtive glances at publicity and success. His approach to the ancient texts was quite natural; he quickly found himself at home in them, gaining first, as he once expressed it in connection with textual criticism, " a very approximate and negative idea of the facts," yet along with this "the vantage points for locating the worthwhile in the wilderness of the useless" (1871:7n.). Once he had before his eyes the exact and positive picture of the facts, he drew it—again omitting the "useless"—with clear bold strokes. The details, such as source division, he gladly let alone when they were without significance for his picture as a whole; those who followed could break their teeth on them. He went quickly on to new fresh problems, however distant from those which had busied him earlier. Seen from this angle the change of Faculty after the completion of the *Prolegomena* was not unwelcome, although his actual motive was quite different and although at the "transition from the Old Testament to the Arabs" it was also his intention "to make the acquaintance of the wild stock onto which the sprig of Yahweh's Torah has been grafted by priests and prophets" (1882:5). He was then "rather fed up" (cf. Schwartz: 19 [347]) with the Old Testament and plunged with delight into the Arabic world with all its color and variety.

But the farewell from ancient Israel was not final. The first lecture in Göttingen in the winter of 1892/93 was devoted to Jewish history after the Babylonian Exile; and out of that developed, advancing the sketch which appeared first under the title "Israel" in the *Encyclopædia Britannica* in 1881, the *Israelitische und jüdische Geschichte* of 1894. This was Wellhausen's principal work of historiography and had originally been envisaged, following the book of 1878, as *Geschichte Israels*, second volume/12/. After devoting his next years mainly to Arabic studies, which ended with the great description of the Umayyad period (1902), Wellhausen changed his field of work once again. He studied the Synoptic Gospels and John and wrote short, aphoristic commentaries on them, followed by analyses of the Revelation of John and the Acts of the Apostles—very impressive testimonies, with after-effects still today, of how little he had won release from the problems of theology/13/.

We turn back to the beginnings, to Greifswald, to the occasion the centenary of which we observe this year. In February 1879, hence a few months after publication of the *Prolegomena*, Wellhausen wrote: "For ten years historical studies have laid exclusive claim on me, Judaism and ancient Israel in their opposition. However, I have reached the end of them"/14/. With these words Wellhausen's whole work up to the *Prolegomena* is summed up under one single heading, the theme "Judaism and ancient Israel in their opposition." For the readers of his first writings this theme was not yet immediately discernible, and even he himself had hardly anticipated the result in anything other than a "very approximate and negative picture." Yet he probably knew roughly what he was aiming at—and that it required a great deal of very basic work. In the curriculum vitae he submitted in 1868 with his application for the tutorial post in the Göttingen Theological Faculty he wrote that he wished to keep silent about his intentions so as not to make himself ridiculous ("Verum consilio rerum gerendarum tacebo, ne ridendus fiam"; cf. Schwartz: 32). And in retrospect on his life he once noted: "I had always simple goals" (cf. Schwartz: 8 [332]). He was accustomed to attacking these goals energetically and without letting himself be deflected even when detours were necessary.

He himself described at the beginning of the *Prolegomena* how his decisive insight was prepared:

> In my early student days I was attracted by the stories of Saul and David, Ahab and Elijah; the discourses of Amos and Isaiah laid strong hold on me, and I read myself well into the prophetic and historical books of the Old Testament Thanks to such aids as were accessible to me, I even considered that I understood them tolerably, but at the same time was troubled with a bad conscience, as if I were beginning with the roof instead of the foundation, for I had no thorough acquaintance with the Law, of which I was accustomed to be told that it was the basis and postulate of the whole literature At last I took courage and made my way through Exodus, Leviticus, Numbers, and even through Knobel's *Commentary* to these books But it was in vain that I looked for the light which was to be shed from this source on the historical and prophetical books On the contrary, my enjoyment of the latter was

marred by the Law. . . . Dimly I began to perceive that throughout there was between them all the difference that separates two wholly distinct worlds. Yet, so far from attaining clear conceptions, I only fell into deeper confusion, which was worse confounded by the explanations of Ewald in the second volume of his *History of Israel*. At last, in the course of a casual visit in Göttingen in the summer of 1867, I learned through Ritschl that Karl Heinrich Graf placed the Law later than the Prophets, and, almost without knowing his reasons for the hypothesis, I was prepared to accept it, I readily acknowledged to myself the possibility of understanding Hebrew antiquity without the book of the Torah. (1885:3f.)

It was through this rather casual information from Professor Albrecht Ritschl, certainly his greatest service to Old Testament scholarship, that Wellhausen as a young graduate became committed to a task that at that time had already lasted more than a half century and which he himself would bring to its ultimate conclusion. W. M. L. de Wette had been the first to see in all its acuteness the problem of the place of the Law in the history of Israel. Through dating Deuteronomy to the seventh century BCE and demonstrating the lack of historical credibility in Chronicles, he furnished important means to its solution. With these means and with the help of Hegel's philosophy of history, Wilhelm Vatke had undertaken in 1835 a first critical presentation of ancient Israelite religious history. However, his study was not read, or not understood, because of its Hegelian language, and in any case it first required verification by the further advances in Pentateuchal criticism. Once there was relative clarity over the separation of the most extensive Pentateuchal source—then called the "Grundschrift" (base document) and later the "Priestly Writing"—K. H. Graf succeeded in 1866 and 1869 in proving that this source, and with it the greater part of the Law in the central books of the Pentateuch, was not more ancient, as de Wette had still believed, but more recent than Deuteronomy and so belonged to a quite late period. To be sure, the nature of this discovery and its great significance had not been quite clear to Graf himself, who died in 1869. It was clearer to the great A. Kuenen (1869-70) in Leiden and after him to the Göttingen lecturer B. Duhm, who in 1875 presented the theology of the prophets utilizing the Grafian discovery/15/. Duhm was at the time a younger friend of Wellhausen and was stimulated by him. So we have to turn again to Wellhausen and depict in a few words the path that reached a temporary stopping-point with the *Prolegomena*.

It was while he was still in Göttingen that the first fruits appeared. After the dissertation of 1870 which placed some Judean lists in Chronicles in the historical geography of the pre- and postexilic period, there followed in 1871 the book on the text of the Books of Samuel, conceived as preparatory to a future critical edition of the Hebrew Old Testament, full of important observations about deteriorations in the original text and possibilities for its reconstruction, but also incidentally about the earlier history of the tradition. These studies did not receive much attention, but A. Kuenen concluded his short review of *Der Text der Bücher Samuelis untersucht* with the sentence: "Unless I am mistaken, scholarship has much to expect from him" (1872). In 1874 there followed in Greifswald *Die Pharisäer und die Sadducäer: Eine Untersuchung zur inneren jüdischen Geschichte*. In it Wellhausen disputes that the opposition between the two Jewish groups was principally dogmatic; it is much more a matter of the difference between two views of life, one party more strongly political and the other more strongly religious. Kuenen this time wrote quite a long review (1875), concluding with the words: "It is with great appreciation that I take leave of 'The Pharisees and the Sadducees,' and also with the wish that we shall often meet Wellhausen again on the ground of Israel's history in its religion."

Kuenen had recognized that Wellhausen's first studies held the prospect of a complete critique of ancient Israel's historiographical tradition, from different sides. A direct attack was immediately launched. In winter 1872/73 Wellhausen investigated Genesis, and the rest of the Hexateuch in winter 1874/75, publishing the results in 1876/77 under the title *Die Composition des Hexateuchs*. In 1878 was added the analysis of the books of Judges, Ruth, Samuel, and Kings (1878b:181-267). The results of these investigations were far from being altogether novel. They recapitulated prevailing literary criticism in purified form, but naturally also advanced it in many respects. Fundamental in the Hexateuch is the identification of two principal components, the Priestly Writing on the one hand and on the other hand the "Jehovist," the latter being a combination of the Yahwist and the Elohist scarcely capable of further unraveling. No claim is made to a consistent source-revision to the last detail; space is left for varied expansions and proliferations. In the books of Judges, Samuel, and Kings we are dealing with a few quite ancient sources, linked together, and along with the Pentateuch finally revised Deuteronomistically, that is, in the spirit of Deuteronomy.

Here too the reaction of A. Kuenen was of the greatest worth. He expressed general agreement with Wellhausen but wrote a series of articles in which he concentrated on working out further the element of later redaction and "diaskeue," which has to be distinguished from the sources/16/. Wellhausen formulated the result of this operation as follows, in a letter of 1880:

> The views I have expressed about the composition of the Hexateuch have not totally endeared themselves to me—but for the axiom that beyond the principal sources there has been a variegated proliferation of material, that the supplementary hypothesis has its justification, that the mechanical mosaic hypothesis is crazy. Kuenen's articles correct me in a manner that concurs with my own intentions; I concede all to him in this regard, even what he has not yet said./17/

These works of Wellhausen are the foundation not only for Kuenen but for all subsequent literary criticism on the first two sections of the canon, even where this is neither known nor welcome. For Wellhausen himself the work was only preliminary. The so-called "Introduction to the

Old Testament" never much interested him as such, only as a means to the reconstruction of the history of ancient Israel. Without this goal he viewed literary criticism—in a favorite expression of his—as a sport or skittle-game. It was obvious to him from the outset that the strata of the historiography represent stages of the history. The task now before him consisted of providing for this insight a coherent realization and drawing its consequences for the history of ancient Israel. That would happen in a two-volume work with the title *Geschichte Israels*. The first volume, the occasion of our jubilee, appeared in 1878, amazingly quickly after the literary-critical publications. The second, the positive presentation of the history, was a long time coming and so brought about the renaming of the first volume to *Prolegomena zur Geschichte Israels*. In the interval between the two volumes Wellhausen once complained to his friend Robertson Smith: "There are few people in Germany who appreciate that I have actually more positive intentions than the criticism of the Pentateuch." But he was able to add: "I am glad that it is different in Britain"/18/.

I am offering no review here of the contents of the *Prolegomena*, not of course to spare those who may not yet have done so the reading of it, rather on the contrary to create an appetite for it. The reader fares with this book as seldom with academic literature. To read it is a pleasure. Its author is able to demonstrate right at the outset that his problem is not just an imaginary one but is actual and urgent (1885:6). It concerns "the place in history of the 'law of Moses;' more precisely, the question to be considered is whether that law is the starting-point of the history of ancient Israel, or not rather for that of Judaism, *i.e.*, of the religious communion which survived the destruction of the nation by the Assyrians and Chaldaeans" (1885:1). The examination is handled in three parts: History of the Cult, History of the Tradition, Israel and Judaism. Its subject is the customs, writings, and basic conceptions of the preexilic/Israelite period on the one side and of the postexilic/Jewish one on the other; it involved—and I mention only a few very familiar catchwords—the multiplicity of cultic sites and Jerusalem, the one place of worship; Yahwist–Elohist and Priestly Writing–Chronicler; oral and written Torah; theocracy as idea and institution. These contrasting pairs are not simply dissected and demonstrated abstractly but are given their locus in the living progress of the history and made comprehensible by it. And so the book treats the basic question as would an expert lawyer in a criminal case—with a synoptical arrangement of the extensive material, never before historically mastered, and with uninterrupted and transparent argumentation. Axiomatic for its method is that, where possible and significant, the argument should be handled in several areas independently. No series of uncertain hypotheses should maintain each other reciprocally; rather, the building should be supported by several independent pillars.

Not the least contribution to the effect of the book was its style. Of highest literary merit, a rare exception among the works of German professors, it is written in a clear and uncomplicated language, fresh and vivid, often pungent and funny. A brilliant element is the serenely cool polemic. It gave pleasure to many readers, but affected some of those concerned with a rage that was all the greater because they were unable to defend themselves with similar weapons. Wellhausen expunged some of this in the edition of 1883. Whoever likes mischievous *bon mots*—certainly a pleasure more for the "old self than the new"—should lay hands on the first edition. For all that, one masterpiece of polemic was added in 1883, in the form of a preface—not repeated in the later editions—in which Wellhausen took issue with his critics. It is the most important document for the earliest history of the book's influence and the author's attitude to it. Later he hardly ever expressed himself about it; others could carry on the struggle.

Against the expectations of author and publisher the book immediately caused a great sensation. It split Old Testament scholars. Some who to that point had not paid much attention to the Grafian hypothesis came over to it with flags flying. Others behaved as if they had always held this opinion; after the event people readily present themselves on the side of the victor. The military image is in fact appropriate; none other than that most incorruptible observer, A. Kuenen, used it when he said of Wellhausen's book: "its publication may be regarded as the 'crowning fight' in the long campaign." And this is how he looked back on his own reaction: "I can hardly describe the delight with which I first read it—a delight such as seldom indeed meets one on the path of learning. At one with the writer *a priori*, not only in principles but in general results, I was able to follow him from beginning to end with almost unbroken assent, and at the same time to learn more than I can say from every part of his work" (1886:xxxix).

On what is this effect based? There were good arguments previously, too. The decisive element must be that Wellhausen had a total view. It was their lack of a total view—church tradition could no longer pass as such, and had been abandoned at important points even by conservative exegetes—which he made a cause of reproach against his opponents (1878a:173f.). But it is also true of most of his predecessors, with the important exception of Vatke whose total view bore all too clearly the imprint of Hegelian philosophy. As Wellhausen became familiar with Vatke's book in 1874, his own view was already formed in its essentials; the report of his visit to Ritschl in 1867 gives a point of reference for how early that had been available to him, at least as a "very approximate and negative picture of the facts." His nature disposed him more strongly than any single other to see this picture and develop it. Free and natural as he was—"In sense of independence he was a match for the proudest peasants of Lower Saxony," reports Eduard Schwartz (30 [360])—he had a strong feeling for similar traits in the Israelites as portrayed in the early tradition. To say it in words much misused yet still pertinent when properly understood: much in this tradition and its concerns was congenial to him. Its immediacy, its freshness, its straightforwardness, its poetry claimed him as in some way kindred, in complete opposition to the prose of the later abstracting, de-individualizing, institutionalizing, dogmatizing revisions. He acknowledged this preference often and willingly. I quote only the sentences from the final chapter on the theocracy, which Martin Buber (67) called the most important part of the whole book:

> . . . the history of the ancient Israelites shows us nothing so distinctly as the uncommon freshness and naturalness of their impulses. The persons who appear always act from the constraining impulse of their nature, the men of God not less than the murderers and adulterers: they are such figures as could only grow up in the open air. Judaism, which realised the Mosaic constitution and carried it out logically, left no free scope for the individual; but in ancient Israel the divine right did not attach to the institution but was in the Creator Spirit, in individuals. Not only did they speak like the prophets, they also acted like the judges and kings, from their own free impulse, not in accordance with an outward norm, and yet, or just because of this, in the Spirit of Jehovah. (1885:412)

To Wellhausen's sympathy for the parts of the Old Testament which have retained the imprint of this world corresponds a clear aversion from the remainder. Πλέον ἥμισυ παντός, "the half is more than the whole"—this phrase from Hesiod is prefaced to the "History of the Tradition" as its motto: when Priestly Writing and Chronicler are omitted, the Old Testament gains. Wellhausen is quite other than a disinterested, nonpartisan historian; on this there can be no doubt. Disliking Leopold Ranke, he liked Theodor Mommsen all the more.

No wonder that his opponents liked to oppose his writing by accusing it of subjectivity and prejudice. It is manifest, the *Neue evangelische Kirchenzeitung* wrote immediately, that the book "is dictated by an unhistorical conception" (1879:84). Wellhausen rejoined that he did not recognize the right of this paper to such a verdict; "the church point of view is not the historical one" (1883:VIIn.). And it is impossible to deny that for all his personal interest Wellhausen was enough of a historian to appreciate fully the achievement of postexilic Judaism in preserving the Israelite heritage. It was popular, too, to place on Wellhausen this or that heretic cap. So the Scottish Reverend Smith got to hear from Professor Delitzsch as he visited him in Leipzig in August 1882 that "Wellhausen's speculations" were "merely applications of Darwinism to the sphere of theology and criticism" (368). Up to our own days there has been a preference on both sides of the Atlantic for calling Wellhausen a Hegelian. "Hegel begat Vatke, Vatke begat Wellhausen" can be read in one (Kegel: 10) of the many, mostly fundamentalist anti-Wellhausen pamphlets; there were so many such attacks that it would take pages to enumerate them. Others said the same in other words and more learnedly, but none produced the proof. That is no accident, for it is impossible to prove. Wellhausen stood at as great a remove from Hegelian speculation as a German historian of the nineteenth century could without falling right out of context/19/. If the authors outside his own discipline who particularly impressed Wellhausen are to be named, then—apart from the German classics, including the two great writers Martin Luther and Otto von Bismarck—they are the already mentioned Theodor Mommsen, Jacob Burckhardt, and, last but not least, Thomas Carlyle, whose *Heroes and Hero-Worship* he gave my father in 1897 as a confirmation present—a characteristic contribution to this Christian festival by a man who was devout in his own way but quite other than an orthodox churchman.

Naturally, alongside the complaints of heresy, there was also serious academic discussion of the *Prolegomena*. It was not very fruitful. Most of it had to do with making the Priestly Writing a little earlier by dating it to the end of the period of the monarchy or by pointing to the age of the material it contained. As far as Wellhausen was concerned the latter suggestion was merely beating the air, for he naturally viewed as very ancient the Jerusalem cult established in the Priestly Writing. For him it was only its literary form, with its own interests and tools, that was first fixed in the postexilic period. The Law—the only form in which it is still available to us—is recent. For the ancient period, what Wellhausen used in the *Prolegomena* as a motto for the "History of the Cult"—"Legem non habentes natura faciunt legis opera" (Rom 2:14)—was valid for the Jerusalem cult, too. About the preliterary stage in the tradition, especially as it concerned narrative materials, he made a few brief remarks that contain the essentials (see, e.g., 1885:326f.). He did not venture on a comprehensive study in this ticklish area or even a methodology for it. That was later Hermann Gunkel's business, with which he introduced a new chapter in the history of the discipline. I cannot now enter further into the not uncomplicated relationship between these two chapters and their representatives, the relation of Gunkel to Wellhausen and of Wellhausen to Gunkel. Permit me only one somewhat apodictic sentence: Gunkel without Wellhausen is a disaster. That, I am certain, would have been Gunkel's own opinion, too.

Wellhausen sometimes reflected on how the chapter which he himself represented in the history of the discipline related to its predecessor. These reflections indirectly concerned the future also and contained a warning for it. He gave them particularly clear expression at the end of a review of the history of Old Testament scholarship which he contributed to F. Bleek's *Einleitung in das Alte Testament*, for whose final editions he was responsible. I conclude my lecture with these sentences in two drafts, the one from the year 1878, the year of the *Prolegomena*, the other from the year 1893. In 1878 Wellhausen speaks of the advances in scholarship based on the abundance of material bestowed by new information about the rest of Semitic and Rabbinic literature, archaeological finds, and travels in the Orient. But, he asks, "who may believe that vis-à-vis the seventeenth century we now find ourselves at the summit? It sounds like a fairy story that Bochart was a pastor and Bentley by profession a theologian. The clock cannot be turned back; but some more philology, some more knowledge, and some more ignorance are not among the impossible wishes" (1878b:656). And then not even two decades later, in 1893, the victory in the Pentateuch question long won and the whole world busy in this field:

> Despite the legitimate interest taken in the Pentateuch question it would still be desirable not to limit attention obstinately to this. People are inclined to deal with the old questions over and over again and run the danger of landing finally in tendentiousness and boredom. It would do Old Testament scholarship good to enlarge its range somewhat, to attack new tasks, for example in the field of the lexicon, linguistics, and antiquities, and not become barren through isolation. And there would be no need to trundle out the work always in the form of commentaries, nor to have the studies swell whenever possible into thick books; less ingenuity, but more learning, more rigor and resignation are urgently needed (1893·627)

Who would dispute that we could put these sentences to good use, *mutatis mutandis*, in 1978 also?

NOTES

° Translated by Dr A Graeme Auld in Edinburgh, to whom my thanks are also due for bibliographical references. Prior to presentation to the Society of Biblical Literature on 20 November 1978, the lecture was delivered in different drafts in October 1978 in Cambridge, Edinburgh, St. Andrews, Durham, Leeds, and Oxford, at the invitation of the universities there. It was preceded in April 1978 by a similar lecture in the Rijksuniversiteit Groningen, which highlighted Wellhausen's relations with Dutch scholarship

/1/ *The British Weekly*, 9 July 1914, 397.

/2/ This is taken from an undated letter of Wellhausen to W. Robertson Smith which may have been written in spring 1881 (Cambridge University Library Add 7449/ D 768).

/3/ Wellhausen to W Robertson Smith on 24 August 1882 (Cambridge University Library Add 7449/ D 772).

/4/ Wellhausen to his mother-in-law on 12 January 1883. For this and further letters in private hands I refer to the promised edition of Wellhausen's correspondence

/5/ See W. A. Irwin; A. Wikgren. The epoch-making character of Wellhausen's work for Old Testament studies is brought out particularly well in English-language presentations. Cf. H F Hahn, 1956; R. E Clements.

/6/ Not so in Israel; cf *Yedioth aharonoth*, 27 April 1978, p. 16.

/7/ The pupil erected a memorial to the teacher. Wellhausen, 1901

/8/ On the Greifswald period, cf A Jepsen.

/9/ Text of the letter in Jepsen: 54 [266f.]

/10/ Letter to W. Robertson Smith of 8 October 1880 (Cambridge University Library Add 7449/ D 756).

/11/   Letter of A. Kuenen to W Robertson Smith of 29 May 1883 (Cambridge University Library Add 7449/ D 341)

/12/   Unfortunately the *Israelitische und Jüdische Geschichte*, which went through nine editions from 1894 to 1958, was never translated into English, in contrast to many much less important books Much false understanding of Wellhausen's historiography—in Germany, too—is a result of the fact that less attention has been paid to this work than to the *Prolegomena*.

/13/   On this I refer to E. Bammel's fine discussion of the academic historical context.

/14/   Letter to J Olshausen of 9 February 1879 (Deutsches Zentralarchiv Merseburg Rep. 92 Justus v Olshausen B I Nr. 7).

/15/   For a general discussion, see R J Thompson.

/16/   These ten articles appeared in the *Theologisch Tijdschrift* from 1877 to 1884. On them cf S. J De Vries.

/17/   Letter to A. Jülicher of 8 November 1880 (Universitatsbibliothek Marburg MS 695).

/18/   Letter to W Robertson Smith of 11 May 1882 (Cambridge University Library Add 7449/ D 770).

/19/   On these problems, see F. Boschwitz, H.-J. Kraus. 240-49, 2nd ed : 260-74; R. Smend; H. F. Hahn, 1959, L. Perlitt; H. Hoffmann For the most recent remarks in the English-language literature, see J. Barr. 145-49; J. Blenkinsopp· 17-23 (cf. W. McKane· 66), R. M. Polzin. 126-49.

WORKS CONSULTED

Anderson, George W.
    1975   "Two Scottish Semitists." Pp ix-xix in *Congress Volume Edinburgh 1974* VTSup 28. Leiden. E. J. Brill.

Bammel, E
    1969   "Judentum, Christentum und Heidentum: Julius Wellhausens Briefe an Theodor Mommsen 1881-1902 " *Zeitschrift für Kirchengeschichte* 80: 221-54

Barr, James
    1977   *Fundamentalism* London. SCM.

Bigger, J L
    1882   "'The Encyclopaedia Britannica'—Wellhausen on Israel." *The Christian Church* 2 (January).

Black, J S., and G. Chrystal
    1912   *The Life of William Robertson Smith* London: A. and C. Black

Blenkinsopp, Joseph
    1977   *Prophecy and Canon: A Contribution to the Study of Jewish Origins* Notre Dame/London. University of Notre Dame.

Boschwitz, Friedemann
    1968   *Julius Wellhausen· Motive und Mass-Stabe seiner Geschichtsschreibung*. Darmstadt· Wissenschaftliche Buchgesellschaft. (Reprint of his 1938 Marburg dissertation)

Buber, Martin
1967   *Kingship of God*. Trans. R. Scheimann from the 3d German edition. London: George Allen & Unwin.

Clements, Ronald E.
1976   *A Century of Old Testament Criticism*. Guildford/London: Lutterworth.

Darlow, T. H.
1925   *William Robertson Nicoll: His Life and Letters*. London: Hodder & Stoughton.

Davies, T. Witton
1901   "Germany through Baptist Eyes." *The Baptist Times and Freeman*, 6 September 1901: 60.

De Vries, Simon J.
1963   "The Hexateuchal Criticism of Abraham Kuenen." *JBL* 82: 31–57.

Duhm, Bernhard
1875   *Die Theologie der Propheten als Grundlage für die innere Entwicklungsgeschichte der israelitischen Religion*. Bonn: Adolph Marcus.

Graf, Karl Heinrich
1866   *Die geschichtlichen Bücher des Alten Testaments: Zwei historisch-kritische Untersuchungen*. Leipzig: T. O. Weigel.
1869   "Die sogenannte Grundschrift des Pentateuch." *Archiv für wissenschaftliche Erforschung des Alten Testaments* 1: 466–77.

Hahn, Herbert F.
1956   *The Old Testament in Modern Research*. London: SCM.
1959   "Wellhausen's Interpretation of Israel's Religious History: A Reappraisal of his Ruling Ideas." Pp. 299–308 in *Essays on Jewish Life and Thought: Presented in Honor of Salo Wittmayer Baron*. Ed. Joseph L. Blau, et al. New York: Columbia University.

Hoffmann, Horst
1967   *Julius Wellhausen: Die Frage des absoluten Mass-Stabes seiner Geschichtsschreibung*. Diss. theol. Marburg. Erich Mauersberger.

Irwin, William A.
1944   "The Significance of Julius Wellhausen." *JBR* 12: 160–73.

Jepsen, Alfred
1956   "Wellhausen in Greifswald." Pp. 47–56 in *Festschrift zur 500-Jahrfeier der Universität Greifswald*, vol. 2. Greifswald: Verlag Volksstimme. = Pp. 254–70 in Jepsen, *Der Herr ist Gott*. Berlin: Evang. Verlagsanstalt, 1978.

Kegel, M.
1923   *Los von Wellhausen!* Gutersloh: Bertelsmann.

Kraus, Hans-Joachim
1956   *Geschichte der historisch-kritischen Erforschung des Alten Testaments*. Neukirchen: Neukirchener Erziehungsverein. 2d ed., 1969.

Kuenen, Abraham
1869–70 *De godsdienst van Israel tot den ondergang van den Joodschen staat*. 2 vols. Haarlem: A. C. Kruseman. = *The Religion of Israel to the Fall of the Jewish State*. 3 vols. London: Williams and Norgate, 1874–75.

1872	Review of J Wellhausen's *Der Text der Bucher Samuelis.* *TTıjd* 6: 95
1875	Review of J. Wellhausen's *Die Pharisäer und die Sadducaer* *TTijd* 9 632-50.
1877-84	"Bijdragen tot de critiek van Pentateuch en Jozua." *TTijd* 11-18.
1886	*An Historico-Critical Inquiry into the Origin and Composition of the Hexateuch* London. Macmillan

McKane, William
| 1979 | Review of J Blenkinsopp's *Prophecy and Canon* *JSOT* 12· 63-69 |

Perlitt, Lothar
| 1965 | *Vatke und Wellhausen: Geschichtsphilosophische Voraussetzungen und historiographısche Motive für die Darstellung der Religion und Geschichte Israels durch Wilhelm Vatke und Julius Wellhausen* BZAW 94. Berlin. Alfred Topelmann |

Polzin, Robert M
| 1977 | *Biblical Structuralism: Method and Subjectivity in the Study of Ancient Texts* Semeia Supplements. Philadelphia. Fortress, Missoula. Scholars Press. |

Schwartz, Eduard
| 1919 | *Julius Wellhausen.* Berlin: Weidmann = Pp 326-61 ın *Gesammelte Schriften*, vol 1 2d ed Berlin de Gruyter, 1963. |

Smend, Rudolf
| 1958 | "De Wette und das Verhaltnis zwischen historischer Bibelkritik und phılosophischem System im 19 Jahrhundert." *TZ* 14· 107-19 |

Smith, Rev.
| 1882 | "Wellhausen and his Position." *The Christian Church* 2. 366-69. |

Taylor, A J P
| 1976 | *Essays in English History*. Harmondsworth/New York· Penguın Books |

Thompson, R J
| 1970 | *Moses and the Law in a Century of Criticism sınce Graf* VTSup 19 Leiden. E. J Brill |

Vatke, Wilhelm
| 1835 | *Die biblische Theologie wissenschaftlich dargestellt* I: *Die Religion des Alten Testamentes nach den kanonıschen Buchern entwickelt.* Berlin· G Bethge. |

Wellhausen, Julius
1870	"De gentibus et familiis Judaeis quae 1 Chr. 2. 4. enumerantur." Theol Liz.-Diss., Gottingen.
1871	*Der Text der Bucher Samuelis untersucht.* Gottingen Vandenhoeck & Ruprecht.
1874	*Die Pharisaer und die Sadducaer: Eine Untersuchung zur ınneren judischen Geschichte* Greifswald· Bamberg
1876-77	"Die Composition des Hexateuchs." *JDT* 21· 392-450, 531-602; 22· 407-79 = Pp 1-208 in *Die Composition des Hexateuchs und der historischen Bücher des Alten Testaments*. 3d ed Berlin· Georg Reimer, 1899
1878a	*Geschichte Israels In zwei Bänden. Erster Band* Berlin· G. Reimer.
1878b	*Einleitung in die Heilige Schrift, Erster Theil: Einleitung in das Alte Testament*, by Friedrich Bleek 4th ed by J Wellhausen Berlin:

	G. Reimer. Pp. 181-267 ("Die geschichtlichen Bucher") reprinted on pp. 208-301 in *Die Composition des Hexateuchs und der historischen Bucher des Alten Testaments.* 3d ed. Berlin. Georg Reimer, 1899
1881	"Israel." *EB*, 9th ed. 13. 396-431.
1882	*Muhammed in Medina: Das ist Vakidi's Kitab alMaghazi in verkürzter deutscher Wiedergabe herausgegeben.* Berlin. G. Reimer.
1883	*Prolegomena zur Geschichte Israels.* 2d ed of *Geschichte Israels* (1878a). Berlin: G. Reimer.
1885	*Prolegomena to the History of Israel.* Translated from the 1883 edition by J. Sutherland Black and Allan Menzies. With Preface by W. Robertson Smith. Edinburgh. Adam & Charles Black. = *Prolegomena to the History of Ancient Israel.* New York: Meridian Books, 1957.
1893	6th ed. of Bleek's *Einleitung* (1878b). Berlin: G. Reimer.
1894	*Israelitische und jüdische Geschichte.* Berlin: G. Reimer. 7th ed., 1914 = 9th ed., Berlin. de Gruyter, 1958.
1898	*Die kleinen Propheten übersetzt und erklärt.* 3d ed. Berlin: G. Reimer.
1901	"Heinrich Ewald." Pp. 61-88 in *Festschrift zur Feier des 150jahrigen Bestehens der Koniglichen Gesellschaft der Wissenschaften zu Göttingen.* Berlin: Weidmann. = Pp. 120-38 in *Grundrisse zum Alten Testament,* ed. R. Smend. TBu 27. Munich. Chr. Kaiser, 1965.
1902	*Das arabische Reich und sein Sturz.* Berlin. G. Reimer.

de Wette, Wilhelm Martin Leberecht
1806   *Beiträge zur Einleitung in das Alte Testament.* I. *Kritischer Versuch über die Glaubwürdigkeit der Bücher der Chronik mit Hinsicht auf die Geschichte der mosaischen Bücher und Gesetzgebung.* Halle: Schimmelpfennig.

Wikgren, Allen
1944   "Wellhausen and the Synoptic Gospels: A Centenary Appraisal." *JBR* 12. 174-80.

WELLHAUSEN AND THE INTERPRETATION OF ISRAEL'S LITERATURE

Douglas A. Knight
Vanderbilt University

ABSTRACT

Wellhausen's interpretation of the literature of the Hebrew Bible was conducted less along the lines of exegesis than in conformity to historiographical method In this he made use of an approach which sought to relate the literary expressions to the respective periods and institutions from which they stemmed. Paramount in this regard was the identification of the presuppositions and *Tendenz* of each piece. For critical reasons he avoided such stages as oral tradition where the historian would be on insecure ground Throughout the *Prolegomena* Wellhausen exhibited a clear preference for the early literature in matters of both style and spirit, and he did not hesitate to criticize forcefully the literary developments of the postexilic period

Beginning especially in the seventeenth century, a shift in mood and indeed in world-view began to occur which encouraged a number of persons to abandon the traditional perspectives on the nature of Scripture in favor of a more humanistic conception (see K. Scholder; H.-J. Kraus; and H. Frei). According to this, the Bible was viewed in much the same light as any other ancient literature, i.e., as essentially a product of human experiences and cultural forces, including the sphere of religion. Such a literary entity could be studied, it was discerned, according to the same principles and methods that would apply for any literature, and the next two centuries found numerous scholars willing to do just this, even when they had their own theological persuasions as well—Richard Simon, Henning Bernhard Witter, Jean Astruc, Johann Salomo Semler, Johann Gottfried Herder, Johann Gottfried Eichhorn, Wilhelm Martin Leberecht de Wette, Eduard Reuss, Wilhelm Vatke, Johann Friedrich Leopold George, Heinrich Georg August Ewald, Hermann Hupfeld, Karl Heinrich Graf, Abraham Kuenen, and many others.

It was proposed by Witter as early as 1711 that distinguishable sources could be isolated in parts of Genesis on the basis of stylistic differences, repetitious content, and alternation between divine names. As it was applied to the whole Hexateuch during the nineteenth century, this source criticism became refined to a delicate art, and an entire system of dividing the Hexateuch into four sources was worked out in detail, culminating with Hupfeld in 1853 and Kuenen in 1861-65. The prevailing opinion, however, was that what we know as the Priestly source came first, having been drafted in the early monarchy, well before the other three. It was therefore a crucial step when Reuss, George, Vatke, and Graf argued that the Priestly law should be placed *after*, not before, J, E, and D/1/. This hypothesis became absolutely fundamental for Julius Wellhausen's *Prolegomena to the History of Israel*.

I. SCOPE OF HIS LITERARY STUDIES

When one considers Wellhausen's overwhelming impact on the study of the Hebrew Bible, it is indeed surprising to find how little exegetical work he actually published, at least in the form of commentaries or shorter studies of individual pericopes. With the New Testament, in contrast, he engaged himself much more exegetically. Perhaps best known among his studies of the Hebrew Bible is the series of three articles published in 1876-77, "Die Composition des Hexateuchs," and later issued separately as a book. From this, the classic literary-critical treatment of the Hexateuch, he derived the bulk of his conclusions about the history of Israel and the history of her religion, as presented in the *Prolegomena*. Its originality lies not so much in the details of the source division—for Wellhausen drew heavily on his predecessors in this regard—but more in the cogency with which the total argument is developed, especially with respect to the JEDP sequence of the documents. But Wellhausen went well beyond mere source criticism and offered enlightening comments also on the meaning of the text itself. It omits numerous exegetical steps which we have come to expect; after all, such methods as form criticism and tradition criticism were at that time still undeveloped. Yet its contributions to the understanding of the Hexateuch and its literary history are undeniable. In 1878 he published a compositional analysis of Judges, Ruth, Samuel, and Kings which was much of the same order (1878b:181-267). His comment on the approach necessary for this literature is noteworthy: "It is obvious that the formal and literary questions cannot be treated apart from the substantive and historical issues" (1878b:181). In comparison, his studies of the books of Samuel in 1871, of the Minor Prophets in 1892, and of the Psalms in 1895 and 1898 are more in the nature of text-critical and philological notes on the texts. And finally, a general discussion of apocalyptic literature (1899) completes the list of explicit treatments of Hebrew texts. Noticeably lacking are any sustained exegetical engagements with the Major Prophets, the wisdom literature, and the Chronicler's history, although the latter received more direct attention in the *Prolegomena*.

By nature the *Prolegomena* is not, of course, an exegetical study. With this volume Wellhausen sought to lay the foundations for writing a history of Israel, and he did this by searching the literary sources for historical clues and by identifying schematic structures for understanding the historical developments within the religious, political, and societal spheres. Yet insofar as this required a critical sifting of the literary materials, Wellhausen was engaging in interpretation, some of it appropriated from his other publications and some of it fresh and new in the *Prolegomena*. Above all, he drew in this regard on the Hexateuch, Judges, Samuel, Kings, Chronicles, and occasionally on the prophets; the Writings received scarcely any notice. Short of thorough exegetical studies, his discussion amounted to what he at one point referred to as "our eclectic pilgrimage through the historical books" (1885:393). Yet one is greatly mistaken if one concludes from this that Wellhausen's textual studies were arbitrary, undisciplined, or inconsequential. Looking back on his work after the decades of the 1960s and 1970s when methodological self-consciousness reached its all-time high point, we must guard ourselves against supposing that his critical method was any less sophisticated or deliberative than today's. Indeed his critical erudition and sensitive understanding of the literature have scarcely a rival—all the more remarkable when one realizes that the *Prolegomena* appeared when he was only thirty-four years of age.

II. PRINCIPLES OF LITERARY INTERPRETATION

In the following we are attempting not to describe Wellhausen's exegetical method but rather to isolate the general principles according to which he approached and critically interpreted the text. These are not to be confused with his historiographical method, even though there will be substantial overlapping between the two. Nor are we here looking for Wellhausen's own philosophical and cultural presuppositions/2/. Rather, how did he approach the literature of the Hebrew Bible, and how did he assess its fundamental characteristics? We will limit ourselves here to evidence from the *Prolegomena*.

1. *The Critical Task*

For the preceding two centuries the critical reading of the Bible had been developed and secured among scholars, and Wellhausen positioned himself consciously within this tradition/3/. While he nowhere discussed at length his understanding of the historical-critical method, one can cull from the *Prolegomena* various comments concerning the posture and task of criticism.

First and most basic to the critical approach, one must in principle suspend traditional notions when one seeks to ascertain the historical state of affairs. The fresh interpretations which Wellhausen was able to offer on individual points throughout the *Prolegomena* were the result of his gaining this distance from conventional ideas. Nowhere, however, is it more evident than on the key issue of the place of the Law in Israel's history. At the very beginning of the book Wellhausen vividly described his breakthrough when, upon hearing Graf's suggestion, he was able to free himself of the view that the Law preceded the prophets (1885:3f.). In contrast, he used hard language against "the defenders of the prevailing opinion" who could not take the same critical step: "To say all in a word, the arguments which were brought into play as a rule derived all their force from a moral conviction that the ritual legislation *must* be old, and *could* not possibly have been committed to writing for the first time within the period of Judaism; that it was not operative before then, that it did not even admit of being carried into effect in the conditions that prevailed previous to the exile, could not shake the conviction—all the firmer because it did not rest on arguments—that at least it existed previously" (1885:11f.).

This led then, secondly, to granting the text, as well as the ancient phenomena in general, their own integrity. This does not mean that one should not study the text critically or attempt to reconstruct the historical course of events differently from that portrayed there. Rather, the critic must quite simply acknowledge the right of antiquity to its own views. As Wellhausen emphasized with respect to Genesis 1, the alternative is that the interpreter "confounds two different things—the value of history for us, and the aim of the writer" (1885:298). And in such a case it has too often happened that "scholars felt themselves responsible for what the Bible says, and therefore like it to come as little as possible in conflict with general culture" (1885:308). This does not mean that one is obliged simply to grant historical veracity to the text's account; Wellhausen himself obviously did not shy away from reconstructing the history quite differently from the biblical witness. But it does require the reader to understand the literature on its own terms—a precondition for historical-critical interpretation. For Wellhausen, this did not imply that one must necessarily find all of it to one's own liking, for as we shall see below he himself did not hesitate to express value judgments on various parts of the literature or the culture.

Third, the historical task of analyzing the literary evidence in order to reconstruct the history of Israel is the primary one for him, although he did not thereby exclude other critical purposes. Quite simply, he followed a strict historical paradigm rather than what we would now call a linguistic paradigm or a synchronic approach (on this distinction see, for example, D. Patte: 9–17; and specifically on Wellhausen, cf. R. M. Polzin: 126–49). He was interested in determining the intentions of the authors, the referents of the textual statements, and the historical sequence and genetic relationship among all the evidence. This he set as the goal of his "literargeschichtliche Untersuchung" (1878a:13; 1885:12f.). Without here elaborating further his historical method (see the chapters in this volume by

J. H. Hayes and P. D. Miller, Jr.; also F. Boschwitz; H. Hoffmann), we can merely emphasize how self-evident this task was for Wellhausen: "history, it is well known, has always to be constructed. . . . The question is whether one constructs well or ill" (1885:367).

Fourth, this very concern led Wellhausen to set a notable limit on his critical task: historians should restrict themselves only to the periods from which there remains adequate literary evidence. This principle lay behind his refusal to investigate the prehistory of the literature at the stage when it was circulating among the people only in the form of oral tradition. It was not that he was opposed to constructing historical hypotheses (see, e.g., his own admissions on 1885:367f.), only that he found it of no value to engage in unfounded speculation. He was preoccupied with tracing the development of written literature. It was Gunkel who extended this critical task to include the preliterary growth as well.

2. *The Rootage of Literature in Society and Religion*

We have already indicated that Wellhausen used biblical literature primarily as a source for the scientific writing of Israel's history. What, for him, did the text represent or reflect? Wellhausen expressed himself frequently on this throughout the *Prolegomena*. Most fundamentally, as he wrote with respect to the legal materials, "the important point is not the matter, but the spirit which is behind it, and may everywhere be recognised as *the spirit of the age* ("Zeitgeist") at one period or another" (1885:366, italics added). Or again: "Under the influence of the spirit of each successive age, traditions originally derived from one source were very variously apprehended and shaped; one way in the ninth and eighth centuries, another way in the seventh and sixth, and yet another in the fifth and fourth" (1885:171). The text, in other words, mirrors this general "spirit of the age" as well as the other specific "active forces" (1885:228) which were at work in society and religion at a given time. Thus he could maintain that in the JE and D legislation it was agriculture, "the basis at once of life and of religion" (1885:91), which made its impress on the laws; or again, that the two contrasting views of the monarchy expressed in the books of Samuel resulted in the one case from the situation of living during the period of the kingdom and in the other from living in the exilic or postexilic age "which had no knowledge of Israel as a people and a state, and which had no experience of the real conditions of existence in these forms" (1885:255); or also, that the ancestral stories in Genesis reflect the naturalness of life in the ninth and eighth centuries, at two main levels: "In the traits of personal character ascribed to the patriarchs they represent substantially the nature and the aspirations of the individual Israelite. The historic-political relations of Israel are reflected with more life in the relations borne by the patriarchs to their brothers, cousins, and other relatives. The background is never long concealed here, the temper of the period of the kings is everywhere discernible" (1885:321f.).

What can be said of the social rootage of the literature applies equally well for its anchorage in religion. In fact, this was so basic to Wellhausen's method that he devoted the entire first part of the *Prolegomena* to examining all literary indications of the religious practices and institutions, with the aim of using these as an aid in understanding the history of the literature and the people. He concluded that in early Israel "worship arose out of the midst of ordinary life" (1885:76) and that this "uncommon freshness and naturalness" (1885:412) of the people made its way from religion into the early literature. A shift occurred in Deuteronomy, however, when the move to centralize all worship in Jerusalem pulled religious practices away from their natural setting in the people's hometowns, and this in turn led to the spiritualization, routinization, and abstraction of worship in the postexilic period at the hand of the Priestly group (see, e.g., 1885:77–82). The three major literary sources—JE, D, and P—correspond directly, then, with these three styles of worship. As is known, Wellhausen did not think highly of the postexilic stage, implying that the Jerusalem priests were acting arbitrarily in making the change represented in P—whereas actually there is no evidence that it was any more out of touch with popular beliefs and values than had been the case in earlier times. But this is a criticism of his results; it does not run counter to his principle that the literature reflects *some* aspect of religion and society. Indeed, Wellhausen deserves the credit for establishing this principle fully. It fell to Gunkel in the next generation to carry it further with his study of the *Sitz im Leben* of individual genres, not only of the contents of the literature.

3. *The Presuppositions of a Literary Stratum*

Wellhausen likewise found it important to inquire of the presuppositions of the biblical authors, and this served for him as a basic historiographical tool. Stated simply, what could the author of a given piece have known from tradition or understood about the current times? Wellhausen assumed quite generally that a later writer would necessarily have been familiar with what had been recorded previously: each prophet knew and built on the preceding prophets; the Priestly writer knew D, and they both had JE before them; Chronicles followed the pattern of the Priestly Writing, whereas the Chronicler's source knew not that but only Deuteronomy (1885:294f.). Actually, the precise configurations of these relationships were the result of his literary-critical investigations. He posed the problem at the very outset in this manner: Is the Law the "basis and postulate of the whole literature" (1885:3)—or only of the postexilic literature? As indicated above, much of Wellhausen's monumental impact on biblical studies resulted from his demonstrating the cogency of Graf's hypothesis that the Law received its present form only in the postexilic period and that therefore the preexilic period and literature, which thus would not have known it, must be understood without it. There are many other examples of this effort to determine what a given writer might have known from before: the unity of Israel is not presupposed in the older "genuine tradition" of Judges but only in the later Deuteronomistic redaction (1885:234); Deuteronomy, in its call for reform rather than restoration, obviously could not have known the exile (1885:404); however, in the Deuteronomistic redaction of Samuel and Kings the fall of Jerusalem is presupposed (1885:277-80); or again, the centralization of the cult is introduced by Deuteronomy, whereas the later Priestly Writing could presuppose it as a given reality (1885:35). This role which Wellhausen assigned to the presuppositions of each writer or period was as crucial for him as it has become for subsequent historical criticism, for by attending to them one can often determine the historical succession of data. "Almost more important to me than the phenomena themselves, are the presuppositions which lie behind them" (1885:368).

4.   *The* Tendenz *of the Literature*

Among Wellhausen's considerable contributions to the study of the biblical literature is his refinement of the method of *Tendenzkritik*. At virtually every point in his study of literary sources throughout the *Prolegomena*, he considered it of paramount importance to determine the writer's *Tendenz*—the intention, including the specific point of view which stands behind it. This, in Wellhausen's view, needs to be identified for each stage in the development of the literature, especially for the later strata which reworked the earlier materials in order to present their own perspectives or achieve their own special purposes. It is a most significant aspect of the historical-critical method, as we can readily recognize in light of its extensive use in literary studies since Wellhausen. For it postualtes that each literary piece—or at least such as we have in the Bible—incorporates an intentionality which gives it purpose and renders it meaningful in its proper historical context.

A few examples of *Tendenzen* may illustrate the point. The Deuteronomistic redaction of the stories of the judges does not present them simply as heroic tales but stresses, for its own generation, the imperative to worship YHWH alone and to avoid the repeated failure of the people in the past to do so (1885:231). While the stories about the monarchy had originally more of a secular purpose, in the Deuteronomistic redaction the intention is to view "the time of the kings as a period past and closed, on which judgment has already been declared" because of unfaithfulness to YHWH, and thus this narrative becomes then "a great confession of sins of the exiled nation looking back on its history" (1885:278). Like many other writings the book of Ezekiel has in its various parts several intentions, such as: to indicate that the exile is Israel's expiation for the enormous sins of the past (1885:279), to call the people to holiness (1885:422), to give the sanction of law to the distinction between priests and Levites (1885:140). In general, the Priestly Writing and Chronicles are both, in Wellhausen's view, laboring at "an artificial revival of the old tradition" in the postexilic period (1885:350), the former by arguing for the "theocratic ideal" and the role of the Law (e.g., 1885:161), and the latter by legitimizing the Jerusalem worshiping community of the Persian period by tracing its roots back to David as founder (e.g., 1885:178). Wellhausen sought primarily among this historical literature for evidences of such a "uniform stamp impressed on the tradition by men who regarded history exclusively from the point of view of their own principles" (1885:293). Ever since Gunkel, however, it has become common practice for form critics to look for intentions also among any other types of literature, whether poetic, prophetic, sapiential, enumerative, or whatever.

5. *The Literature as Historical Source*

In light of the above characteristics of biblical literature, one might well wonder to what extent Wellhausen could consider that these sources might retain reliable historical information. The answer is that Wellhausen proceeded very cautiously and discriminatingly on this question of historicity. The kind of myth present in the opening chapters of Genesis, in Wellhausen's view, is "not true, but it is honest" (1885:318), and these traditions—especially those of JE—are in fact of considerable historical value with respect to our understanding the ancient people's views of reality. With the ancestral stories of Genesis we meet graphically Wellhausen's principle of historical projection: "The materials here are not mythical but national, and therefore more transparent, and in a certain sense more historical. It is true, we attain to no historical knowledge of the patriarchs, but only of the time when the stories about them arose in the Israelite people; this later age is here unconsciously projected, in its inner and its outward features, into hoar antiquity, and is reflected there like a glorified mirage" (1885:318f.). Wellhausen supposed that only certain isolated statements may be historically correct (1885:360n.).

In contrast to Genesis, however, the "epic tradition" of Moses and Joshua is more credible, at least insofar as there probably are factual kernels underlying some of the elements; this is because the tradition could draw on a source from the premonarchic period, rather than being completely projected back in time as were the ancestral legends (1885:360). For the Deuteronomistic literature, the historicity is generally discounted wherever the redactor's hand can be observed, while elsewhere the stories may well have some basis in fact even though they will likely have become embellished with time. Thus in Judges the chronological framework, the four-stage religious cycle of events (rebellion, affliction, conversion, peace), and the command for exclusive worship of YHWH are considered later additions (1885:229–32). The transition to the monarchy related in Samuel is also Deuteronomistic (1885:248), for example, as are various religious views basic to Kings (1885:281). The situation changes considerably in the postexilic period, however. Wellhausen's global judgment is worth citing in full:

> It is not the case that the Jews had any profound respect for their ancient history; rather they condemned the whole earlier development, and allowed only the Mosaic time along with its Davidic reflex to stand; in other words, not history but the ideal. The theocratic ideal was from the exile onwards the centre of all thought and effort, and it annihilated the sense for objective truth, all regard and interest for the actual facts as they had been handed down. It is well known that there never have been more audacious history-makers than the Rabbins. But Chronicles affords evidence sufficient that this evil propensity goes back to a very early time, its root the dominating influence of the Law, being the root of Judaism itself (1885.161, see also the chapter by L H. Silberman in this volume)

Wellhausen was not quite so harsh with the Priestly Writing as he was with the Chronicler, of whose literature he added: "It is indeed possible that occasionally a grain of good corn may occur among the chaff, but to be conscientious one must neglect this possibility of exceptions, and give due honour to the probability of the rule. For it is only too easy to deceive oneself in thinking that one has come upon some sound particular in a tainted whole" (1885:224). In a word, historicity is not to be expected at all in Chronicles.

Two observations are worth making in this regard. First, subsequent scholars have generally tended to attribute more credibility to the biblical literature. The ancestral traditions are commonly used as a source for some historical information about the premonarchic consolidation period, if not earlier; the sources of the Deuteronomistic History are thought to be early; and especially the Priestly Writing but also the Chronicler are held to contain more early material than Wellhausen had reckoned. Second, with his principle of projection Wellhausen in fact found more historical information in the biblical literature than he admitted. Even if he repudiated the accuracy of a given piece for the period it was describing (e.g., the Chronicler's account of David), he used it to gain an understanding of the period in which it was written. In other words, JE—putatively about the pre-Mosaic and Mosaic ages—was for him a source about the ninth and eighth centuries, and even earlier. Similarly, the Deuteronomistic redactional work gives us insight on the exilic period. And it can hardly be overlooked that he seized the Priestly and Chronicler literatures as the best windows on the postexilic religious community. A literary piece, it is clear, can be a historical source in more than one way. In Wellhausen's own words: "of course, no fancy is pure fancy; every imagination has underlying it some elements of reality by which it can be laid hold of, even should these only be certain prevailing notions of a particular period" (1885:161).

6.   *The Inaccessibility of Oral Tradition*

As a matter of principle, Wellhausen considered the preliterary developments of the traditions to be irrecoverable, and consequently for historiography he focused the entirety of his literary analyses on the written stages/4/. However, while attributing primary responsibility to those who wrote JE, D, P, the prophetic literature, and any other documentary materials, he readily acknowledged that they were often not the creators of all which they composed. Especially the earlier of these drew heavily on oral traditions, ordered and connected them through various means, and thereby produced their compositions. Yet Wellhausen was and remained a literary critic in that he restricted his analysis to only these written stages of composition and redaction. The oral period was too elusive to study. And when Gunkel in *Schöpfung und Chaos* made the first massive effort to do so less than two decades after the first appearance of the *Prolegomena*, Wellhausen responded adamantly that such investigation of the preliterary origins "is perhaps of antiquarian interest but is not the task of the theologian and the exegete" (1899:233). What is of importance is the literary history and the meaning of the materials in the present text.

However, Wellhausen did venture numerous comments about what the nature of the oral tradition must have been. In the mouth of the people one can expect only detached narratives; it takes a literary artist or a poet to weave them together into an extended, connected whole (1885:296). In fact, not much enumerative material (chronologies, lists of numbers, catalogues of names, dates, measurements) can be retained orally at all (1885:337). On the other hand, oral traditions are likely to display vivid local color and the pathos of everyday life. For the ancestral traditions, Wellhausen noted, "the clearer the traces they display of love and hatred, jealousy of rivals and joy in their fall, the nearer are we to the forces which originated the tradition about early times" (1885:333). Moreover, the narratives are often attached to particular localities, as can be adduced from their references to places (1885:325). In the case of some of the stories in Judges, those stemming from "independent oral material" are very vague in their historical reminiscences, are freely overgrown with legend, and display "greater art and more naïveté"; furthermore, the general principle regarding the religious tenor is that "the nearer history is to its origin the more profane it is" (1885:244f.). In light of the numerous variations and repetitions of the same stories in Genesis, Wellhausen was of the opinion that the oral traditions were still very "plastic and living" in the ninth and eighth centuries (1885:327). However, on the question of historical credibility he saw little hope for the historian: "The longer a story was spread by oral tradition among the people, the more was its root concealed by the shoots springing from it" (1885:326). Only certain main features and general presuppositions of the stories about the early period may not be fictitious (1914:10).

Wellhausen largely restricted his discussion of oral tradition to the materials retained in JE, Joshua, and Judges. For the rest of the historical literature he reckoned almost exclusively with written documents and written transmission, almost as if the mouth of the people were stopped shut once the sources were recorded. This question, just as also the issue of historical credibility, has received considerable attention during the following century, not the least among numerous Scandinavian scholars (see Knight: passim), and it has become commonplace to extend widely the scope of oral tradition in light of form-critical and traditio-historical indications. Wellhausen himself may indeed have provided an opening for this, for he stipulated that the priests as well as the prophets functioned throughout this time on the basis of a traditional authority and through the means of oral teaching and proclamation (1885:392-410). It remained then only for his successors to develop a method for probing such spheres and relating them to the texts which resulted from them.

7.   *Style and Vocabulary*

As hypothetical as Wellhausen's historical and literary work is often held to be, one must certainly credit him throughout for his effort to found his views on the concrete data provided by the text. A clear evidence of this is his attention to style and vocabulary, especially as these are related to the *Tendenz* of a given literary piece. Recognizing that the study of the history of the Hebrew language was very much in its infancy in the latter part of the nineteenth century, he perceived correctly that a given author or period could have a distinct style, characteristic terminology, syntactical peculiarities—all of which could be set apart from the way other authors used language, with the comparative data then set in chronological sequence (1885:390). Note, for example how he described these characteristics of the Priestly Writing: The style is marked by "an indescribable pedantry" which classifies, draws plans, enumerates, describes to excess, repeats the obvious again and again. "What is interesting is passed over, what is of no importance is described with minuteness, his exhaustive clearness is such as with its numerous details to confuse our apprehension of what is in itself perfectly clear" (1885:350f.). We find in it technical terms, repeated formulae, and a "great poverty of language" (1885:386f., 332f.). All of this confirms, in Wellhausen's opinion, the conclusion reached on other grounds that this Priestly Writing can be dated only in the postexilic period. If it had been authored much earlier, e.g. before JE, it would have had an influence on the subsequent history of language But we find, rather, that the style and vocabulary of the Priestly Writing bear similarities only with other postexilic pieces such as late elements inserted into the Deuteronomistic History, Ezekiel, the postexilic prophets, Psalms, Qohelet, and Chronicles. The language of JE, on the other hand, shares more in common with the earlier historical narratives, Amos, Isaiah, and Micah (1885:386). In it one observes a naturalness, a closeness to life, and poetic color. In all such cases this linguistic evidence confirms well, according to Wellhausen, the postulated intention and point of view of the literature in question.

8. *Literature and Values*

It is readily acknowledged today that literature incorporates or gives expression to values of different types—aesthetic, moral, religious, social, and more (see, for example, R. Wellek and A. Warren: passim). This is true for the Hebrew Bible no less so than for any other type of literature. Wellhausen saw this clearly and did not hesitate to side with whatever he found there to be in conformity to his own tastes or viewpoints. Even the most casual reader of the *Prolegomena* cannot help but be struck by the frankness with which Wellhausen passed judgment on the materials. A number of examples may aid us in distinguishing both some of these diverse values represented in the Bible and also Wellhausen's opinion on them.

In very general terms, Wellhausen differentiated early Israel from the postexilic times in this regard: the ancient Israelites acted according to "the uncommon freshness of their impulses" with the divine power imbuing them as individuals, whereas after the exile the outward norms and the established institutions overwhelmed the vitality of the individuals (1885:412). In his own personal character Wellhausen exhibited simplicity, independence, and warmth, and he quite predictably was drawn to the early Israelites and repelled by the postexilic developments (see E. Schwartz; H. F. Hahn). For the ancient period he scarcely went further than to criticize it for its "naïveté" in certain religious practices and viewpoints (e.g., 1885:61f.). The color, vibrancy, directness, passion, earthiness, imagination were all much more in its favor, making JE, the early historical narratives, and the early prophets all the more interesting to him. In contrast, the later literature, especially the Priestly and the Chronicler, drew his constant fire. The Priestly Writing could contain certain "refinements" vis-à-vis its ancient predecessors (1885:67f.), but in its basic advocacy of the "Mosaic theocracy" it amounts to "an immense retrogression" (1885:422). Wellhausen's judgments were the harshest when the subject was the ways in which the later writers appropriate the earlier source materials, even though he rightly recognized that the manner of apprehension is not done out of malice but because of the spirit of each new age (1885:171). As the historical narratives are being handed down, Wellhausen noted, frequently "the new forces have not caused the old root to send forth a new stock, or even so much as a complete branch; they have only nourished parasitic growths" (1885:228). The Deuteronomistic revision can be so alien to its sources that it "does violence to them" (1885:280). Most disturbing of all for Wellhausen was the Chronicler's work: "a very transparent mutilation of the original narrative" about David (1885:173); "its perversion of 2 Kings xii" (1885:200); concerning the end of the kingdom of Judah, "inventions of the most circumstantial kind have arisen out of this plan of writing history, as it is euphemistically called" (1885:207); "the free flight of the Chronicler's law-crazed fancy" (1885:195); the "evil propensity" of the "audacious history-makers" (1885:161). At the very base of Wellhausen's opinion about such "distortions" of past history was his own anti-institutional posture, which turned him against the postexilic intentions—as he identified them—and drew him to the free spirit which he saw at play in the early period. Nowhere did he seem to recognize that the very life and survival of the postexilic community may well have been due to precisely those values it was expressing in its literature.

Throughout his interpretation of the biblical literature Wellhausen's keen, discerning, creative mind advanced critical understandings to a degree scarcely to be matched. This is perhaps so not only because of his analytical skill. It is due also to the fact that he found it impossible to take a dispassionate approach to it. He addressed this ancient document with all the acumen and personal engagement which the text itself deserves. Any interpreter who wishes to differ with him must do no less.

NOTES

/1/   In his first edition (1878a.4) Wellhausen attributed the hypothesis to Graf (1866), George (1835), and Vatke (1835), but in the second edition he credited Reuss with being the originator of it in 1833, although the latter's work was not published until 1879. Wellhausen cited Reuss's twelve theses in 1883.4f (also 1885·4)

/2/   Wellhausen has been and still is commonly charged with presupposing a Hegelian view of history, supposedly mediated to him by Vatke For a sound refutation of this notion, see L. Perlitt

/3/   Wellhausen did not refer frequently to other scholarly publications, especially not in his *Prolegomena* He certainly evinced no compulsion—often evident in more recent academic studies—to fill his pages with needless lists of secondary sources The object of his examinations was antiquity, and he tended to cite other critical scholarship only at those points where it proved instructive in his understanding of the ancient phenomena or where he wanted to distinguish his position from other views. There is every indication, however, that he was well versed in the academic literature of his time, although more so for what was published in Germany than elsewhere. For a brief overview of the history of Old Testament scholarship, see his 1878b 644–56

/4/   For a more detailed discussion of the rise of traditio-historical research and Wellhausen's place in it, see D. A Knight 39–68.

WORKS CONSULTED

Boschwitz, Friedemann
1968 *Julius Wellhausen. Motive und Mass-Stabe seiner Geschichtsschreibung.* Darmstadt: Wissenschaftliche Buchgesellschaft. (Reprint of his 1938 Marburg dissertation.)

Frei, Hans W.
1974 *The Eclipse of Biblical Narrative: A Study in Eighteenth and Nineteenth Century Hermeneutics.* New Haven/London. Yale University.

George, Johann Friedrich Leopold
1835 *Die älteren judischen Feste, mit einer Kritik der Gesetzgebung des Pentateuch.* Berlin: E. H. Schroeder.

Graf, Karl Heinrich
1866 *Die geschichtlichen Bucher des Alten Testaments. Zwei historisch-kritische Untersuchungen.* Leipzig: T. O. Weigel.

Gunkel, Hermann
1895 *Schöpfung und Chaos in Urzeit und Endzeit: Eine religionsgeschichtliche Untersuchung uber Gen 1 und Ap Joh 12.* Gottingen. Vandenhoeck & Ruprecht.

Hahn, Herbert F.
1959 "Wellhausen's Interpretation of Israel's Religious History. A Reappraisal of his Ruling Ideas." Pp. 299–308 in *Essays on Jewish Life and Thought: Presented in Honor of Salo Wittmayer Baron.* Ed. Joseph L. Blau, et al. New York: Columbia University.

Hoffman, Horst
1967 *Julius Wellhausen: Die Frage des absoluten Mass-Stabes seiner Geschichtsschreibung.* Diss. theol. Marburg: Erich Mauersberger.

Hupfeld, Hermann
1853 *Die Quellen der Genesis und die Art ihrer Zusammensetzung.* Berlin

Knight, Douglas A.
1975 *Rediscovering the Traditions of Israel.* Revised ed. SBLDS 9. Missoula: Scholars Press

Kraus, Hans-Joachim
1969 *Geschichte der historisch-kritischen Erforschung des Alten Testaments.* 2d ed. Neukirchen-Vluyn. Neukirchener Verlag.

Kuenen, Abraham
1861–65 *Historisch-kritisch onderzoek naar het ontstaan en de verzameling van de boeken des Ouden Verbonds.* 3 parts. Leiden. (English translation in 1886.)

Patte, Daniel
1976 *What is Structural Exegesis?* Guides to Biblical Scholarship. Philadelphia. Fortress

Perlitt, Lothar
1965 *Vatke und Wellhausen: Geschichtsphilosophische Voraussetzungen und historiographische Motive für die Darstellung der Religion und Geschichte Israels durch Wilhelm Vatke und Julius Wellhausen.* BZAW 94. Berlin: Alfred Topelmann

Polzin, Robert M.
1977 *Biblical Structuralism: Method and Subjectivity in the Study of Ancient Texts.* Semeia Supplements. Philadelphia: Fortress; Missoula. Scholars Press.

Reuss, Eduard
1879 *L'histoire sainte et la loi (Pentateuque et Joshue).* 2 vols Paris: Sandoz et Fischbacher

Scholder, Klaus
1966 *Ursprunge und Probleme der Bibelkritik im 17. Jahrhundert· Ein Beitrag zur Entstehung der historisch-kritischen Theologie* Forschungen zur Geschichte und Lehre des Protestantismus, X/33 Munich. Chr. Kaiser.

Schwartz, Eduard
1919 *Julius Wellhausen.* Berlin· Weidmann. = Pp 326–61 in *Gesammelte Schriften,* vol. 1 2d ed Berlin. de Gruyter, 1963.

Vatke, Wilhelm
1835 *Die biblische Theologie wissenschaftlich dargestellt.* I. *Die Religion des Alten Testamentes nach den kanonischen Büchern entwickelt.* Berlin: G Bethge.

Wellek, René, and Austin Warren
1975 *Theory of Literature.* 3d ed. New York/London: Harcourt Brace Jovanovich.

Wellhausen, Julius
1871 *Der Text der Bucher Samuelis untersucht* Gottingen. Vandenhoeck & Ruprecht.
1876–77 "Die Composition des Hexateuchs." *JDT* 21· 392–450, 531–602; 22. 407–79 = Pp. 1–208 in *Die Composition des Hexateuchs und der historischen Bücher des Alten Testaments.* 3d ed. Berlin· Georg Reimer, 1899
1878a *Geschichte Israels. In zwei Banden. Erster Band* Berlin: G. Reimer.
1878b *Einleitung in die Heilige Schrift, Erster Theil: Einleitung in das Alte Testament,* by Friedrich Bleek. 4th ed. by J Wellhausen. Berlin. G Reimer.
1883 *Prolegomena zur Geschichte Israels.* 2d ed. of *Geschichte Israels* (1878a). Berlin· G Reimer.
1885 *Prolegomena to the History of Israel.* Translated from the 1883 edition by J Sutherland Black and Allan Menzies. With Preface by W. Robertson Smith. Edinburgh· Adam & Charles Black. = *Prolegomena to the History of Ancient Israel.* New York: Meridian Books, 1957
1892 *Skizzen und Vorarbeiten,* vol. 5: *Die kleinen Propheten ubersetzt, mit Noten.* Berlin: Georg Reimer
1895 *The Book of Psalms.* The Sacred Books of the Old Testament: A Critical Edition of the Hebrew Text, Printed in Colors, with Notes· Part 14. Leipzig: Hinrichs, Baltimore: The Johns Hopkins Press, London· David Nutt
1898 *The Book of Psalms* The Sacred Books of the Old and New Testaments A New English Translation with Explanatory Notes and Pictorial Illustrations. Part 14. London· James Clarke, New York: Dodd, Mead, and Co.

1899 "Zur apokalyptischen Literatur." Pp. 215–49 in his *Skizzen und Vorarbeiten*, vol 6 Berlin. Georg Reimer
1914 *Israelitische und judische Geschichte*. 7th ed Berlin. Georg Reimer

Witter, Henning Bernhard
1711 *Jura Israelitarum in Palaestinam*. Hildesiae.

WELLHAUSEN AS A HISTORIAN OF ISRAEL

John H. Hayes
Emory University

ABSTRACT

Wellhausen's historical work was founded on a careful analysis of the literary sources, on the basis of which he drew explicit implications for reconstructing the course of Israel's history. The evidence from the history of religious ordinances proved especially important for this task Similarly, special apologetic interests and ideological purposes in certain of the sources were weighed for their historical worth, whether for the period which they were describing or the period in which they were produced. For Wellhausen the history of Israel fell into three stages, each quite distinct from the other in mood, religious structures, and literary expressions. preexilic, Deuteronomic, and postexilic. His influence in method and historical reconstruction has been considerable down to the present, even if his work is to be criticized in several respects.

I. THE LAW AND THE QUEST

Three developments which were to have enormous consequences for the reconstruction of ancient Israelite history were reaching an advanced stage at the time Wellhausen entered the arena of Old Testament studies. These were (a) the dating of the various strata of the Pentateuchal traditions, (b) the isolation and exposition of the theological tendencies and perspectives not only of the Pentateuchal traditions but also those of the historical books, and (c) the desire to produce a history of Israel that was neither theological nor apologetical in character.

(a) The dating of Deuteronomy to the time of Josiah and the dating of the Priestly document or the levitical tradition of the Pentateuch to the post-Deuteronomic period were the most radical results of nineteenth-century Pentateuchal studies. Such a late dating for these sources carried with it the general assumption of the sources' historical unreliability. These conclusions were first expounded by Wilhelm Martin Leberecht de Wette in 1805, Eduard Reuss in 1833, Wilhelm Vatke in 1835, Johann Friedrich Leopold George in 1835, Karl Heinrich Graf in 1866, Abraham Kuenen in 1869–70, and John William Colenso in 1862–65, among others.

As early as 1833, Reuss, Graf's teacher at Strasbourg, had formulated twelve theses which already provided the basic arguments for the lateness of the priestly laws and which pointed to the implications of such a late date for writing the history of Israel/1/. His theses were as follows:

(1) The historical element in the Pentateuch can and must be examined apart from and not be confused with the legal element. (2) Both were able to exist without written documentary form. The mention, in some ancient writings, of certain patriarchal or Mosaic traditions does not prove the existence of the Pentateuch, and a nation can have customary law without a written code. (3) The national traditions of the Israelites appear earlier than the laws of the Pentateuch, and the writing down of the former is prior to that of the latter. (4) The principal interest of the historian should focus on the date of the laws because this is the area in which there is the best chance of arriving at certain results. Consequently, it is necessary to proceed through an interrogation of the evidence. (5) The narrated history, in the books of Judges and Samuel, and partially that which comprises the books of Kings, is in contradiction with the dictates of Mosaic law; thus the latter was unknown at the time of the composition of these books, a very strong argument that they did not exist at the time these books describe. (6) The prophets of the 8th and 7th centuries did not know anything of the Mosaic code. (7) Jeremiah is the first prophet who knew of the written law, and his quotations agree with Deuteronomy (8) Deuteronomy (4:45-28:68) is the book which the priests pretended to have found in the temple at the time of King Josiah. This code is the oldest part of the edited legislation now comprising the Pentateuch. (9) Israelite history, insofar as it is a question of national development determined by the written law, may be divided into two periods, before and after Josiah (10) Ezekiel is older than the composition of the ritual code and the law which definitely organized the hierocracy. (11) The book of Joshua is not, as far as can be known, the most recent part of the entire work. (12) The author of the Pentateuch is to be clearly distinguished from the ancient prophet Moses.

The consequences of such perspectives were first developed in the area of the religion of ancient Israel by Kuenen and Bernhard Duhm. The task of delineating the consequences for the reconstruction of ancient Israelite history was left to Wellhausen.

(b) The recognition of the theological orientation and tendencies within the Pentateuchal sources and historical books meant, of course, that these materials could be used in reconstructing Israelite history only after a proper assessment of how their orientation and tendencies had influenced their presentation of the course of events. Gradually, it was becoming clear that the historical materials in the Hebrew Bible were as much products as portrayals of historical developments. The history of Israel and its religious institutions was slowly recognized as being as determinative for the history of the documents as the documents were depictive of the history of Israel. De Wette's critical essays on the credibility of the books of Chronicles and the Mosaic history (1806-7) were important harbingers of future developments in pre-Wellhausenian times.

(c) The nineteenth has been designated as the century of historical inquiry. The remarkable advances made in recovering and reconstructing the past—especially Greek and Roman history—could not but eventually influence the reconstruction of Israelite history. Writing as late as 1863, A. P. Stanley noted the following:

> The Jewish History has suffered from causes similar to those which still, within our own memory, obscured the history of Greece and of Rome Till within the present century, the characters and institutions of those two great countries were so veiled from view in the conventional haze with which the enchantment of distance had invested them, that when the more graphic and critical historians of our time broke through this reserve, a kind of shock was felt through all the educated classes of the country The same change was in a still higher degree needed with regard to the history of the Jews. Its sacred character had deepened the difficulty already occasioned by its extreme antiquity (viii–ix)

On 10 February 1835, the classicist Thomas Arnold wrote the diplomat-theologian Christian Carl Josias von Bunsen that "what [Friedrich August] Wolf and [Barthold Georg] Niebuhr have done for Greece and Rome seems sadly wanted for Judaea" (in Stanley, 1844:355). The application of historiographic rigor to the history of Israel was not as easily done as its counterpart in classical study. The older histories of Humphrey Prideaux (1717–18; the Schürer of the eighteenth century) and Samuel Shuckford (1728–30) with their strong apologetic flavor and anti-deistic polemic continued to be the standard English works into the nineteenth century. When Henry Hart Milman, in 1829, published his moderately critical *History of the Jews*, it met with widespread opposition. In his preface to the second edition (1830), he sought to defend his wish "to avoid the tone of a theological treatise" in his presentation of the history and his tendency to describe Jewish history in rather naturalistic terms as a gradual process of development. He wrote:

> Nothing is more curious, or more calculated to confirm the veracity of the Old Testament history, than the remarkable picture which it presents of the gradual development of human society: the ancestors of the Jews, and the Jews themselves, pass through every stage of comparative civilization. The Almighty Ruler of the world, who had chosen them as conservators of the knowledge of his Unity and Providence, and of his slowly brightening promises of Redemption, perpetually interferes, so as to keep alive the remembrance of these great truths, the object of their selection from mankind; and which nothing less, it should seem could have preserved through so many ages. In other respects the chosen people appear to have been left to themselves to pass through the ordinary stages of the social state, and to that social state their habits, opinions, and even their religious notions, were in some degree accommodated. (1829/1834·v–vi)

When the history of Israel written by Heinrich Georg August Ewald began to appear in 1843, many felt that he had finally done for Israel what Wolf and Niebuhr had done for Greece and Rome. However, Ewald's verbose and passionate effort, which "closed rather than opened an epoch" (J. W. Thompson: 578), was overly dominated by a theological program, viz., to demonstrate that the aim of Israelite history was the attainment of Perfect Religion.

> The beginning and end of the history of this people turn on this one high aim; and the manifold changes, and even confusions and perversities, which manifest themselves in the long course of the threads of its history, always ultimately tend to the solution of this great problem, which the human mind was to work out here. The aim was lofty enough to concentrate the highest efforts of a whole people for more than a thousand years, and to be reached at length as the prize of the noblest struggles. And as, however the mode of the pursuit might vary, it was this single object that was always pursued, till finally attained only with the political death of the nation, there is hardly any history of equal compass that possesses, in all its phases and variations, so much intrinsic unity, and is so closely bound to a single thought pertinaciously held, but always developing itself to higher purity. The history of this ancient people is in reality the history of the growth of true religion, rising through all stages to perfection; pressing on through all conflicts to the highest victory, and finally revealing itself in full glory and power, in order to spread irresistibly from this centre, never again to be lost, but to become the eternal possession and blessing of all nations (1869:4–5)

Few works have received more back-handed praise than Ewald's history: ". . . the present work, even in its introductory portions, claims to be a History of Israel; although no such lucid and connected narrative will be found in it as is generally associated with that term. . . . We read Ewald, page after page, and seem to come across no clear and distinct event . . ." (Russell Martineau, in his "Preface" to Ewald, 1869:viii–ix). "I must confess that I read Ewald ever with increasing wonder at his unparalleled ingenuity, his surpassing learning, but usually with decreasing conviction. I should like an Ewald to criticise Ewald" (Milman, 1829/1874:1.30).

The question of "the place in history of the 'law of Moses'" was a major concern for both Milman and Ewald just as it was the starting point for Wellhausen in the *Prolegomena*. For both, the question of whether the laws of the Pentateuch and the formation of the Israelites into a theocratic community were to be assigned to the wilderness or pre-settlement period had to receive an affirmative response. One can see Milman is struggling with this issue in the following passage:

> . . the Israelites wind along the defiles of this elevated region, till at length they come to the foot of the loftiest peak in the whole ridge, that of Sinai Here after the most solemn preparations, and under the most terrific circumstances, the great lawgiver of the Jews delivered that singular constitution to his people, which presupposed their possession of a rich and fertile territory in which as yet they had not occupied an acre, but had hitherto been wandering in an opposite direction, and not even approached its borders The laws of a settled and civilized community were enacted among a wandering and homeless horde who were traversing the wilderness, and more likely, under their existing circumstances, to sink below the pastoral life of their forefathers, than advance to the rank of an industrious agricultural community Yet, at this time, judging solely from its internal evidence, the law must have been enacted. Who but Moses ever possessed such authority as to enforce submission to statutes so severe and uncompromising? yet, as Moses incontestibly died before the conquest of Canaan, his legislature must have taken place in the desert To what other period can the Hebrew constitution be assigned? To that of the judges? a time of anarchy, warfare, or servitude! To that of the kings? when the republic had undergone a total change! To any time after Jerusalem became the metropolis? when the holy city, the pride and glory

of the nation, is not even alluded to in the whole law! After the building of the temple? when it is equally silent as to any settled or durable edifice! After the separation of the kingdoms? when the close bond of brotherhood had given place to implacable hostility! Under Hilkiah? under Ezra? when a great number of the statutes had become a dead letter! The law depended on a strict and equitable partition of the land At a later period it could not have been put into practice without the forcible resumption of every individual property by the state; the difficulty, or rather impossiblity, of such a measure, may be estimated by any reader who is not entirely unacquainted with the history of the ancient republics. In other respects the law breathes the air of the desert. Enactments intended for a people with settled habitations, and dwelling in walled cities, are mingled up with temporary regulations, only suited to the Bedouin encampment of a nomad tribe. There can be no doubt that the statute book of Moses, with all his particular enactments, still exists, and that it recites them in the same order, if it may be called order, in which they were promulgated (1829/1834:78-79)

In later editions of his history, in which he shows thorough familiarity with Old Testament scholarship, Milman refused to budge from his position. As is well known, Ewald, who designated the main document of the Pentateuch (P) "The Book of Origins," argued that the theocratic community was founded in the wilderness period and that the literary deposit of the theocracy was composed in the tenth century BCE.

The reconstructed history of Israel in the works of Milman and Ewald, given the latter's reassignment of Deuteronomy to the seventh century and both's acceptance of the general non-historicity of Genesis 1–11, differed from the general flow of the Old Testament presentation itself only in degree and not in kind. Both, however, reflect the early nineteenth-century drive toward a quest for the historical Israel which would tell "what really happened" (Ewald, 1869:13) rather than merely retell the Old Testament narrative with academic *midrash*.

II. WELLHAUSEN AND LITERARY CRITICISM

All three of the developments sketched above came to a focus in the work of Wellhausen. In the opening sentences of the *Geschichte Israels*, he stated the issue rather bluntly to demonstrate that literary conclusions about the Old Testament, especially the Pentateuch, have far-reaching consequences for understanding Israelite history. The literary history of the Pentateuch could not be rewritten (or written) without a simultaneous rewriting of the history of Israel. He stated:

Das vorliegende Buch unterscheidet sich von seinesgleichen dadurch, dass die Kritik der Quellen darin einen ebenso breiten Raum einnimmt als die Darstellung der Geschichte Warum es so angelegt worden, wird es selber ausweisen; hier soll nur gesagt werden, um was es sich in diesem ersten, kritischen Teile handelt. Die Frage ist, ob das mosaische Gesetz der Ausgangspunkt sei für die Geschichte des alten Israel oder fur die Geschichte des Judentums, d. h der Sekte, welche das von Assyrern und Chaldaern vernichtete Volk uberlebte. (1878a.1)

Elsewhere, while describing the course of Pentateuchal criticism prior to the advent of "two Hegelian writers" (Vatke and George), Wellhausen made the same point in different terms:

> Critical analysis made steady progress, but the work of synthesis did not hold even pace with it; this part of the problem was treated rather slightly, and merely by the way. Indeed the true scope of the problem was not realized; it was not seen that most important historical questions were involved as well as questions merely literary, and that to assign the true order of the different strata of the Pentateuch was equivalent to a reconstruction of the history of Israel. (1885b:508)

His main criticism of Graf focused on the same issue:

> He (Graf) brought forward his arguments somewhat unconnectedly, not seeking to change the general view which prevailed of the history of Israel For this reason he made no impression on the majority of those who study these subjects; they did not see into the root of the matter, they could still regard the system as unshaken, and the numerous attacks on details of it as unimportant. (1885a:368)

For Wellhausen, literary criticism and historical reconstruction went hand in hand. The significance and impact of the former necessitated the latter, and for him the former was in service to and prerequisite to the latter. His Old Testament work moved primarily in three stages: from literary analysis, to the consequences of such analysis, to historical reconstruction demanded by the consequences of the literary analysis. His dissertation was a study in Chronicles (1870). This was followed by an investigation of the text of Samuel (1871), a study of the composition of the Hexateuch (1876a–77), and an analysis of the books of Judges, Ruth, Samuel, and Kings (1878b). His works of literary and textual analysis were never pedantic. He was primarily interested in the broader questions of source analysis and theological tendency rather than minute matters of detail. He was basically interested in what he called "the literary process."

> Criticism has not done its work when it has completed the mechanical distribution [of the sources]; it must aim further at bringing the different writings when thus arranged into relation with each other, must seek to render them intelligible as phases of a living process, and thus to make it possible to trace a graduated development of the tradition. (1885a:295)

Thus he was content to speak (following Theodor Nöldeke) of three main strata in the Pentateuch: Deuteronomy, the Jehovist (the Yahwist with extracts from the Elohist), and the Priestly Code/2/. Such a matter as the dating of the Jehovist was discussed in rather general terms: "the period of the kings and prophets which preceded the dissolution of the two Israelite kingdoms by the Assyrians" (1885b:508).

III. THE *PROLEGOMENA*

The *Prolegomena* provides not only a presentation of the results of Wellhausen's literary analyses of the Hexateuch and the historical books but also his description of the consequences of such analyses for the reconstruction of the history of Israel. The first part of this book is called "History of the Ordinances of Worship." His program in this section can be seen in his criticism of the earlier work of Friedrich Bleek and Ewald who had failed to undertake what Wellhausen pursued:

> [Bleek] never thought of instituting an exact comparison between them [the priestly laws] and the Deuteronomic law, still less of examining their relation to the historical and prophetical books   [Ewald] too neglected the task of a careful comparison between the different strata of the Pentateuchal legislation and the equally necessary task of determining how the several laws agreed with or differed from such definite data of the history of religion as could be collected from the historical and prophetical books. He had therefore no fixed measure to apply to the criticism of the laws. . . . (1885b.508)

Wellhausen described his own method of approaching the issue of the history of religious ordinances in the following way:

> After laboriously collecting the data offered by the historical and prophetical books, we constructed a sketch of the Israelite history of worship, we then compared the Pentateuch with this sketch, and recognised that one element of the Pentateuch bore a definite relation to this phase of the history of worship, and another element of the Pentateuch to that phase of it. (1885a 367)

The primary element of the Pentateuch which had not been associated with its proper phase of history and the historical consequences drawn therefrom was, according to Wellhausen, the Priestly Code.

> There are in the Pentateuch three strata of law and three strata of tradition, and the problem is to place them in their true historical order So far as the Jehovist and Deuteronomy are concerned, the problem has found a solution which may be said to be accepted universally, and all that remains is to apply to the Priestly Code also the procedure by which the succession and the date of these two works has been determined—that procedure consisting in the comparison of them with the ascertained facts of Israelite history. (1885a.366)

The five chapters in the first section, on the place of worship, sacrifice, the sacred feasts, the priests and levites, and the endowment of the clergy, sought to demonstrate that the order of the documents was Jehovist, Deuteronomy, and Priestly Code and that the latter was post-Deuteronomic and thus the foundation of life in postexilic Judaism, not in preexilic Israel. For Wellhausen, the issue of the centralization of worship was the pivotal point in the history of the ordinances of worship.

> The turning-point in the history of worship in Israel is the centralization of the cultus in Jerusalem by Josiah (2 Kings xxii , xxiii.) (1885b.509)

> I differ from Graf chiefly in this, that I always go back to the centralisation of the cultus, and deduce from it the particular divergences My whole position is contained in my first chapter ["The Place of Worship"]. there I have placed in a clear light that which is of such importance for Israelite history, namely, the part taken

> by the prophetical party in the great metamorphosis of the worship, which by no means came about of itself. Again I attach much more weight than Graf did to the change of ruling ideas which runs parallel with the change in the institutions and usages of worship. . . . Almost more important to me than the phenomena themselves, are the presuppositions which lie behind them. (1885a:368)

With methodological regularity, Wellhausen outlines the nature of the religious ordinances as these are reflected in the historical and prophetical books and compares these with the various legal strata to demonstrate how these legal strata reflect the conditions of three historical epochs: the period before Josiah (Jehovist), the transition period introduced by Josiah's reform (Deuteronomy), and the period after the exile (Priestly Code). The accompanying chart summarizes how Wellhausen viewed the development in five main areas of the history of the ordinances of worship.

In the second main section of the *Prolegomena*, "History of Tradition," Wellhausen set out to demonstrate that "the history of the tradition leads us to the same conclusion as the history of the cultus" (1885a:294). He discusses, first of all, Chronicles, then Judges, Samuel, and Kings, and finally the narrative of the Hexateuch. Chronicles (with Ezra–Nehemiah), whose composition Wellhausen placed in the early Hellenistic period (1885a:171), embodies a history of the cultus which is very similar to that found in the Priestly Code. The unreliability of the historical portrait contained in Chronicles had to be demonstrated as a prerequisite for dating the priestly legislation in the post-Deuteronomic period. In his chapter on Chronicles, Wellhausen supported this position which had first been systematically advocated by de Wette (1806). Wellhausen argued for three basic conclusions about Chronicles: (1) The material and emphases found in Chronicles but not in the other canonical books are not the result of Chronicles' having possessed preexilic traditions, reliable nonbiblical sources, or a better text of Samuel and Kings. (2) Chronicles is the product of a particular historical epoch and the result of rewriting history viewed through the lens of the priestly tradition.

> When the narrative of Chronicles runs parallel with the older historical books of the canon, it makes no real additions, but the tradition is merely differently coloured, under the influence of contemporary motives. In the picture it gives the writer's own present is reflected, not antiquity But neither is the case very different with the genealogical lists prefixed by way of introduction in I Chron. i –ix.; they also are in the main valid only for the period at which they were drawn up—whether for its actual condition or for its conceptions of the past. (1885a:211)

> The alterations and additions of Chronicles are all traceable to the same fountainhead—the Judaising of the past, in which otherwise the people of that day would have been unable to recognise their ideal. (1885a:223)

> Thus whether one says Chronicles or *Midrash* of the Book of Kings is on the whole a matter of perfect indifference; they are children of the same mother, and indistinguishable in spirit and language, while on the other hand the portions which have been retained verbatim from the canonical Book of Kings at once betray themselves in both respects. (1885a:227)

	Place of Worship	Sacrifice	Sacred Feasts	Priests and Levites	Endowment of the Clergy
Jehovist	Multiplicity of altars, shrines, high places, and sacred sites	Assumed to be pre-Mosaic; spontaneous and related to ordinary life	Main form of worship; agricultural thanksgiving festivals; times of joyous gladness; three in number	No limitation of cultus to special class or family	Gifts presented to Jehovah; priestly shares and dues not regulated
Deuteronomy	Single sanctuary commanded; other centers to be destroyed	Very similar to Jehovist; some regulation in light of centralization	Very similar to Jehovist; some historical dressing	Priests are organized class; all Levites have priestly functions	Some regulations and stipulation of priestly dues
Priestly Code	Limitation of worship to one sanctuary presupposed and assumed from the Mosaic period	Mosaic in origin; regulated by statute; sin and propitiation stressed	Fixed dates; denaturalization; additional feast days	Sharp division between priests and Levites; fully developed hierocracy under high-priest	Sacred dues paid to priests, special possessions assigned to priests, increased share of sacrifices

(3) Chronicles, therefore, cannot be used in reconstructing the history of Israel in preexilic times.

> With what show of justice can the Chronicler, after his statements have over and over again been shown to be incredible, be held at discretion to pass for an unimpeachable narrator? In those cases at least where its connection with his "plan" is obvious, one ought surely to exercise some scepticism in regard to his testimony; but it ought at the same time to be considered that such connections may occur much oftener than is discernible by us, or at least by the less sharp-sighted of us It is indeed possible that occasionally a grain of good corn may occur among the chaff, but to be conscientious one must neglect this possiblity of exceptions, and give due honour to the probability of the rule. For it is only too easy to deceive oneself in thinking that one has come upon some sound particular in a tainted whole. (1885a: 224)

If the tradition in Chronicles has been recast in the form of *midrash* ("like ivy it overspreads the dead trunk with extraneous life, blending old and new in a strange combination" [1885a:227]), the situation is different in the case of Judges, Samuel, and Kings.

> ... in Judges, Samuel, and Kings even, we are not presented with tradition purely in its original condition; already it is overgrown with later accretions. Alongside of an older narrative a new one has sprung up, formerly independent, and intelligible in itself, though in many instances of course adapting itself to the former. More frequently the new forces have not caused the old root to send forth a new stock, or even so much as a complete branch; they have only nourished parasitic growths; the earlier narrative has become clothed with minor and dependent additions. To vary the metaphor, the whole area of tradition has finally been uniformly covered with an alluvial deposit by which the configuration of the surface has been determined. It is with this last that we have to deal in the first instance; to ascertain its character, to find out what the active forces were by which it was produced Only afterwards are we in a position to attempt to discern in the earlier underlying formation the changing spirit of each successive period. (1885a·228)

This "alluvial deposit" or the "uniform in which [the original contents of the tradition] is clothed" (1885a:231) is the Deuteronomistic revision. "This means no more than that it came into existence under the influence of Deuteronomy, which pervaded the whole century of the exile" (1885a:280). This Deuteronomistic (distinguishable from Deuteronomic) overlay, which preserved "only so much of the old tradition . . . as those of a later age held to be of religious value" (1885a:281), is characterized by a strong religious perspective, the idea of a central place of worship, a Judean point of view, and a chronological schematization. This Deuteronomistic redaction of the older material had also a very specific purpose.

> The writer looks back on the time of the kings as a period past and closed, on which judgment has already been declared. Even at the consecration of the temple the thought of its destruction is not to be restrained; and throughout the book the ruin of the nation and its two kingdoms is present in the writer's mind. This is the light in which the work is to be read, it shows why the catastrophe was unavoidable. It was so because of the unfaithfulness to Jehovah, because of the utterly perverted

tendency obstinately followed by the people in spite of the Torah of Jehovah and His prophets. The narrative becomes, as it were, a great confession of sins of the exiled nation looking back on its history. (1885a:278)

The Deuteronomistic overlay is found from Judges, where it occurs with a monotonous beat reminding one of "Hegelian philosophy" in the scheme of "rebellion, affliction, conversion, peace; rebellion, affliction, conversion, peace" (1885a:231), through the books of Samuel and Kings, where it appears most prominently in speeches and "at every important epoch in sermon-like discourses" (1885a:247,274).

Within the books, especially Judges, Wellhausen argued that between the original form of the tradition and the Deuteronomistic redaction an earlier effort at editorial redaction can be seen. The historian in him sought to move behind the Deuteronomistic redaction (and post-Deuteronomistic additions and retouching), through the earlier supplementation and additions, to the original form of the traditions. What emerged in the book of Judges was a number of individual narratives without the scheme of historical continuity or succession and without the peculiar theocratic emphasis.

In these [original narratives] Israel is a people just like other people, nor is even his relationship to Jehovah otherwise conceived of than is for example that of Moab to Chemosh (chap xi 24) (1885a:235)

The period of the Judges presents itself to us as a confused chaos, out of which order and coherence are gradually evolved under the pressure of external circumstances, but perfectly naturally and without the faintest reminiscence of a sacred unifying constitution that had formerly existed (1885a.5)

In the books of Samuel, Wellhausen isolates the double accounts of Saul's rise to kingship (1 Samuel 7; 8; 10:17ff.; 12 and 9:1-10:16; 11), the narrative of David's rise to power (1 Sam 14:52-2 Sam 8:18) which now contains some interruptions and alterations, and the narrative of "occurrences at the court of Jerusalem" and how "Solomon reached the throne" (2 Samuel 9-2 Kings 2, minus 2 Samuel 21-24). The latter "affords us a glance into the very heart of events, showing us the natural occasions and human motives which gave rise to the different actions" (1885a:262).

According to Wellhausen, in Kings one finds that the redaction "is essentially uniform with that of the two historical books which precede it" (1885a:277)—that is, its selection of materials, depiction of events, and evaluations are based on the perspectives of Deuteronomy and show no acquaintance with the Priestly Code. The main core of the original tradition of Kings is a secondary compilation made from annalistic records and provides evidence for reconstructing the history of Israel.

The final chapter in section two is an analysis of the narrative of the Hexateuch. Here he comments on the primitive world history, the history of the patriarchs, and the Mosaic history in the two strata of the Hexateuch and seeks to demonstrate their parallel structure and the priority of the Jehovist to the Priestly Code. Genesis 1–11 are treated as mythical. In his discussion of the patriarchal materials, Wellhausen reaches a number of conclusions which are later reflected in his historical reconstructions. (1) The patriarchs are primarily ideal prototypes of the true Israelite—peace-loving shepherds. (2) The patriarchal stories do not provide us with the history of individuals but at best are representative of ethnological groups. (3) Of the partriarchal traditions, those of Abraham are the most enigmatic.

> Abraham alone is certainly not the name of a people like Isaac and Lot. he is somewhat difficult to interpret. That is not to say that in such a connection as this we may regard him as a historical person; he might with more likelihood be regarded as a free creation of unconscious art. He is perhaps the youngest figure in the company, and it was probably at a comparatively late period that he was put before his son Isaac. (1885a:320)

(4) The patriarchal traditions are more informative of the age in which they developed than of the age they purport to describe.

> The materials here are not mythical but national, and therefore more transparent, and in a certain sense more historical. It is true, we attain to no historical knowledge of the patriarchs, but only of the time when the stories about them arose in the Israelite people; this later age is here unconsciously projected, in its inner and outward features, into hoar antiquity, and is reflected there like a glorified mirage. (1885a:318–19)

(5) In the stage of oral tradition, the narratives existed as separate and independent stories which could be understood in their individuality apart from the rest, were associated with and reflective of particular locales (many were cultus-myths), and were still plastic and living in the ninth and eighth centuries. The weaving together of the detached narratives with chronological and other connections was the work of the poetical or literary artist when being collected and reduced to writing.

In discussing the Mosaic tradition, Wellhausen again stresses the differences in perspective between the Jehovistic and Priestly materials. In doing so, he points to a number of factors of consequence for the writing of Israelite history. (1) Sinai played no role in the earliest form of the tradition in the Jehovist.

> In the Jehovist, one form of the tradition may still be discerned, according to which the Israelites on crossing the Red Sea at once proceeded towards Kadesh, without making the detour to Sinai. We only get to Sinai in Exod. xix., but in Exod. xvii. we are already at Massah and Meribah, *i.e.*, on the ground of Kadesh . . The story of the manna and the quails occurs not only in Exod. xvi., but also in Num. xi.; and the rocky spring called forth by Moses at Massah and Meribah is both in Exod. xvii. and Num xx. In other words, the Israelites arrived at Kadesh, the original object of their wanderings, not after the digression to Sinai but immediately after the Exodus, and they spent there the forty years of their residence in the wilderness. Kadesh is also the original scene of the legislation [see Exod 15.25]. (1885a.342–43)

(2) The Jehovist was originally a pure history-book, and it was only at a

secondary stage that legal material was taken up into the history-book. (3) The original role of Moses is best seen in the earliest form of the Jehovist. (4) The "main stock" (*Grundschrift*) of the Priestly material (see note /2/) ended with the death of Moses and cannot be traced in the book of Joshua although extensive sections in the second half of Joshua belong to the Priestly Code, that is to the final edited form of the "main stock" or Book of the Four Covenants. (5) There are three different accounts of the conquest in the Bible, and Judges 1 is vastly nearer the facts.

> The priestly narrator represents all Canaan as reduced to a *tabula rasa*, and then makes the masterless and unpeopled land be divided by lot. The first lot falls to Judah, then come Manasseh and Ephraim, then Benjamin and Simeon, and lastly the five northerly tribes, Zebulon, Issachar, Asher, Naphtali, Dan. "These are the inheritances which Eleazar the priest and Joshua the son of Nun and the heads of the tribes of Israel apportioned by lot at Shiloh before Jehovah at the door of the tabernacle " According to the Jehovist (Josh. xiv. 6) Judah and Joseph seem to have had their portions assigned to them while the Israelite headquarters were still at Gilgal—but not by lot—and to have gone forth from Gilgal to take possession of them A good deal later the rest of the land was divided by lot to the remaining tribes at Shiloh, or perhaps, in the original form of the narrative, at Shechem (Josh xviii. 2-10), Joshua casts the lots and makes the assignments alone, Eleazar is not associated with him. The absolute uniformity in the method of the division of the land to all the tribes is in some degree given up in this account; it is still more strongly contradicted by the important chapter, Judges i. Fragments of this chapter are found also in the book of Joshua, and there is no doubt that it belongs to the Jehovistic group of narratives, in common with which it speaks of the Angel of Jehovah It is in truth not a continuation of but a parallel to the book of Joshua, presupposing the conquest of the lands east of the Jordan, but not of western Canaan. (1885b.512–13)

The third and final section of the *Prolegomena* contains three chapters: "Conclusion of the Criticism of the Law," "The Oral and the Written Torah," and "The Theocracy as Idea and as Institution." In this part of the volume, Wellhausen defends the literary-critical approach, notes some differences between himself and other scholars, and discusses the relationship of Jehovist, Deuteronomy, Ezekiel, Law of Holiness, and Priestly Code. His most significant comments are found in the chapter on oral and written torah. Here he is concerned to demonstrate that, in spite of the fact that "the law of Moses" is the starting-point for the history of Judaism, "ancient Israel was certainly not without God-given bases for the ordering of human life; only they were not fixed in writing" (1885a:393). This "God-given bases" was not only the unwritten laws of custom but also the torah, the "special Torah of Jehovah, which not only sets up laws of action of universal validity, but shows man the way in special cases of difficulty, where he is at a loss" (1885a:394). This torah was the product of priestly teaching and instruction, including the giving of oracles, "but it continued to be an oral decision and direction. . . . There is no torah as a ready-made product, as a system existing independently of its originator and accessible to everyone: it becomes actual only in the various utterances, which naturally form by degrees the basis of a fixed tradition" (1885a:395). The prophets, in early Israel, were men of God who also gave torah or teaching: "the Torah of the priests was like a spring which runs always, that of the prophets like a spring which is intermittent, but when it does break forth, flows with all the greater force" (1885a:397).

> There is thus a close relation between priests and prophets, *i.e.*, seers; as with other peoples (1 Sam. vi. 2, 1 Kings xviii. 19, compare with 2 Kings x 19), so also with the Hebrews. In the earliest time it was not knowing the technique of worship, which was still very simple and undeveloped, but being a *man of God*, standing on an intimate footing with God, that made a man a priest, that is one who keeps up the communication with heaven for others; and the seer is better qualified than others for the office (1 Kings xviii. 30 seq.). There is no fixed distinction in early times between the two offices; Samuel is in 1 Sam. i.–iii. an aspirant to the priesthood; in ix x. he is regarded as a seer (1885a:396–97)

The writing down of the torah and its fixity as law developed as a process. The earliest deposit of such torah is found in the legal deposit (Exodus 19–24; 32–34) taken up into the Jehovist which was originally "a pure history-book" (1885a:345). With the promulgation of Deuteronomy (Deuteronomy 12–27), a radically new dimension is introduced.

> Deuteronomy persupposes earlier attempts of this kind, and borrows its materials largely from them, but on the other hand it is distinguished from them not only by its greater compass but also by its much higher claims. It is written with the distinct intention not to remain a private memorandum, but to obtain public authority as a *book*. The idea of making a definite formulated written Torah the law of the land, is the important point: it was a first attempt and succeeded at the outset beyond expectation. (1885a:402)

> After the solemn and far-reaching act by which Josiah introduced this law, the notion of covenant-making between Jehovah and Israel appears to have occupied the central position in religious thought: it prevails in Deuteronomy, in Jeremiah, Ezekiel, in Isaiah xl –lxvi , Lev. xvii.–xxvi , and most of all in the Book of the Four Covenants. (1885a:418–19)

Wellhausen saw the appearance of the law as the end of the old freedom, the creation of an objective authority, and the death of prophecy. Deuteronomy was primarily a program of reform which "took for granted the existence of the cultus, and only corrected it in certain general respects" (1885a:404). The later codes—Ezekiel, Holiness, and Priestly—were attempts at restoration.

> . . the temple was now destroyed and the worship interrupted, and the practice of past times had to be written down if it was not to be lost Thus it came about that in the exile the *conduct of worship* became the subject of the Torah, and in this process reformation was naturally aimed at as well as restoration. . . . Ezekiel was the first to take this step which the circumstances of the time indicated In the last part of his work he made the first attempt to record the ritual which had been customary in the temple of Jerusalem. Other priests attached themselves to him (Lev xvii.–xxvi), and thus there grew up in the exile from among the members of

this profession a kind of school of people who reduced to writing and to a system what they had formerly practised in the way of their calling After the temple was restored this theoretical zeal still continued to work, and the ritual when renewed was still further developed by the action and reaction on each other of theory and practice; the priests who had stayed in Babylon took as great a part, from a distance, in the sacred services, as their brothers at Jerusalem who had actually to conduct them The latter indeed lived in adverse circumstances and do not appear to have conformed with great strictness or accuracy to the observances which had been agreed upon. The last result of this labour of many years is the Priestly Code. It has indeed been said that we cannot ascribe the creation of such a work to an age which was bent on nothing but repristination Granted that this is a correct description of it, such an age is peculiarly fitted for an artificial systematising of given materials, and this is what the originality of the Priestly Code in substance amounts to.

The Priestly Code, worked into the Pentateuch as the standard legislative element in it, became the definite "Mosaic law." (1885a.404-5)

It was Ezra who, in 444 BCE, introduced and published the Pentateuch in its final form as the authoritative law and norm of life in written code. "What distinguishes Judaism from ancient Israel is *the written Torah*. The water which in old times rose from a spring, the Epigoni stored up in cisterns" (1885a:410).

The theocratic ideas and goals of postexilic Judaism—the community as a church which "was merely a spiritualised survival of the nation" (1885a:256)—represented a religion and cultus that were estranged from their own roots. The older impulses were now replaced with a new emphasis—"exactly according to prescription: at the right place, at the right time, by the right individuals, in the right way" (1885a:424).

in the Mosaic theocracy the cultus became a pedagogic instrument of discipline. It is estranged from the heart; its revival was due to old custom, it would never have blossomed again of itself It no longer has its roots in childlike impulse, it is a dead work, in spite of all the importance attached to it, nay, just because of the anxious conscientiousness with which it was gone about At the restoration of Judaism the old usages were patched together in a new system, which, however, only served as the form to preserve something that was nobler in its nature, but could not have been saved otherwise than in a narrow shell that stoutly resisted all foreign influences (1885a.425)

IV. RECONSTRUCTING EARLY ISRAELITE HISTORY

In his preface to the English edition of the *Prolegomena*, W. Robertson Smith wrote: "The Old Testament does not furnish a history of Israel, though it supplies the materials from which such a history can be constructed" (1885a:vii). Wellhausen published four works demonstrating how "a history can be constructed" in light of the consequences of the issues raised and solutions proposed in his literary analyses. The foundation document (one is tempted to say *Grundschrift*) of these works was his article "Israel" first published in the *Encyclopædia Britannica* (1881). This work, in a shorter German form, was distributed by Wellhausen at Christmastime in 1880/3/. An expanded form of the *EB* article was published in German in 1884/4/. His fullest treatment of Israelite and Judean history was first published in 1894 with the title *Israelitische und jüdische Geschichte*/5/.

In his treatment of "Die Anfänge des Volkes," one finds no "Patriarchal Age" in the traditional sense, for "die Erzählungen über die Erzväter in der Genesis gehn von ethnologischen Verhältnissen und von Kultuseinrichtungen der Königszeit aus und leiten deren Ursprünge aus einer idealen Vorzeit her, auf die sie in Wahrheit nur abgespiegelt werden" (1894/1958:10). The origins of the people are located among the Hebrews, a group to which the ancestors of the Ammonites, Moabites, and Edomites belonged. Israelite ancestors also had connections with the Arameans as well as the nomadic and seminomadic Arabian tribes of the Sinai peninsula (Ishmaelites, Midianites, Kenites, Amalekites, and Kenizzites). From the steppes of southern Palestine, one of these Hebrew groups moved into the land of Goshen, a traditional "Besitz von Nomaden" (1894/1958:10)/6/. Here they continued their life as shepherds and goatherds, retaining their language and style of life (1894/1958:10-11)/7/. This is about the extent of Wellhausen's utilization of the narrative material of Genesis, and practically all of this could have been derived or deduced from other Old Testament texts.

Wellhausen reconstructs the wilderness period or Mosaic epoch in the following manner. About 1250 BCE, the group of Hebrews fled Egypt, maybe undergoing some special event at the "sea" (Exod 14:31: "auf die der Natur der Sache nach kein Verlass ist" (1894/1958:11). The group made its way to Kadesh where it stayed for some time/8/. Here the Rachel group (Joseph) and the Leah group (Reuben, Simeon, Levi, Judah, Issachar, and Zebulon; probably none of these had been in Egypt) came to a sense of tribal unity. This unity of the seven tribes was based on kinship ties ("Alle *legitime* Gemeinschaft ist Blutgemeinschaft. . . . die natürliche Gemeinschaft, die des Blutes, ist die heilige" [1894/1958:22]) and religious community ("Yahve der Gott Israels, Israel das Volk Jahves" [1894/1958:23]). In this tribal relationship, warfare and military concepts played a significant role ("Der Krieg ist es, was die Völker macht. . . . Das Kriegslager, die Wiege der Nation, war auch das älteste Heiligtum. Da war Israel und da war Jahve" [1894/1958:23-24])/9/. Moses' role was that of priestly functionary and judicial authority at the sacred center of Kadesh and was viewed by Wellhausen in terms of his understanding of priesthood and torah in early Israel (see above)/10/. Thus it is proper to speak, in a certain sense, of Moses as the originator of Israelite religion. The Israelites left Kadesh for the Transjordan in response to the need of their kinsmen, the Ammonites and Moabites whose territory was being overrun by the Amorite, King Sihon of Heshbon.

Wellhausen reconstructs the main features of this period without recourse to much of the narrative tradition of the Pentateuch: there is little if any uniqueness to the history of the Israelite ancestors, no desert theocracy, no monotheistic faith, no law set once and for all, no unified experience of all the tribes in Egypt, no covenant theology. "Die Israeliten waren eine Nation wie andere Nationen" (1894/1958:19). "The religious startingpoint of the history of Israel was remarkable, not for its novelty, but for its normal character" (1885a:437).

In the traditions about the settlement in Palestine and its immediate aftermath, Wellhausen found much to use in reconstructing the history of the ancient Israelites. According to him, there were two movements across the Jordan. The first, by Judah, Simeon, and Levi, was not overly successful. The second by Joseph and related groups under the leadership of Joshua moved into the area later occupied by the Benjaminites/11/. These movements across the Jordan and the settlement north and south led to a new division of the tribes—Israel and Judah—replacing the older Leah–Rachel division/12/. Many cities and much territory were captured although "Ai, Jericho und andere Städte scheinen allerdings nicht erst durch die Israeliten zerstört zu sein, sondern schon vor deren Einbruch in Trümmern gelegen zu haben" (1894/1958:25 n.1). The final act of Joshua was to lead the Israelites to victory over a coalition of forces under Jabin.

In addition to his emphasis on the military aspects of the settlement, Wellhausen also stressed the lack of wholesale conquest and the limited geographical occupation which occurred in spite of the disintegrated state of the enemy. The effort led by Sisera was the last major attempt of Canaanites to stem the tide. The Israelite victory is celebrated in the song of Deborah, "dem frühesten Denkmal der hebräischen Literatur," in which, however, "Israel ist kein Organismus . . . ; Israel is nur eine Idee" (1894/1958:37). As a rule, however, the tribes operated on their own: "the period of the Judges presents itself to us as a confused chaos . . ." (1885a:5)/13/. Many of the individual stories in the book of Judges were seen as reflecting historical but not chronologically successive events: the migration of the tribe of Dan, the struggles with the Moabites under Eglon, the defeat of the Midianites, and the attempt of Abimelech the son of Jerubbaal to establish himself as king over Israel (Ephraim and Manasseh). For Wellhausen, the most significant features of the period of the judges were the invaders' amalgamation with the indigenous population and their adaptation of an agricultural way of life. Religious practices, customs, and beliefs were not excluded from such amalgamation.

In Wellhausen's reconstruction of this period of Israelite history, one can see that he utilized what he considered to be the earliest stage of the traditions, after the various "alluvial deposits" with their religious coloration/14/, chronological cohesiveness, and all-Israel orientation have been removed, in order to describe what seemed to have the greatest probability of having happened.

For Wellhausen, the really pivotal period in the formation of Israel was the time of the early monarchy. Although he spoke of the community and commonality of the tribes ("kriegerischer Bund," "kriegerische Eidgenossenschaft") during the invasion and settlement, Wellhausen saw the establishment of kingship as the most decisive event in Israelite history since even postexilic and theocratic Judaism was a spiritualized survival of monarchical structures.

> Saul and David first made out of the Hebrew tribes a real people in the political sense (Deut xxxiii. 5). David was in the eyes of later generations inseparable from the idea of Israel; he was the king par excellence: Saul was thrown into the shade, but both together are the founders of the kingdom, and have thus a much wider importance than any of their successors. It was they who drew the life of the people together at a centre, and gave it an aim; to them the nation is indebted for its historical self-consciousness. All the order of aftertimes is built up on the monarchy; it is the soil out of which all the other institutions of Israel grow up. In the time of the judges, we read, every man did that which was right in his own eyes, not because the Mosaic constitution was not in force, but because there was no king in those days The consequences were very important in the sphere of religion as well. since the political advance of the people brought the historic and national character of Jehovah to the front again. . . This was the result of Israel's becoming a kindom the kingship of Jehovah, in that precise sense which we associate with it, is the religious expression of the fact of the foundation of the kingdom by Saul and David (1885a:413-14)

Wellhausen understood the establishment of the monarchy as the people's response to the threat of outside pressure, primarily from the Philistines from the west but also from the Ammonites from the east/15/. With Philistine pressure, there developed a "widespread exaltation of religious feeling," led by "troops of ecstatic enthusiasts" (1885a:449; 1894/1958:50-51). The old seer Samuel, although himself not a *nabi*, recognized from the neighboring peoples the advantages that could accrue from the consolidation of the tribes and families into a kingdom, utilized the spirit of the times, and discovered the man capable of meeting the needs of the hour. It was a time when "religion and patriotism were then identical" (1885a:449)/16/. The monarchy is thus described as a popular and natural development unattended by any immediate clash with the old orders. "What contributed more than anything else to David's elevation to the throne was the general recognition of the fact that he was the man best fitted on the whole to overtake the labour it brought with it, viz., the prosecution of the war with the Philistines, a war which was as it were the forge in which the kingdom of Israel was welded into one" (1885a:453; see 1894/1958:59).

The above short discussion of Wellhausen's reconstruction of the history of ancient Israel—from the beginnings through the early monarchy—must suffice. At any rate, his methodology can best be seen in this area, and many aspects of the later period have been noted in the analysis of the *Prolegomena* in section III above.

V. EVALUATION AND CRITIQUE

Three factors about Wellhausen's reconstruction of Israelite history cannot be overstressed. (1) He was the first to produce a history of Israel in which there was a thorough integration of literary criticism and historical reconstruction. The two movements were not viewed as two separate activities but as two aspects of a single activity. Regardless of the results of Wellhausen's endeavor, or one's opinion of them, to disagree with his program and intent is difficult if not impossible. It was this aspect of his work which struck certain forms of Old Testament study such a devastating blow and put a generation of scholars on the defensive. (2) In his reconstruction as in his literary analysis, Wellhausen was interested in total perspectives, presuppositions, the larger meaning, the living process, and the interconnectedness of events, movements, and literary expressions. It was this aspect of his work which gave his writings their attractiveness and wide popularity. (3) Wellhausen sought to produce a secular or profane history of Israel which would sketch its developments in naturalistic terms. This does not mean that he disregarded the theological and religious interests of the Old Testament writings—in fact and in many ways these were the heart of his work—but that he did not utilize the theological perspectives of the Old Testament as elements in his historiographical methodology. It was this aspect of his work which frequently antagonized and sometimes traumatized religious believers of his and subsequent times.

Perhaps no scholar's work has been more scrutinized and criticized than his. Many of his critics, however, have confused denunciation with dialogue, repudiation with refutation, and malicious malignment with substantive argumentation (see R. J. Thompson; L. Perlitt). Most are shots at targets in non-existent firing ranges. This, however, does not mean that his work is not open to criticism.

The following are offered as critiques of his reconstruction of Israelite history. (1) Wellhausen's own sentiments, personal character, and individualism led him to an idealization of early Israelite life and to an almost total disdain for religious structures and cultic institutions. His emphases on the freshness and naturalness of early Israelite impulses, the freedom of a less institutionalized culture, and the goodness of primitive forms led him not only to overplay these in his reconstruction but also to fail to see that the function of law (even written law) in a culture need not lead to oppressive and stifling forms of existence/17/. (2) Wellhausen's obsession with "the place in history of the 'law of Moses,'" although understandable in the context of nineteenth-century scholarship, not only created a certain tunnel vision which overlooked other matters but also led to an overemphasis on the importance of legal codes in Israelite history. (3) His radical distinction between preexilic Israel and postexilic Judaism, partially fed by his distinction between pre- and post-Deuteronomic traditions, led to his caricaturing of Judaism (see L. H. Silberman's essay in this volume). (4) Wellhausen overemphasized the importance and role of the prophets in the life of ancient Israel/18/. To see the preaching of the prophets as the impetus which eventually led to the complete reformation and centralization of religion—a movement which resulted in the tragic end of prophecy—is greatly to overstress the role of prophecy. Again Wellhausen shared in the nineteenth-century rediscovery of prophecy, and his overzealousness can be understood in this light. Further, however, one feels that the prophets were Wellhausen's heroes and that he sensed himself as a modern counterpart/19/. (5) Finally, Wellhausen did not sufficiently appreciate the importance of the monarchy and monarchial politics and interests for developments in Israelite life—even centralization of the cult. There is a certain naïveté about his treatment of royal politics and even the origin and nature of the monarchy. Surely the dominant Judean figures in the eighth and seventh centuries were the kings—not the prophets Isaiah and Jeremiah.

NOTES

/1/   First published in 1879:23–24. These are reprinted in Wellhausen, 1885a:4, and in his 1885b:508–9. I am indebted to my wife Sarah for the translation of the French.

/2/   In 1885:8 n. 2, Wellhausen describes his use of terminology in the following way. "In the following pages the Jehovistic history-book is denoted by the symbol JE, its Jehovistic part by J, and the Elohistic by E, the 'main stock' pure and simple, which is distinguished by its systematising history and is seen unalloyed in Genesis, is called the Book of the Four Covenants and is symbolised by Q [=*quatuor*; see 1876a:392 and now also Lou H Silberman]; for the 'main stock' as a whole (as modified by an editorial process) the title of Priestly Code and the symbol RQ (Q and Revisers) are employed."

/3/   This "Geschichte Israels," issued in manuscript form, contains sections 1–9 of "Israel" (1881:396–417), covering the period down to the exile, although with some passages omitted (on 1881.399–401, 403, 406, 414). This work has now been reissued in 1965:13–64.

/4/   The *EB* article of 1881 was reprinted as a separate work at least three times with the title *Sketch of the History of Israel and Judah* (3d ed 1891). The *Sketch* contains an appendix, "Judaism and Christianity," which is the translation of a section from the *Abriss* (1884) which was not in the original *EB* article. The *EB* article was reprinted in the English edition of *Prolegomena* (1885:427–548) with "Judaism and Christianity" as section 11 (1885:499–513). Quotations and pagination from "Israel" in the present article are from the reissue in the *Prolegomena* (1885).

/5/   1st ed., 342 pp , 2d ed., 1895, 378 pp.; 3d ed , 1897, 388 pp.; 4th ed., 1901, 395 pp., 5th ed , 1904, 395 pp , 6th ed., 1907, 386 pp.; 7th ed , 1914, 372 pp., with subsequent reprints. Quotations in the present article are from the 9th ed (1958), a reprint of the 1914 edition.

/6/   In "Israel," Wellhausen gives the general reference "some fifteen centuries before our era" (1885a:429), but in *Geschichte* he offers no date for the descent. One can see at many points where the positions taken in "Israel" have been modified in *Geschichte*.

/7/   Cf 1885a:429, where he says that "forced labour was exacted of them for the construction of new public works in Goshen," which does not appear in *Geschichte*

/8/ In "Israel" (1885a:430), he spoke of a visit to Sinai prior to arrival at Kadesh.

/9/ In "Israel," he wrote. "Jehovah is to be regarded as having originally been a family or tribal god, either of the family to which Moses belonged or of the tribe of Joseph, in the possession of which we find the ark of Jehovah, and within which occurs the earliest certain instance of a composite proper name with the word Jehovah for one of its elements (Jeho-shua, Joshua). No essential distinction was felt to exist between Jehovah and El, any more than between Asshur and El, Jehovah was only a special name of El which had become current within a powerful circle, and which on that account was all the more fitted to become the designation of a national god" (1885a:433 n 1) "Jehovah was the warrior El, after whom the nation styled itself" (1885a.434). See 1894/1958·23 and also 25: "So ausserte sich Jahve vorzugsweise in den grossen Krisen der Geschichte; seine 'Tage' waren, wie die Tage der Araber, Schlachttage."

/10/ ". . . if Moses did anything at all, he certainly founded the sanctuary at Kadesh and the torah there, which the priests of the ark carried on after him, thus continuing the thread of the history of Israel, which was taken up again in power by the monarchy" (1885a:397 n. 1) See also his article on Moses (1883).

/11/ Reuben (and Gad?) remained behind in Transjordan (1894/1958:34) "It is probable that Manasseh's migration to the territory eastward of Jordan took place from the west, and later than the time of Moses" (1885a·455 n 1)

/12/ Many of the tribes such as Ephraim and Benjamin were formed and acquired their names only after the settlement

/13/ "Der kriegerische Bund der Stamme zerfiel unter den friedlichen Verhältnissen, die Ansiedlung zerstreute die durch das Lager- und Wanderleben Geeinigten" (1894/1958.48).

/14/ "It may stand as a general principle, that the nearer history is to its origin the more profane it is" (1885a:245).

/15/ "Aus freier Notwendigkeit war das Konigtum erwachsen" (1894/1958·52)

/16/ Samuel was "der patriotische Prophet in Sonderheit" (1894/1958:51).

/17/ Here one can see not only Wellhausen's personal disposition but also a tendency going back to Herder and the earlier deists and romantics. See Friedemann Boschwitz; Herbert F. Hahn.

/18/ In his review of Duhm's *Die Theologie der Propheten*, Wellhausen (1876b) criticized Duhm for overemphasizing the role of the prophets at the expense of the priests in the origin and formation of Old Testament law.

/19/ It is probably no accident that Thomas Carlyle's book on heroes could serve as a confirmation present from Wellhausen.

WORKS CONSULTED

Boschwitz, Friedemann
    1968   *Julius Wellhausen: Motive und Mass-Stäbe seiner Geschichtsschreibung.* Darmstadt: Wissenschaftliche Buchgesellschaft. (Reprint of his 1938 Marburg dissertation)

Colenso, John William
1862–65   *The Pentateuch and Book of Joshua Critically Examined.* 5 vols London. Longmans, Green, and Co.

Duhm, Bernhard
1875   *Die Theologie der Propheten als Grundlage fur die innere Entwicklungsgeschichte der israelitischen Religion.* Bonn: Adolph Marcus.

Ewald, Heinrich Georg August
1843–55   *Geschichte des Volkes Israel bis Christus.* 5 vols. Göttingen: Dieterich'sche Buchhandlung.
1869   *The History of Israel.* Vol. 1. 2d ed. London. Longmans, Green, and Co

George, Johann Friedrich Leopold
1835   *Die alteren jüdischen Feste, mit einer Kritik der Gesetzgebung des Pentateuch.* Berlin. E. H. Schroeder.

Graf, Karl Heinrich
1866   *Die geschichtlichen Bucher des Alten Testaments: Zwei historisch-kritische Untersuchungen.* Leipzig: T. O. Weigel.

Hahn, Herbert F.
1959   "Wellhausen's Interpretation of Israel's Religious History. A Reappraisal of his Ruling Ideas." Pp. 299–308 in *Essays on Jewish Life and Thought: Presented in Honor of Salo Wittmayer Baron.* Ed. Joseph L. Blau, et al. New York: Columbia University.

Kuenen, Abraham
1869–70   *De godsdienst van Israël tot den ondergang van den Joodschen staat.* 2 vols. Haarlem: A. C. Kruseman. = *The Religion of Israel to the Fall of the Jewish State.* 3 vols. London: Williams and Norgate, 1874–75

Milman, Henry Hart
1829   *The History of the Jews: From the Earliest Period to the Present Time.* 3 vols. London. John Murray. 2d ed., 1830. Harper's Family Library edition; New York: Harper & Brothers, 1834. New edition; New York: W. J. Widdleton, 1874

Perlitt, Lothar
1965   *Vatke und Wellhausen: Geschichtsphilosophische Voraussetzungen und historiographische Motive für die Darstellung der Religion und Geschichte Israels durch Wilhelm Vatke und Julius Wellhausen.* BZAW 94. Berlin: Alfred Töpelmann.

Prideaux, Humphrey
1717–18   *The Old and New Testament Connected in the History of the Jews and Neighboring Nations, from the Declension of the Kingdoms of Israel and Judah to the Time of Christ* 2 vols. London R Knaplock.

Reuss, Eduard
1879   *L'histoire sainte et la loi (Pentateuque et Joshue).* 2 vols. Paris· Sandoz et Fischbacher.

Shuckford, Samuel
1728–30   *The Sacred and Profane History of the World Connected, from the Creation of the World to the Dissolution of the Assyrian Empire at the Death of Sandanapalus, and to the Declension of the Kingdoms*

of Judah and Israel under the Reigns of Ahaz and Pekah. 2 vols London: R. Knaplock & J. Tonson.

Silberman, Lou H.
1979 "Whence *Siglum* Q? A Conjecture." *JBL* 98· 287–88.

Stanley, Arthur Penrhyn
1844 Ed., *The Life and Correspondence of Thomas Arnold* Vol 1. New York· Charles Scribner's Sons.
1863 *Lectures on the History of the Jewish Church, Part I: Abraham to Samuel.* New York. Charles Scribner's Sons.

Thompson, J W
1942 *A History of Historical Writing* New York. Macmillan

Thompson, R J
1970 *Moses and the Law in a Century of Criticism since Graf.* VTSup 19 Leiden· E J Brill.

Vatke, Wilhelm
1835 *Die biblische Theologie wissenschaftlich dargestellt.* I· *Die Religion des Alten Testamentes nach den kanonischen Büchern entwickelt.* Berlin. G. Bethge.

Wellhausen, Julius
1870 "De gentibus et familiis Judaeis quae 1. Chr. 2 4. enumerantur." Theol. Liz.-Diss., Gottingen.
1871 *Der Text der Bucher Samuelis untersucht* Gottingen: Vandenhoeck & Ruprecht.
1876a–77 "Die Composition des Hexateuchs " *JDT* 21 (1876): 392–450, 531–602; 22 (1877): 407–79. Reissued separately. *Skizzen und Vorarbeiten*, vol. 2. *Die Composition des Hexateuchs* Berlin. Georg Reimer, 1885
1876b Review of B. Duhm's *Die Theologie der Propheten. JDT* 21: 152–58
1878a *Geschichte Israels. In zwei Banden. Erster Band.* Berlin· G Reimer. 2d ed and henceforth under the title. *Prolegomena zur Geschichte Israels* Berlin. G. Reimer, 1883.
1878b "Die geschichtlichen Bucher [Richter, Ruth, Samuelis, Konigel." Pp. 181–267 in *Einleitung in die Heilige Schrift, Erster Theil: Einleitung in das Alte Testament*, by Friedrich Bleek. 4th ed by J. Wellhausen. Berlin· G. Reimer Reprinted, pp. 208–301 in *Die Composition des Hexateuchs und der historischen Bücher des Alten Testaments* 3d ed Berlin· Georg Reimer, 1899.
1880 "Geschichte Israels " Privately published as manuscript at Christmastime, Greifswald Reprinted in 1965:13–64
1881 "Israel." *EB*, 9th ed. 13. 396–431 (expansion of 1880). = 1885a·427–548 (with addition of section 11, "Judaism and Christianity," from 1884) = (with minor changes) *Sketch of the History of Israel and Judah* 3d ed. London/Edinburgh A. & C. Black, 1891.
1883 "Moses." *EB*, 9th ed. 16· 860–61.
1884 *Skizzen und Vorarbeiten*, vol. 1. I, *Abriss der Geschichte Israels und Juda's*. Berlin G Reimer. (Expansion of 1880 and 1881)
1885a *Prolegomena to the History of Israel.* Translated from the 2d ed. of 1878a by J. Sutherland Black and Allan Menzies. With Preface by W Robertson Smith Edinburgh. Adam & Charles Black. = *Prolegomena to the History of Ancient Israel* New York: Meridian Books, 1957.

1885b	"Pentateuch and Joshua." *EB*, 9th ed. 18: 505–14.
1894	*Israelitische und jüdische Geschichte.* Berlin: G. Reimer. 7th ed., 1914. = 9th ed., Berlin: de Gruyter, 1958.
1965	*Grundrisse zum Alten Testament.* Ed. Rudolf Smend. TBü 27 Munich: Chr. Kaiser.

de Wette, Wilhelm Martin Leberecht

1805	*Dissertatio critico-exegetica qua Deuteronomium a prioribus Pentateuchi libris diversum.* Jena. Etzdorf.
1806–7	*Beiträge zur Einleitung in das Alte Testament. I: Kritischer Versuch uber die Glaubwürdigkeit der Bücher der Chronik mit Hinsicht auf die Geschichte der mosaischen Bucher und Gesetzgebung. II: Kritik der mosaischen Geschichte.* 2 vols. Halle: Schimmelpfennig und Compagnie.

WELLHAUSEN AND THE HISTORY OF ISRAEL'S RELIGION

Patrick D. Miller, Jr.
Union Theological Seminary in Virginia

ABSTRACT

In his historical studies of ancient Israel Wellhausen assigned a special position to the history of the religion itself While examining changes in the institutional aspects of religion, he was also attentive to the religious moods which they reflected among the people According to his schematization, this history moved from a religious orientation toward nature, to one toward history, and finally to one toward law. In ascertaining Wellhausen's current impact upon the discipline it is instructive for us to examine several specific issues. place(s) of worship, sacrifice, history of priesthood, covenant, and early Yahwism.

Wellhausen's *Prolegomena to the History of Israel* is genuinely that. His ultimate interest and aim were to write a history of Israel; what he produced was a critical study of the sources as a foundation for that history—i.e., prolegomena. The critical analysis, insofar as it is a history at all, is partly history of Israel's religion and partly history of tradition. The history of Israel is really a history of the ordinances of worship, which Wellhausen saw as "rude and colorless," but the implications of that history of worship were clearly much broader. The patterns discerned in the understanding and enactment of the ordinances of worship as they are characterized in the documents of the Pentateuch are significant clues to the spirit of the age in which the documents were written. Thus, for example, one can discern from the ritual practices in one of the sources that life was much more loosely organized, relationships established on natural bases, institutions more flexible and free without significant centralization of political and religious activities. Another source reveals a general picture of highly structured, institutionalized cultus in a period where the individual's essential task is to follow the moral demands.

I. HISTORICAL DEVELOPMENT OF ISRAELITE RELIGION

With regard to the history of the religion itself Wellhausen saw in the documents different understandings of the practices of worship pointing to definite changes that took place in that history as it moved from the free to the fixed, from the simple to the formal, from the natural to the ceremonial and institutional. In the JE tradition and the narratives reflecting the early period there are many sanctuaries where worship may legitimately take place; sacrifice is simple, naïve (1885a:61), related to ordinary life, accompanied by a meal (1885a:76), and the only real concerns are the quantity and quality of the gifts (1885a:61) and the one to whom sacrifice is offered (1885a:53), which is the only way Israelite sacrifice is any different from Canaanite sacrifice (1885a:54). The festivals are not precisely fixed on certain days (1885a:90): they are agricultural, and the fruitful soil is the object of religion (1885a:91). There is no fixed, hereditary priesthood or legislative prescription for such.

By the time of Deuteronomy these practices and their assumptions have changed or are in the process of changing significantly. One central sanctuary is prescribed as the legitimate sanctuary, a demand expressed as an "aggressive novelty" (1885a:33). Sacrifice is cut from its natural roots, placed in the daily life of the people, and formalized at a single place under priestly responsibility (1885a:76–77). The festivals, while still resting upon an agricultural base, begin to be historicized (1885a:91); priests become more prominent and constitute a clerical order, hereditary in numerous families with a levitical priesthood beginning to emerge dominant in Jerusalem. Then in the Priestly document and thus in the postexilic era the one central sanctuary commanded in Deuteronomy is now presupposed (1885a:35). It is the tabernacle, of course, which "rests on an historical fiction" (1885a:39) according to Wellhausen. Sacrifice becomes now completely ritualized and formalized so that "technique was the main thing and strict fidelity to rubric" (1885a:78); the use of incense begins, and the concerns of sin and propitiation are to the fore (1885a:80). In the time of P the festivals become completely historicized. New ones are instituted; Passover assumes a central role; and the Sabbath rest is intensified in a way unmatched previously. As for the priesthood, it is fully in charge in a theocracy under the dominance of the Aaronids; the Levites are now Temple servants.

What is present in all this is a schema that preceives salvation or Israel's understanding of her relation to God as shifting from *nature*, i.e., soil, life and death, and fertility, to *history*, i.e., victory over enemies and establishing of a community, to *law*, ritual celebration and correctness to ensure God's blessing. Such a movement was not progress in Wellhausen's view. Unlike many scholars of more recent vintage, Wellhausen did not see the increasingly historical emphasis in Israel's religion as an especially positive move, and the final stage—the Priestly move into a theocratic, hierocratic, legal community—was clearly a large step backward. In fact, one of the things that is always startling in reading Wellhausen is that along with the wealth of data he marshalled to argue his case there is a significant amount of value judgment running throughout the *Prolegomena*. He sees, for example, Deuteronomy as creating a situation in which the Israelite would "lose oneself in a large community" over against the positively viewed small family context of earlier worship (1885a:77), and he says of the Priestly cultus:

> The warm pulse of life no longer throbbed in it to animate it; it was no longer the blossom and the fruit of every branch of life; it had its own meaning all to itself It symbolised worship, and that was enough The soul was fled; the shell remained, upon the shaping out of which every energy was now concentrated   The sacred action [sacrifice] came to be regarded as essentially perfect by virtue of its own efficacy in being performed by the priest even though no one was present.... The connection of all this with the Judaising tendency to remove God to a distance from man   is clear (1885a.78-79)

As if realizing how far he had ventured in making a theological judgment with the last statement, Wellhausen added a long footnote to indicate that a value comparison with earlier stages was not intended. He only succeeded in confirming that it was.

Having characterized Wellhausen's schema as a view of Israel's religion developing out of a shift from nature to history to law, I must acknowledge that all too often Wellhausen is dealt with simplistically and hastily by ascribing such a system of stages to his portrayal of the history of that religion and letting it go at that. One understands that tendency even while wanting to avoid it, for Wellhausen seems in fact to have wanted to schematize that history. He was in that respect a child of his times, seeing in the historical process stages in a development, although of course not always the same stages that others perceived. There was for Wellhausen a period in Israel's religion when it was natural, familial, local, and free, when God was for Israel a God of the people and not a universal God, when matters of law and morals were governed by the relationship with deity but were not the whole of religious concern nor even primary over cultus, and when the people were not prepared for an "enlightened conception of God" (1885b: 437). There came a later stage under the prophets which grew out of the earlier period and happened at "an opportune period and not too suddenly" (1885b:474; Wellhausen saw this as the providence of God) when there was a significant breakthrough in the move toward the universal and the ethical. Or as Wellhausen put it: "As God of the righteousness which is the law of the whole universe, Yahweh could be Israel's God only in so far as in Israel the right was recognised and followed. The ethical element destroyed the national character of the old religion" (1885b:474).

The problem with such an approach is that when the schematic framework becomes shaky the whole edifice is in danger. If the data do not fit the schema, then the more detailed parts of the analysis go by the board even when they may in fact often be on target. That, I think, has been the case with Wellhausen.

If one tries to elaborate Wellhausen's scheme as reflected in the *Prolegomena* and elsewhere, specifically his essay "Israelitisch-jüdische Religion" (1905), several points can be noted, although any brief summary excludes important dimensions. Wellhausen saw no possibility of reaching behind Moses to an earlier stage of patriarchal religion because there was a dark age between the patriarchs and Moses and because in the time of settlement in the land the people projected their present worship back into hoary antiquity in order to sanctify it and to strip off the actual heathen (i.e., Canaanite) origin of it. The time of Moses was the "properly creative period in Israel's history" and set the pattern and norm for all that followed. The religious center was the conviction that Yahweh was the God of Israel and Israel the people of Yahweh. While later this would be referred back to a definite act of covenant-making, it originally was valid and functioned naturally and not contractually or as capable of dissolution. The war camp was the cradle of Israel's childhood and constituted the primitive sanctuary, i.e., where Yahweh's ark was found. Yahweh, originally a God of the thunderstorm, was much identified with Baal (and vice versa) and fought for Israel in heaven and on earth. The theocracy of the ancient time was nothing less than a hierocracy but without any high priest or priest king. No real distinction between sacred and secular existed. Yahweh was never designated king in the early history, nor did the deity have anything to do with the individual human being or with the world, only with a definite circle held together by blood.

The end of the period of the Judges was not a decline but an upswing. Kingship arose out of a patriotism made active by crisis and need. And patriotism was at that time religion since Yahweh went hand in hand with the nation. Enmity toward kingship was only a later development. Without the kingdom and the king as Yahweh's anointed even Yahweh would not have survived. Kingship and the religious developments attendant with it were important and necessary steps although the building of the temple was a crucial preparation for centralization—a religious development neither present nor envisaged at its creation.

In the ninth century "a new stage" in the religious history began with Elijah, who "thought of (Yahweh) as a great principle which cannot coexist in the same heart with Baal. To him first was it revealed that we do not have in the various departments of nature a variety of forces worthy of our worship, but that there exists overall but one Holy One and one Mighty One, who reveals Himself not in nature but in law and righteousness in the world of man" (1885b:462). In a sense all that follows was derivative from this, but in his penchant for stages and phases Wellhausen saw in Amos "the founder, the purest type, of a new phase of prophecy" (1885b:472) in which the ethical and the universal "destroyed the national character of the old religion" (1885b:474).

Deuteronomy was the clearest expression of the fundamental religious thought of prophecy, but the result of the reform was the death of prophecy when its precepts became laws (1885b:487–88). The final outcome was mainly the limitation of the Yahwistic cultus to Jerusalem, which led to the great increase in the importance of the Solomonic temple and the influence of the priests of Jerusalem, the sons of Zadok, thus paving the way for the postexilic hierocracy which received its greatest impetus from Ezekiel and its main charter in the developing Priestly legislation, without the "hard and ossified forms" (1885b:497) of which Judaism would probably not have survived in the chaos and turmoil of the Graeco-Roman Empire.

When one seeks to assess Wellhausen's interpretation of the history of Israel's religion, the verdict is mixed. His schema is too simplistic and at points simply wrong. For example, the notion of the kingship and universal rule of Yahweh was not a religious conviction that came in slowly with the monarchy and culminated with the eighth-century prophets. It is found at earlier stages in the ancient Yahwistic poetry and was rooted in pre-Israelite developments. Indeed the rise of human kingship apparently posed a problem early on because it was perceived by some as an encroachment on the kingship of God, and prophecy arose in large part to ensure the kingship of Yahweh over the human king. Or to take another example that demonstrates the complexity of Israelite religion at any point against an overly simple schema, the realm of nature and natural dimensions of the relationship with Yahweh have a vigorous play in Hosea even as he uses covenantal language and imagery. Wellhausen's overly negative judgment on the later history of Israel's religion leads to a somewhat skewed presentation of it. Nevertheless much of what he wrote about that religion holds good, and some of his conclusions look stronger now than they once did (see below). Criticisms of Wellhausen are properly more muted than even in the recent past. There are many points at which he was on the right track and laid the groundwork for a continuing reading of Israel's religious history.

Two major flaws undercut the overall validity of his work and have kept it from being of even more lasting value as a guide to the history of Israel's religion. One of these was the result of a methodological enthusiasm; the other, an accident of history. In the first case his zeal to demonstrate—correctly—that a literary document or source may reflect the general picture of the era of its final composition kept him from acknowledging that significant elements of the source may go back to an earlier period. He was not unaware of this possibility—he regarded the war laws of Deuteronomy 20 as in part quite ancient despite their absence in earlier documents, and he knew that the Priestly circle did not discover the significance of purity and impurity in religious matters—but it did not play a large role in his interpretation of Israel's religion. The accident of history was the fact that Wellhausen wrote his *Prolegomena* just as the flood of Near Eastern materials, which now almost overwhelms us, was only beginning. While it is good to celebrate the centennial of Wellhausen's *Prolegomena*, and perhaps to discover his worth anew, in terms of lasting impact on the history of Israel's religion, and all other areas for that matter, it might have been more appropriate to commemorate the centennial of George Smith's paper on "The Chaldean Account of the Deluge" read to the Society of Biblical Archaeology in 1872 or the publication of his book *The Chaldean Account of Genesis* in 1876. For the mass of data from the ancient Near East has rendered many of Wellhausen's analyses and conclusions obsolete—although some would say, and with vigor, prematurely so.

In his 1905 essay "Israelitisch-jüdische Religion," Wellhausen showed at that time that he was neither unaware of nor totally disinterested in the growing mass of literary and artifactual remains from the ancient Near East. "Israelite antiquity can no more be isolated; one sees too clearly how closely it is bound on all sides with the near and distant environment" (1965:65). Perhaps a *Prolegomena* written 10 years after that would have looked quite different. But he felt also the danger of a kind of leveling of the religions of the ancient Near East and would not allow the notion that there was nothing special in Israelite religion. "One may not with regard to the similarities of beginnings and the analogy of the development overlook the difference in end result" (1965:66). Wellhausen was just as concerned—indeed clearly more so—with the *development* of that religious history and the comparison of its various stages. The history of religion is both a *comparative* and a *historical* discipline, i.e., interested (a) in how the religious phenomena of the milieu have influenced or affected the religion under examination, in this case Israel's, and how they illumine our understanding of that religion even where they have not directly influenced it, as well as (b) in the historical development of that religion, what it looked like in its long course, what changes took place, what aspects continued fundamentally the same and provided a continuing thread, what tensions and strains arose in the course of that history.

Wellhausen clearly seized hold of one end of that methodological pole, the historical. And while the comparative emphasis and data have led to a continuing challenge of his synthesis of the religion, two things can be learned from Wellhausen's emphasis on historical development—one out of his works and the other against his work. First, his insistence on the investigation of the historical movement of Israel's religion is a proper admonition to those who continue to take up this task and a warning against the dangers of a comparative analysis that picks any point or item in the milieu of the ancient Near East and easily relates it to any point in Israel's religion as if the latter were one and the same at all times. A patternism as a way of seeing Israel's religion in relation to the ancient Near East would have been anathema to Wellhausen if it did not take account of the nuances and changes of that history, which could not be simply leveled out. In his sense of the historical development he could see that the conflict of Yahwism with

Baal takes place in Elijah's time despite apparent indications in the literature of an earlier struggle. Second, against Wellhausen but in the light of his work we realize that variety and complexity in Israel's religion did not arise simply out of the historical progress or development of that religion but may have been and indeed were present at all points. The dimension of complexity, tension, and dialectic is present along the way—and not merely in the setting or contrasting of one phase against another.

II. CURRENT VIEWS ON SPECIFIC ISSUES

It has been suggested that Old Testament scholarship in general may be closer to Wellhausen at the centennial of the *Prolegomena* than it was at the eightieth anniversary. That conclusion is not without some validity, so it may be appropriate to take a few major issues in Wellhausen's work and see to what extent that may or may not be the case when one looks at various trends or points of view in contemporary Old Testament scholarship.

1. *Place(s) of Worship*

Wellhausen was certainly correct in arguing for a strong move toward centralization of Israel's worship. Twenty years ago, however, there was considerable consensus that a central sanctuary of some sort existed long before Deuteronomy and in fact reached back to the early days of the tribal confederation, even though the location of the sanctuary may have changed from time to time. While other sanctuaries existed for local worship, the league had a sacred center for the great festivals, and it is out of this long-standing tendency in Israel that the Deuteronomic central sanctuary developed as the final stage.

The increasing criticisms of Martin Noth's amphictyonic hypothesis, however, have shattered that consensus. The most recent works on this period and this problem have nearly all argued against the notion of a premonarchical central shrine (see, e.g., A. D. H. Mayes; S. Herrmann; R. de Vaux; J. H. Hayes and J. M. Miller). On this issue the pendulum has clearly shifted in Wellhausen's direction.

With regard to the specific institution of the tabernacle Wellhausen understood this to be a historical fiction projected back from the postexilic period, although he thought there was probably some sort of tent for the ark (2 Sam 6:17). In this regard he referred frequently to the silence of the non-Priestly Pentateuchal and historical traditions on the tabernacle and the absence of any reference to it in connection with the temple. He understood the tent references in 2 Samuel 7 to refer to the tent David set up for the ark.

While there are some aspects of that analysis that may be on the right track, the work of Frank Cross, Richard Clifford, and others, particularly in light of the Ugaritic texts, has challenged his overall conclusion, suggesting instead that the tabernacle described by P goes back to the tent of David or of Shiloh, originally conceived as formed on the pattern of the abode of El. The Priestly description obviously draws from the most elaborate and highest development of that institution (with allowance also for P exaggeration and the influence of the temple), but it probably also reflects a telescoping of tradition so that the desert tent, the Shiloh structure (here Cross assumes a central or common cultus and shrine of some sort), and the tent of David all represent the one continuous religious institution of early Israel, and may with some justification be called "the tabernacle" (so Cross). Whatever modifications may be necessary in such an analysis, it remains a significant counter in part to Wellhausen's understanding of the tabernacle particularly and the P work in general.

2.   *Sacrifice*

Wellhausen saw the heart of the matter as a move from a primitive, naïve, joyous practice of sacrifice to a legal, prescribed, complicated ritual of sacrifice divorced from daily life. Such a complex pattern was to be found in P—a reflection of the time and *Zeitgeist* of the Second Temple. Again one may judge Wellhausen correct in seeing in P a system that represents end stages of a development, yet one should also question his assumption that *only* a picture of the final stage is reflected here.

The absence of any real comparative data in Wellhausen's analysis of sacrifice has often been noted. There is now a great deal of such data that will have to be taken into account both with regard to the conception of sacrifice (here Wellhausen is probably correct in seeing that sacrifice early and generally was primarily understood as gift and was similar to Canaanite sacrifice) and the practice of it. One of the things that is apparent is the fact that sacrifice can be and is quite complex and ritualized all along the way, as the Hittite, Assyrian, and Ugaritic ritual texts testify. But the biblical materials themselves suggest in various ways that order and prescription are not confined to the latest stages. 1 Sam 2:12ff., while not reflecting P regulations, points to a prescribed and complex priestly ritual for sacrifice at an early stage in Israel's history. Furthermore, the order of sacrifice in the ritual texts in Leviticus may reflect much earlier conceptions and practices. Anson Rainey has made the cogent suggestion that the liturgical sequence of offerings in Leviticus 9 reflects actual temple practice as suggested not only for Hezekiah's time (2 Chr 29:20–36) but even for the Solomonic era and the dedication of the temple (1 Kgs 8:5, 64). The sequence of sacrifices in Amos 5:22 corresponds to the first three types of offerings in Leviticus 1–6. The order and relationship of these sacrifices were apparently not a Priestly creation but were familiar from the practices and conceptions of a much earlier period. Indeed Amos may have had in mind the whole sequence of sacrifices in Leviticus 1–6, i.e., the sin offering and the guilt offering, if his oracle reflected a kind of ABC abbreviated list that stood for the whole catalogue of offerings.

3.   *History of Priesthood*

Wellhausen divided the history of the priesthood into three phases: (a) an early stage without a fixed hereditary priesthood or legislative prescription for such; (b) growth of influence, power, and centralization of the priesthood under the monarchy, with the priests in the late monarchy constituting a clerical order, hereditary in numerous families; (c) in the postexilic period, the picture of which is preserved in P, a theocracy under priests and Levites with the Aaronid priests dominating, the Levites generally becoming temple servants, and the high priest functioning as head of worship and head of the nation.

This analysis in general still governs the various formulations of that history—with continuing debate over particular points, such as the nature and degree of difference between priest and Levite in Deuteronomy and the late monarchy. Notice has been taken of the growing evidence for high priests, hereditary craft, and military guilds among the peoples surrounding Israel at the early period. But one cannot easily extrapolate information for Israel's early priesthood from the often fragmentary data from Canaan and Phoenicia. That there was a head of priests at earlier stages or among other peoples does not invalidate Wellhausen's recognition that the Priestly characterization of this office represents the postexilic period for the most part or an idealization of that position.

A recent significant attempt to build upon and correct Wellhausen has been made by Frank Cross in his study of the priestly houses of Israel. He thinks Wellhausen is probably correct in seeing Moses as the dominant priestly figure of the older traditions while Aaron originally played little or no role. On the basis of various kinds of data but especially the stories of conflict in the wilderness, evidence which has not figured prominently in the studies of the Israelite priesthood, Cross posits an ancient and prolonged strife between two priestly houses: the Mushite (i.e., Mosaic) priesthood which was present at the sanctuaries of Shiloh and Dan and an allied Mushite-Kenite priesthood of the local shrines at Arad and Kadesh opposed to the Aaronite priesthood of Bethel and Jerusalem. Recognizing the presence, power, and conflict between these houses, David wisely chose two priests, one from each line: Abiathar from the Mushite (Shiloh) line (against the genealogy of 1 Chronicles 24) and Zadok from the Aaronid line (against Wellhausen). With such a reconstruction Cross assumes some of Wellhausen's conclusions; but over against his presuppositions about a free early period devoid of fixed hereditary institutions playing any major role Cross contends that there are strong pointers to the existence of two great rival priestly families whose strength and following were such that even in David's time both had to be taken into account.

4. *Covenant*

The significance of covenant in the history of Israel's religion is one of the areas in which the present picture suggests a larger or wider affinity for Wellhausen's perspective than was the case twenty years ago. The natural character of the relationship between Israel and Yahweh precluded any possibility of a formal covenantal structure embodying moral and legal stipulations. Such was unnecessary and therefore did not arise until a later time when the existence of the nation was threatened by outside forces and the circumstances led "such prophets as Elijah and Amos [to] raise the Deity high above the people, sever the natural bond between them, and put in its place a relation depending on conditions, conditions of a moral character" (1885a:417). Only after this and out of this did the notion of a contractual relationship expressed in a covenant or treaty arise. The major step in that direction was the Josianic reform and the promulgation of the Deuteronomic law. From that time on "the notion of covenant-making between Jehovah and Israel appears to have occupied the central position in religious thought" (1885a:419). The postexilic hierocracy carried this notion in an increasingly cultic and legalistic direction.

The work of G. E. Mendenhall, K. Baltzer, and many others in the 1950s and afterwards radically challenged this view, again in the light of extrabiblical data as well as biblical. On the basis of analogy with ancient Near Eastern treaties, the argument was made that the covenantal structure of the Yahweh-Israel relationship was there at very early stages, it was of a treaty character, and moral and legal stipulations sanctioned and guarded by this formal structure were at its very center. Without going into detail on the extensive covenantal discussion (see McCarthy, 1963 and 1972b), one may say that the extrabiblical data have in fact altered the context and basis for decision without settling the matter. The work of Mendenhall and those following his point of view has come under considerable criticism on the grounds of both historical and form-critical method. In recent times a position in many respects closely akin to that of Wellhausen and in some respects going beyond it (see McCarthy, 1972a) has been vigorously and ably put forth by Lothar Perlitt. His definition of *berît* as "obligation," i.e. for Israel the law, is not far from that of Wellhausen although the latter seems to have understood the term to be capable of referring to a relationship, a notion which Perlitt essentially rejects. Even more important is Perlitt's conclusion, with which a number of other scholars have in recent years agreed, that the term *berît* and the notion of covenant arose in the Deuteronomic era and under the impulse of prophecy. Whether such a position will finally carry the day is uncertain. The writer is inclined to agree with McCarthy (1972a) that the recognition by Wellhausen, and more recently by Perlitt and others, of the significant role of covenant in Deuteronomy and Deuteronomic theology is on target, but the Deuteronomists were not the creators of the covenantal idea nor did it simply arise out of prophecy. In any event, however, the pendulum of scholarly investigation of this subject has swung rather heavily toward Wellhausen in the last decade, and he is getting a wider hearing than before.

5. *Early Yahwism*

Wellhausen was very weak on the pre-Yahwistic stages of Israelite religion, tending always to see here a primitive understanding and maintaining that we cannot know much about these stages anyway. The work of Albrecht Alt especially, but also that of F. M. Cross, has changed the situation quite significantly. They have discerned in the patriarchal narratives the worship of the high god El (so Cross) and the tutelary clan deity of the patriarchs (so Cross and Alt), deities which are related to each other and to the gods of the ancient Near East.

With regard to the early Yahwistic stages Wellhausen saw much more clearly than he is often given credit—and better than some of his successors—the nature of Israel's religion in that early period. That may have been because of his romantic bias toward the early stages or because of a careful sifting of data. Whatever the reason we are in a better position now to assess and confirm some of the briefly stated conclusions of Wellhausen.

His recognition that the foundation upon which early Israel's unity rested was religious and that the heart of the matter may be summed up in the formula, Yahweh is the God of Israel and Israel is the people of Yahweh, was essentially correct. The first point may seem self-evident, but in fact it is not always assumed even though John Bright, George Mendenhall, and others keep reminding us of the religious element as the fundamental factor that bound the tribes together in the earliest stage. Rudolf Smend (1970) in recent times has made a strong case for seeing the formula and relationship of Yahweh as the God of Israel and Israel as the people of Yahweh as the center of the Old Testament. He has done this in self-conscious dependence upon and affirmation of Wellhausen (Smend: 52). Wellhausen's conclusion that Yahweh was only a special name of El (1885b:433) has been worked out in some detail by Cross from a particular point of view and in the light of data unavailable to Wellhausen. In like manner this writer has sought to make the case that Yahweh reflects the warrior El in continuity with Wellhausen's understanding of the character of Israel's god in the early period (Miller, 1968; 1973). Indeed Wellhausen's insistence on the war camp as central to Israel's early history and religion and the Divine Warrior imagery as basic to the religious conceptuality of ancient Israel was on target, as is reflected in much scholarly research during the last two decades. Finally, Wellhausen correctly perceived the relationship between Yahweh and Baal as initially one of co-existence, with Yahweh's absorbing elements and functions of Baal until the ninth century, by which time such co-existence and the ever-increasing worship of Baal had become intolerable for Yahweh's prophets, particularly Elijah, and a minority within the Northern Kingdom.

The specific aspects of Israelite religion cited above are only illustrative and do not allow one to cite a clear trend. They do suggest that some of Wellhausen's positions have received more of a hearing in recent times or have received some degree of confirmation as well as modification even if that has not always been the intention of those who have produced such confirmation. Surely his influence—in general and in particular—is not at an end. Contemporary investigation of the history of the religion of Israel will use his work critically and cautiously, but cannot ignore it.

WORKS CONSULTED

Alt, Albrecht
1929   *Der Gott der Väter*. BWANT III/12. Stuttgart· W. Kohlhammer. = Pp. 1–78 in *Kleine Schriften zur Geschichte des Volkes Israel*, vol. 1. Munich. C. H. Beck, 1953. = "The God of the Fathers." Pp. 1–77 in *Essays on Old Testament History and Religion*. Oxford: Basil Blackwell, 1966.

Baltzer, Klaus
1960   *Das Bundesformular*. WMANT 4 Neukirchen: Neukirchener Verlag. 2d ed., 1964. = *The Covenant Formulary in Old Testament, Jewish, and Early Christian Writings*. Trans. D. E. Green Philadelphia: Fortress, 1971.

Bright, John
1972   *A History of Israel*. 2d ed. Philadelphia: Westminster.

Clifford, Richard J.
1971   "The Tent of El and the Israelite Tent of Meeting." *CBQ* 33: 221–27.

Cross, Frank Moore
1973   *Canaanite Myth and Hebrew Epic: Essays in the History of the Religion of Israel*. Cambridge: Harvard University.

Hayes, John H., and J. Maxwell Miller, eds.
1977   *Israelite and Judaean History* Philadelphia· Westminster.

Herrmann, Siegfried
1973   *Geschichte Israels in alttestamentlicher Zeit*. Munich. Chr. Kaiser = *A History of Israel in Old Testament Times*. Trans. John Bowden Philadelphia: Fortress, 1975.

McCarthy, Dennis J.
1963   *Treaty and Covenant: A Study in Form in the Ancient Oriental Documents and in the Old Testament* AnBib 21. Rome: Pontifical Biblical Institute. 2d ed., 1978.
1972a   "$b^e rit$ in Old Testament History and Theology." *Bib* 53: 110–21.
1972b   *Old Testament Covenant: A Survey of Current Opinions*. Richmond: John Knox.

Mayes, A D H
1974   *Israel in the Period of the Judges* London· SCM.

Mendenhall, George E
1954   "Law and Covenant in Israel and the Ancient Near East." *BA* 17: 26–46, 49–76.

Miller, Patrick D , Jr
1968   "El the Warrior " *HTR* 50: 411–32
1973   *The Divine Warrior in Early Israel*. Cambridge: Harvard University.

Noth, Martin
1930   *Das System der zwolf Stamme Israels*. BWANT IV/1. Stuttgart: W. Kohlhammer Reprint, Darmstadt: Wissenschaftliche Buchgesellschaft, 1966.

Perlitt, Lothar
1969   *Bundestheologie ım Alten Testament* WMANT 36 Neukirchen-Vluyn. Neukirchener Verlag.

Rainey, Anson F.
1970   "The Order of Sacrifices in Old Testament Ritual Texts." *Bib* 51: 485–98

Smend, Rudolf
1970   *Die Mitte des Alten Testaments* TS 101. Zurich. EVZ-Verlag.

Smith, George
1873   "The Chaldean Account of the Deluge." *Transactions of the Society of Biblical Archaeology* 2· 213–34. (Read to the Society in 1872.)
1876   *The Chaldean Account of Genesis*. London: S. Low, Marston, Searle and Rivington.

de Vaux, Roland
1971–73   *Histoire ancienne d'Israël*. 2 vols Etudes bibliques. Paris. Gabalda. = *The Early History of Israel*. Philadelphia: Westminster, 1978.

Wellhausen, Julius
1885a   *Prolegomena to the History of Israel*. Translated from the 2d German edition by J. Sutherland Black and Allan Menzies. With Preface by W. Robertson Smith Edinburgh· Adam & Charles Black. = *Prolegomena to the History of Ancient Israel*. New York: Meridian Books, 1957.
1885b   "Israel." Pp 427–548 in *Prolegomena* (1885a). Originally published in *EB*, 9th ed., 1881 13: 396–431.
1965   "Israelitisch-jüdische Religion." Pp. 65–109 in his *Grundrisse zum Alten Testament*, ed R Smend. TBü 27. Munich. Chr. Kaiser. Reprinted from pp. 1–38 in *Die Kultur der Gegenwart*, ed P Hinneberg, 1/4. Berlin/Leipzig: B. G. Teubner, 1905.

WELLHAUSEN AND JUDAISM

Lou H. Silberman
Emeritus, Vanderbilt University

ABSTRACT

In his *Prolegomena* Wellhausen took a decided stance against Judaism. This occurred in conjunction with his view that the written Law, created by the postexilic Jewish community, constituted a radical move away from the dynamic religion of earlier Israel. Such a notion has more in common with the religious sentiments of Wellhausen's own time than with the ascertainable religious developments of Israelite and Jewish antiquity itself

In an address entitled "Higher Criticism—Higher Anti-Semitism," delivered on 26 March 1903, Solomon Schechter said: "Wellhausen's Prolegomena and History are *teeming with aperçus* full of venom against Judaism" (36). He went on to suggest, in keeping with the title, that Wellhausen's being awarded a decoration by the German government was proof that he was an anti-Semite. On the basis of the testimony of my own teacher, Jacob Z. Lauterbach, who studied with Wellhausen in Göttingen at the turn of the century, I find it necessary to reject Schechter's conclusion. Wellhausen was no vulgar anti-Semite. Nonetheless, the evidence drawn from the *Prolegomena* calls for the conclusion that it, like practically everything written by German Protestant theologians of the period and many subsequently and to this day, is a work of anti-Judaism/1/.

The central theme and thesis of the *Prolegomena* is Pauline antinomism as exacerbated by Luther: Law is the creation of Judaism. "Thus the possibility that the law of Judaism was as well its product cannot be preemptorily dismissed . . ." (1878:3). "The question is whether the Mosaic law is the starting point for the history of ancient Israel or for the history of Judaism, that is, the sect that survived the destruction of the people by the Assyrians and Chaldeans" (1878:1)/2/. Yet one may ask: Is that, presuming it to be true, such a negative statement? Is it merely a matter of fact, or does it intend a judgment? The beginning of an answer is to be found in a paragraph occurring in the first edition only. Part III, entitled "Israel und das Judentum," has a motto on its title page attributed to Vatke: "Das Gesetz ist zwischenein getreten." The first paragraph of chapter 9, "Abschluss der Kritik des Gesetzes," reads: "Paul certainly did not mean the statement in Rom 5:20 in exactly the same sense in which it is used as a motto for this section. Yet for one who hears the voice of prophecy in the judgment of Abraham, Gen 15:6 (Hab 2:4), the reinterpretation is still close to it, particularly since the law that the Apostle wished to remove as central was for him the Law of Judaism. νόμος παρεισῆλθεν—Judaism projects itself deeply into the Old Testament, into the tradition concerning ancient Israel. Our investigation thus far has given us the right to take our stand on this base and to survey the scene from it" (1878:379). Wellhausen has admittedly pushed Paul beyond what Paul said, that legalism sidled in. For him νόμος is not law nor legalism but *the Law*, with the definite article and a capital letter. παρεισῆλθεν, it has sidled in where it has no place/3/.

"The Law," wrote Wellhausen, "is the key to the understanding of the alteration of the tradition. All of the various characteristics of the narrative of the Priestly collection are to be connected with its influence. Theory, rule, judgment assert themselves everywhere. What was asserted about cult previously may be repeated verbatim for saga. It may be compared to a green tree that in olden times grew out of the soil as it would and could; subsequently it became dried-out timber that was cut to pattern with compass and square. Pharisaic deuterosis (*Pharis. und Sadd.*, pp. 124ff.) and the Koran exercised the same influence on the historical tradition. An old Arabic proverb said of devout Moslems that they excelled in falsifying history" (1878:362f.)/4/. Although the concluding sentences are omitted from later editions, the spirit they breathe is found elsewhere: "It is well known that there never have been more impudent inventors of history than the Rabbins. But Chronicles offer sufficient evidence that this evil propensity reaches back to very early times, for its root, the dominating influence of the Law, is the root of Judaism itself" (1878:166)/5/.

Yet it is not merely the Law but the written Law that has caused this "alteration of the tradition." Chapter 10 bears the title "Die mündliche und die schriftliche Thora" and begins: "What importance writing, the book of the Law, possessed for the Jews, we all know from the New Testament. Of ancient Israel, on the contrary, it is said in the introductory poem of *West-östlicher Divan* that the word was so important there because it was a spoken word. The contrast which Goethe evidently perceived is indeed characteristic and deserving of further evaluation" (1878:403f.). Whether Goethe "evidently perceived" the contrast is not here the point. Wellhausen perceived it and laid great weight upon it.

It is to the explication of this presumed contrast between the oral and the written, between Israel and Judaism, that Wellhausen turned. The pages immediately following the lines just quoted are among the most eloquent he wrote. He began by arguing that ancient Israel did not lack "divinely ordained foundations for the ordering of human life" (1878:408).

There were universally known requirements of Deity in force. Additionally there was the particular Torah of Israel, oracular decisions that had been freed from heathenistic devices. Yes, even the Torah of the priests, although of a legal ("rechtlich") character, was a spoken Torah, "a living power, equal to the occasion and never-failing" (1878:410f.). There was, too, another expression of Torah, that of the seers, originally related to that of the priests, eventually becoming that of the prophets. Although the Torah of the priests necessarily developed a tradition and institutional status, the latter, even though intermittent, broke forth with greater force. At the end when "the spirit of the ancient men of God . . . had been banished into institutions, it [had] sought and found a new outlet in the prophets. The old fire, like a volcano, broke through the hardened deposits" of the past (1878:413).

The next passage must be quoted in its fullness, for it is the key to our understanding of Wellhausen's attitude toward the Law:

> The native element of the prophets is the storm of world history that sweeps away the establishments of men, in which the rubbish heap of the generations together with the houses built upon it shake apart so that all that remains is the ground that needs no grounding When the earth quakes, then do they triumphantly proclaim that the Lord alone remains, exalted
> They do not preach from set texts; they speak out of the spirit that judges all and is judged by none. Where and when do they ever depend on any authority other than experience? When and where, on any foundation other than their own certainty? In prophetic, in true revelation, the Lord, ignoring all institutional mediation, makes himself known to the *individual*, the one called, in whom the mysterious, unanalyzable rapport, wherein godhead stands with man, becomes energized. There is no prophecy *in abstracto*, apart from the prophet It exists in his human–divine I (John 10:35). Thus is an apparent contradiction resolved in a synthesis. the subjective in the highest sense, stript of all structures, is in truth objective It proves itself to be such through the consent of the general conscience upon which the prophets count, just as does Jesus in the Gospel of John, in all their polemics against the traditional form of worship. They desire to proclaim nothing new, only ancient truth Involved in the most creative activity, they feel themselves passive. For them, *homo tantum et audacia*—which may be rightly applied to persons like Elijah, Amos, Isaiah—means the same as *deus tantum et servitus*. But their credo is not in a book. It is barbarous to deface the countenance of such a phenomenon with the Law. (1878:413f.)/6/

νόμος παρεισῆλθεν—das Gesetz ist zwischenein getreten—the Law sidled in. It is not a natural development. It was the Babylonian Exile that "evidently tore the nation from its native soil for a half century—a breach of historical continuity, a greater than which it is scarcely possible to conceive." The next generation had no natural, only an artificial relation to the past. "Only the pious, who with trembling obeyed the Lord's word, provided the remnant and had the strength, amid the motley of peoples surrounding them, to preserve Jewish particularity. There returned from the exile not a nation but a religious sect." What did they bring back from the forgetfulness of the exile? ". . . That the one God had only one center for worship," the remembrance of the Deuteronomic reformation. What did they create? A centralized cult. They apparently knew nothing else of their past, or what they knew they despised. "The Jews of the restoration did not have any respect for their ancient history." "From the exile onward the theocratic ideal was central to all thought and deed and annihilated the meaning of objective truth." There were, of course, some elements of reality, for "no phantasy is pure phantasy." But what did phantasy do with even those elements of realty? The history of tradition, Wellhausen argued, makes it evident. Taking as his example 1 Chronicles 22-29, he wrote that the whole section was "a free construction, a horrible example of the statistical phantasy of the Jews which revels in vast sums of money on paper (22:14), in artificially devised regiments of names and numbers (chs. 23-27), in the enumeration of mere subjects without predicates, that simply stand on parade doing nothing, meaning nothing, the monotony broken occasionally by unctuous speeches that never come to life"/7/.

There is more, of course, that may be educed, but we have come, only now, to the heart of the matter. Wellhausen's portrayal of Judaism was, it seems clear, motivated by interests that had little or nothing to do with what happened in Judea restored in the sixth or fifth centuries BCE. The real Judaizers were not of the past; they were alive and flourishing in the nineteenth century. They were those who had failed to recognize "prophetic revelation in which the Lord, ignoring all institutional mediation, makes himself known to individuals" (1878:414).

The key to this is found in two passages. In one toward the end of a sharp critique of Riehm and Dillmann for their admiration of the purity and faithfulness of the Priestly Codex as exhibited in the stage of religious development, Wellhausen wrote: "One can find pleasure in these merits only if one believes that the religion was originally natural and 1500 years before Christ became *positiv*" (1878:360)/8/. It is this last word that tells us much. It is not to be translated vaguely into English as "positive," for its reference is to the theological development in German Protestantism in the nineteenth century. "*Positiv*" is the self-designation of conservative tendencies in church and theology, meant to accuse opponents of being negative and negating, overcritical and destructive, while at the same time claiming itself to be constructive. The Priestly Codex, the Law, Judaism are for Wellhausen the prime examples of "*positiv*." It is, at the same time, none other than the ecclesiastical establishment that while not attacking him made it impossible for him to retain his theological professorship in Greifswald. Eduard Schwartz's description of Wellhausen as "überhaupt kein Parteimann," as one who was interested exclusively in philological matters and had no interest in ecclesiastical politics, is wide of the mark/9/.

If it be suggested that I am reading more into this word than is proper and making it bear too great a burden of interpretation, then let us look at the second passage (1878:427): "In Wahrheit ist Mose etwa in dem gleichen Sinne der Urheber der 'mosaischen Verfassung', wie unser Herr Jesus Christus der Stifter der Niederhessischen Kirchenordnung." ("In truth, Moses is the originator of the 'Mosaic constitution' in about the same sense that our Lord Jesus Christ is the founder of the ecclesiastical establishment of Lower Hesse.") Not for the first time nor the last was Judaism invented in one's image of one's theological opponents so that they could be tarred with the brush of "Judaizers." The Judaism that in the sixth and fifth centuries BCE invented the Law that sidled in was invented in the nineteenth century by German biblical scholarship of which Wellhausen was the most influential spokesman/10/.

One final matter. Wellhausen's demonstration that Judaism was the inventor of νόμος παρεισῆλθεν—the Law that sidled in, interrupting the true spiritual development of Israel—made it unnecessary for liberal Protestant thought in Germany to reassess any traditional judgment of Judaism. Indeed, as Leo Baeck showed in his critical review of Harnack's *Das Wesen des Christentums*, Judaism could continue to be for the liberal Protestant the dark background against which the incandescence of the religion of Jesus could ever more brightly shine, once it had been purged of the dross of dogma/11/. What had been dogmatic was now scientific. Of the consequence of this I shall not write.

NOTES

/1/ The Lauterbach comments were made in personal conversation. Lauterbach said that it was Wellhausen who urged him to devote himself to rabbinic literature instead of becoming an Arabist "Anyone," he quoted Wellhausen as saying, "can be an Arabist." See also G F. Moore; F E Talmadge; and Charlotte Klein

/2/ It is to be emphasized that this paper deals only with Wellhausen's portrayal of Judaism in his publication of 1878. Nonetheless, while there are important shifts of nuance in subsequent editions and in other writings (see the discussion by Hans Liebeschutz), it was the attitude here taken that remained decisive for biblical scholarship All references are to the first edition of what was latterly called *Prolegomena zur Geschichte Israels* but was originally entitled *Geschichte Israels*, published in 1878 It was planned as the first of two volumes; the second never appeared but was apparently replaced by *Israelitische und Judische Geschichte* (1894) The translations in this paper are mine, made from the first edition. They, however, occasionally reflect the English translation (1885) made from the second German edition (1883). In the passage cited above, the term "sect" was used in the first edition It was changed subsequently (see the English translation and the 1899 edition) to "Religionsgemeinde," "religious communion "

/3/ The motto, "Das Gesetz ist zwischenein getreten," is found in the first (1878.377) and second (1883.385) editions with the citation. "Vatke S 183 " It is still found in the 1899 edition, but without the citation. Actually the words from Rom 5:20, νόμος δὲ παρεισῆλθεν, are not quoted exactly in Wilhelm Vatke (183) but are given a paraphrastic interpretation "Die tiefe Idee des Neuen Testaments, dass das Gesetz zwischen die Verheissungen und deren Erfüllung hineingetreten sei, lässt sich dessenungeachtet historisch rechtfertigen, da der Pentateuch in seine Vollendung in der That später fallt, als die Verheissungen der meisten Propheten." The first paragraph of chapter 9 which makes clear both the meaning of the motto and the reference to Vatke is found only in the first edition Why Wellhausen omitted it from all subsequent editions is difficult to determine, for it contains the operative concept—taken from Vatke—of the whole work. The meaning of παρεισῆλθεν is given by Sanday and Headlam as: "come in to the side of a state of things already existing" (143). This is exactly what the verb "to sidle" means, yet it has not been used in any English translation See now C. E. B. Cranfield's commentary where a non-disparaging meaning is suggested (291f.). Yet note 3 on page 291 insists· "That the OT law is meant [by νόμος] may be regarded as certain. To infer from the absence of the article that the meaning is more general is quite unjustified."

/4/ "Das Gesetz ist der Schlussel zum Verstandnis der Umgestaltung der Überlieferung." The English translation from the second edition reads· "The law is the key to the understanding even of the narrative of the Priestly Code" (1885·361). The impact of the sentence is quite other than the original. The translation of "Codex" by "code" certainly distorted the understanding of English-reading students, for it seems to emphasize the nature of P as a formal structure of laws to the exclusion of all else. "Codex" in Wellhausen's usage meant a collection of materials not necessarily legal in nature. The reference "Pharis. und Sadd." is to Wellhausen's earlier work of 1874. For a recent critique of this work, see Liebeschütz; cf. also note /9/ below.

/5/ In the English translation (1885:161), the phrase "dreistere Geschichtsmacher," which I have translated "impudent inventors of history," is rendered "audacious history-makers," which conveys or may convey something quite different.

/6/ It is interesting to note that Wellhausen avoids "Gesetz" and "gesetzlich" in this passage, except in a quotation, saving it for his thunderous conclusion.

/7/ 1878:29ff , 38, 166. Wellhausen's completely negative judgment of Chronicles and its authors continued to surface. See his discussion of "the Midrash of the Book of Kings" (1878·236f.), with its self-confident evaluation of midrash as "the result of holding sacred the relics of the past, an entirely idiosyncratic resurrection of dead bones in an artificial manner, primarily to provide labels, as the predilection for names and numbers evidences." Since Wellhausen never bothered to learn rabbinic Hebrew (see Liebeschutz: 248f), the judgment here rendered can hardly be based on an acquaintance with rabbinic midrash. As to midrash within Scriptures, see Renée Bloch. Wellhausen, at this point, turned again to the simile of the dead tree in describing midrash—as a surrogate for Judaism: "Wie der Efeu umgrunt derselbe den angestorbenen Stamm mit fremdartigem Leben, Altes und Neues in sonderbarer Vereinigung mischend" (1878.237).

/8/ In the second edition (1883.358f.; see also 1885:339, and 1899:343) the passage has been recast Riehm and Dillmann are no longer referred to, instead it is said: "Now, until a short time ago, there was a great inclination (no one will be found at this date to acknowledge that he felt it) to admire the sobriety and faithfulness of the Priestly Code." For the sentence quoted from 1878:360, the English translation has "naturalistic" in place of my "natural " The German has "naturalistisch." The fifth edition (1899:343) has substituted "rationalistisch" for "naturalistisch." Both refer, of course, to the Enlightenment idea of natural religion. For a discussion of "positiv" see H. Mulert.

/9/ Of Schwartz's address Liebeschütz wrote (253): "dieser ausführliche Nachruf des durch seine kirchengeschichtlichen Studien ausgezeichneten Altphilologen . . . , eine Göttinger Akademierede von 1918, ist wohl das Beste, was uber W.'s Werk und Person geschrieben worden ist " I read Liebeschutz's chapter only after I had completed this paper. Although it is a thoughtful contribution, it ignored the *Prolegomena* and dealt only with the essay *Pharisäer und Sadducäer* (1874) and with *Israelitische und judische Geschichte* (1894). The *Prolegomena* is mentioned but once, and that in connection with Wellhausen's acknowledgment of his indebtedness to Vatke Because of this, Liebeschütz did not recognize that for Wellhausen the traditional position, that Judaism, i.e., "das Gesetz," was an intruder between prophecy and gospel, was now, in Vatke's words, "historically justified." The portrait of Wellhausen as a scholar without interest in the theological struggles of the time, limned by Schwartz and accepted by Liebeschutz, who adds to it evidence from a letter to Dillmann dated 7 April 1872 that Wellhausen had no sympathy for theological liberalism (250), is not that of the author of the first edition of the *Prolegomena*, although changes in subsequent editions suggest that Wellhausen, after a brief sally into the field, beat a measured retreat. As Liebeschutz indicated in connection with the letter to Dillmann, Wellhausen was "Privatdozent" in Gottingen at the time, and his call to Greifswald, a stonghold of conservatism, was "in der Schwebe." As pointed out in note /8/ above, the critique, in the first edition, of Dillmann, recipient of the 1872 confidence concerning liberalism, has vanished in the second edition. Concerning Wellhausen's influence upon his Jewish contemporaries, see Liebeschütz. 254ff. It is interesting to note that in his mention of Wellhausen's influence on Harnack Liebeschutz (230 and note 30) accuses the latter of going beyond Wellhausen's intention, without reference to Leo Baeck's strictures against that influence.

/10/ In the second edition (1883.436, English translation, 1885.412) the topical reference is withdrawn, and in its place one reads· "Petrus der Stifter der Romischen Hierarchie." On the "invention" of Judaism see Lou H Silberman, 1957, on the tarbrush of "Judaizers" see Lou H. Silberman, 1962: especially 358f.

/11/ See also the citation from Vatke in note /3/, above, and its influence on Wellhausen, note /9/, above.

WORKS CONSULTED

Baeck, Leo
1901 "Harnack's Vorlesungen uber das Christentum." *MGWJ* 45· 97–120.

Bloch, Renée
1957 "Midrash " *DBSup* 5: 1263–81 = "Midrash " Pp. 29–50 in *Approaches to Ancient Judaism: Theory and Practices* Ed. W. S. Green. BJS 1. Missoula Scholars Press, 1978.

Cranfield, C. E. B.
1975 *A Critical and Exegetical Commentary on the Epistle to the Romans.* Vol 1. ICC. Edinburgh. T & T. Clark

Harnack, Adolf
1900 *Das Wesen des Christentums* Leipzig: J. C Hinrichs.

Klein, Charlotte
1978 *Anti-Judaism in Christian Theology.* Philadelphia· Fortress

Liebeschutz, Hans
1967 *Das Judentum im deutschen Geschichtsbild von Hegel bis Max Weber.* Tubingen. J. C. B. Mohr (Paul Siebeck).

Moore, George Foot
1921 "Christian Writers on Judaism." *HTR* 14. 197–254

Mulert, Hermann
1930 "Positiv." *RGG*, 2d ed 4.1357f.

Sanday, William, and Arthur C. Headlam
    1902   *A Critical and Exegetical Commentary on the Epistle to the Romans.*
                            5th ed. ICC Edinburgh· T. & T. Clark.

Schechter, Solomon
    1915   *Seminary Addresses, and Other Papers.* Cincinnati. Ark Publishing Co.

Schwartz, Eduard
    1963   "Julius Wellhausen." Pp. 326–61 in *Gesammelte Schriften*, vol. 1. 2d ed. Berlin. de Gruyter (First published in 1918)

Silberman, Lou H.
    1957   "'Judaism' and the Christian Theologian." *JR* 37: 246–52.
    1962   "Survey of Current Theological Literature: Jews, Christians, Germans." *Judaism* 11: 357–63.

Talmadge, F. E.
    1975   *Disputation and Dialogue.* New York: Ktav

Vatke, Wilhelm
    1835   *Die biblische Theologie wissenschaftlich dargestellt.* I. *Die Religion des Alten Testamentes nach den kanonischen Büchern entwickelt.* Berlin: G. Bethge.

Wellhausen, Julius
    1874   *Die Pharisäer und die Sadducäer: Eine Untersuchung zur inneren jüdischen Geschichte.* Greifswald: Bamberg.
    1878   *Geschichte Israels.* Erster Band. Berlin: G. Reimer.
    1883   *Prolegomena zur Geschichte Israels* 2d ed of 1878 Berlin· G. Reimer
    1885   *Prolegomena to the History of Israel.* Translation of 1883 edition by J. S. Black and A. Menzies. Edinburgh: A. & C. Black.
    1894   *Israelitische und judische Geschichte.* Berlin. G. Reimer.
    1899   *Prolegomena zur Geschichte Israels.* 5th ed. Berlin. G. Reimer.

WELLHAUSEN IN ENGLISH

Brevard S. Childs
Yale University

ABSTRACT

Wellhausen's critical studies of the Old Testament first drew attention in the English-speaking world as a result of the controversy surrounding W. Robertson Smith. The negative response to Wellhausen occurred partly because of a distrust of German theological scholarship, partly because of his historical skepticism, and partly because of his polemical style. After 1891 his work became increasingly accepted by scholars abroad, although numerous critics since the 1930s have suspected him of Hegelianism, a charge which has been soundly refuted.

An important aspect in the history of biblical interpretation which has often been neglected is the transmission and reception of a writer's work into a foreign language. During much of the nineteenth century the particular selection of German theological books for English translation and the neglect of others had a significant impact on the shape of American theology. In relation to biblical studies one only has to recall the enormous influence of the T. & T. Clark series "The Foreign Theological Library" which made widely available the commentaries of Hengstenberg, Delitzsch, and J. P. Lange, but left untranslated those of de Wette, Schleiermacher, and J. C. K. von Hofmann. Therefore, it seems appropriate for the Wellhausen centennial briefly to pursue the process by which Wellhausen was rendered into English.

The name of Julius Wellhausen first became known to a wide English-speaking audience through a series of articles on the Old Testament which began to appear in the 9th edition of *The Encyclopædia Britannica* (1875–89), and from the outset his name was linked with that of W. Robertson Smith. One only has to recall the highly charged religious atmosphere of Britain in the third quarter of the century to understand the crisis in biblical studies which shortly erupted. In 1859 Darwin's *Origin of Species* appeared. It was followed by *Essays and Reviews* in 1860 which had an even greater impact on the Anglican establishment. Two years later the celebrated and nasty controversy over Bishop Colenso's interpretation of the Pentateuch further polarized the parties. Finally, the translation of Renan's *Life of Jesus* in 1864 exerted a greater influence on the broad public than had the earlier and more radical books of the Germans.

The role of W. Robertson Smith as the catalyst in the explosion is well known and need not be repeated in detail/1/. Appointed in 1870 as Professor of Oriental Languages and Old Testament Exegesis at the Free Church College in Aberdeen, Smith's articles in *The Encyclopædia Britannica*, particularly the one on the "Bible" in volume 3, evoked an immediate storm in the General Assembly of the Free Church. In the ensuing trial Smith was at first vindicated but in 1881 was removed from his chair. His famous lectures of 1880–81 forced the issue of biblical criticism to every corner of the English-speaking world. It is obvious that the English translation of Wellhausen's *Prolegomena* which appeared in 1885 with its preface by Smith was seen as an integral part of the same battle for a historical-critical reading of the Bible. This peculiar background explains in part the different reception of Wellhausen's book to that afforded earlier to the books of Ewald.

In the heated debate over historical criticism of the Old Testament which was waged both in Britain and America between the years 1875 and 1890, Wellhausen's book was given little attention at first. That is to say, the primary issue in the English-speaking world turned on the legitimacy of the critical method in itself rather than on Wellhausen's thesis respecting the Pentateuch. Thus the controversy differed sharply from that within Germany where the right of critical studies had already been firmly established.

The evidence for this description can be clearly seen in the major American debate which was carried out between 1881 and 1883 in the *Presbyterian Review* and involved a cross section of the leading biblical scholars. W. H. Green represented the traditional conservative position, S. I. Curtiss and H. P. Smith a mediating position, and C. A. Briggs a liberal, critical stance. (See also F. L. Patton.) Significantly, Briggs, in his defense of critical study of the Old Testament, distanced himself from Wellhausen whom he placed on the far left of the spectrum. In time Briggs drew much closer to Wellhausen, but at first he viewed him as a threat to his attempt to gain acceptance of cautious criticism. This initial reaction to Wellhausen began to change significantly with S. R. Driver's *Introduction* of 1891 which expressed a general acceptance of the postexilic dating of the Priestly source.

There are several clear reasons for the initially negative response to Wellhausen's *Prolegomena* within the English-speaking world. In the first place, there remained a distrust of German theological scholarship, particularly in England. In a characteristic response Prime Minister William Gladstone responded in a letter to the Rev. W. L. Baxter who had written a rebuttal of Wellhausen. Gladstone wrote: "I thank you sincerely for your criticism of Wellhausen, whose works, in a rather slight acquaintance, I have all along mistrusted" (quoted in Baxter). He then went on to express his irritation that a German would be set up as a guide in *The Encyclopædia Britannica* for the British public.

Again, Wellhausen's approach to the Bible shared little of the religious idealism which had tempered the criticism of the earlier Germans. A. P. Stanley had been able to popularize the *History of Israel* by Ewald with its heterodox theories by finally appealing to the spiritual mystery which enveloped Israel. In contrast, Wellhausen cut through the smoke screen and appeared as an iconoclast who discounted much of the Old Testament's historicity.

Finally, there is no doubt that Wellhausen's style offended his English and American readers. One finds constant reference to Wellhausen's manner of polemic which was thought sarcastic and anti-clerical. H. P. Smith complained of the harshness of his attack (367). S. I. Curtiss thought his style was "profane and irreverent." He wrote: "It seems as though the author delights in wounding the sensibilities of his Christian readers" (84). However, this reaction was not confined to the church. E. G. Hirsch, writing in *The Jewish Encyclopedia*, acknowledged Wellhausen's brilliance, but complained of an "unmistakable anti-Jewish bias" which pervades his writings.

The period between 1891 and 1925 marked an increased acceptance of Wellhausen's work. A younger generation of English-speaking scholars, such as B. W. Bacon, T. H. Robinson, J. A. Bewer, and R. H. Pfeiffer championed his position, usually in a slightly modified form (cf. J. B. Harford). The majority of popular textbooks of this period, such as those of C. F. Kent, represented some form of Wellhausen's position.

Interestingly enough, the impact of Wellhausen's New Testament work has always been different from his Old. Although never translated into English, his commentaries on the Gospels were widely used by scholars and called forth far less outright opposition. Because the right of Gospel criticism had long been established in Britain, and the quality of Wellhausen's criticism did not stand out as especially radical when compared with that of Strauss or Wrede, the reception of his New Testament books was far less controversial.

In these years there was also an effort to soften Wellhausen's image. In a notable article A. R. Gordon sought to portray to his English audience the spirit of true reverence which Wellhausen had for the character of Jesus. He cited Wellhausen's description of Jesus as one living "a simple and open life, free from all earthly care," who delighted in children, birds and flowers. The impression given was that anyone who appreciated nature—whether Jesus or Wellhausen—could not be all bad.

Ironically, during the same period in which Wellhausen's work was gaining a wide acceptance in the English-speaking world, a major attack on his literary-critical method had been launched in Germany which was associated with the followers of Gunkel. In a carefully balanced article of 1930 W. Baumgartner summed up the criticism. He concentrated on the new attitude toward oral tradition and to the new data provided by the opening up of the ancient Near East. Baumgartner was highly appreciative of Wellhausen's contribution while at the same time pointing out the limitations of his approach from the perspective of Gunkel.

However, during the 1930s and 1940s a different charge began increasingly to be levelled against Wellhausen, chiefly from the side of W. F. Albright (88) and his students. Albright voiced some of the same criticisms as had Baumgartner—his isolation from the world of the ancient Near East, his dependence upon Arabic parallels rather than the earlier cuneiform material—but he added a new item in claiming that Wellhausen's dependence upon Hegelian philosophy had been the determining element in his critical reconstruction. This same construction was soon picked up by others; however, it is to Y. Kaufmann's credit that he dealt with Wellhausen in a far more serious way than had Albright. Unfortunately, in spite of L. Perlitt's massive rebuttal of this charge, it continues to be passed on uncritically in many textbooks.

Some thirty-five years ago at the celebration of Wellhausen's birth, two significant articles appeared out of Chicago assessing Wellhausen, one by W. A. Irwin and another by A. Wikgren. Both articles were critical of some aspects of his work. Yet both articles were aware of his lasting contribution and thus reflected well the modern assessment of him. I suspect that Wellhausen would have particularly enjoyed Allen Wikgren's concluding characterization: "a great New Testament scholar with a most excellent Old Testament background."

NOTE

/1/ The best source remains J S. Black and G. Chrystal. Cf. also the excellent article by Warner M. Bailey.

WORKS CONSULTED

Albright, William Foxwell
    1957   *From the Stone Age to Christianity*. 2d ed. New York: Doubleday & Co.

Bailey, Warner M.
    1973   "William Robertson Smith and American Biblical Studies." *Journal of Presbyterian History* 51: 285–308.

Baumgartner, Walter
    1930   "Wellhausen und der heutige Stand der alttestamentlichen Wissenschaft." *Theologische Rundschau* NF 2: 287–307.

Baxter, William Lang
    1896   *Sanctuary and Sacrifice: A Reply to Wellhausen*. London. Eyre & Spottiswoode

Black, J. S., and G. Chrystal
    1912   *The Life of William Robertson Smith*. London· A. & C. Black.

Briggs, Charles A
    1883   "A Critical Study of the History of the Higher Criticism with Special Reference to the Pentateuch." *PR* 4. 69–130

Colenso, John William
    1862–65   *The Pentateuch and Book of Joshua Critically Examined* 5 vols. London· Longmans, Green, and Co.

Curtiss, Samuel I.
    1882   "Delitzsch on the Origin and Composition of the Pentateuch." *PR* 3: 553–88.

Driver, S R.
    1891   *An Introduction to the Literature of the Old Testament*. Edinburgh: T & T. Clark.

Ewald, Heinrich Georg August
    1867–74   *The History of Israel* 5 vols. London: Longmans, Green, and Co (German original in 1843–55.)

Gordon, A R
    1905   "Wellhausen." *The Expositor* VI/11: 177–94, 257–75.

Green, W. Henry
    1882   "Professor Robertson Smith on the Pentateuch." *PR* 3· 108–56.

Harford, J Battersby
    1925   "Since Wellhausen." *The Expositor* IX/4. 4–26, 83–102, 164–82, 244–65, 323–49, 403–29

Hirsch, Emil G
    1905   "Julius Wellhausen." *The Jewish Encyclopedia* 12: 501.

Irwin, William A
    1944   "The Significance of Julius Wellhausen." *JBR* 12· 160–73.

Kaufmann, Yehezkel
    1960   *The Religion of Israel: From Its Beginnings to the Babylonian Exile*. Translated and abridged by Moshe Greenberg. Chicago. University of Chicago.

Patton, F. L
    1883   "The Dogmatic Aspect of Pentateuchal Criticism." *PR* 4· 344–410

Perlitt, Lothar
    1965   *Vatke und Wellhausen. Geschichtsphilosophische Voraussetzungen und historiographische Motive für die Darstellung der Religion und Geschichte Israels durch Wilhelm Vatke und Julius Wellhausen* BZAW 94. Berlin: Alfred Töpelmann.

Smith, Henry P.
    1882   "The Critical Theories of Julius Wellhausen." *PR* 3· 357–88.

Smith, William Robertson
    1878   "Bible." *The Encyclopædia Britannica*. 9th ed. 3: 634–48.

1881	*The Old Testament in the Jewish Church: Twelve Lectures on Biblical Criticism.* Edinburgh· A & C Black.

Stanley, Arthur Penrhyn
1863–76	*Lectures on the History of the Jewish Church.* 3 vols London: J. Murray.

Wellhausen, Julius
1885	*Prolegomena to the History of Israel* Trans. J. S. Black and A. Menzies. Edinburgh. A. & C. Black. (1st German edition in 1878.)

Wikgren, Allen
1944	"Wellhausen and the Synoptic Gospels: A Centenary Appraisal." *JBR* 12: 174–80

WELLHAUSEN ON THE NEW TESTAMENT

Nils A. Dahl
Emeritus, *Yale University*

ABSTRACT

In his later years Wellhausen devoted a main part of his scholarly efforts to the study of the New Testament, especially the Gospels. The present essay first draws attention to the characteristic form of his publications and refers briefly to his pioneering work on the Aramaic background of the Gospels and his interest in textual criticism. His critical analysis of the Gospels, Acts, and the Johannine apocalypse illustrates how Wellhausen used literary source analysis as a tool for historical source criticism. He found that the crucifixion of Jesus as king of the Jews explained the contrast between the Jewish and the Christian Messiah and, thereby, provided a clue to the origins of Christianity and a criterion for historical criticism of the Gospels. The four Gospels attest, each in its own way, the Christian faith in Jesus as the crucified and risen Christ, and even most of the sayings attributed to Jesus presuppose this faith. Only scattered fragments of historical information have been preserved in the earliest source, the Gospel of Mark, and still less elsewhere.

The radical criticism prepared for a pointed discussion of key historical issues. Wellhausen found it increasingly difficult to answer the question of whether and in what sense Jesus regarded himself as the Messiah His general conclusion was that the person of Jesus is only known to us as it is reflected by the medium of Christian faith As a basis for religion the historical Jesus is a poor substitute for the Christian faith. Jesus was a Jew, Christianity orginated with the faith in the resurrection of the crucified Messiah, as a sudden mutation of the practical monotheism of the Bible. The first period of Christian history was one of gradual emancipation from Judaism, without much influence from Greek or syncretistic ideas. Conflict with the Roman empire marked the beginning of a second period.

Wellhausen's contributions to the study of the New Testament never made an impact comparable to his *Prolegomena* and other works on Israelite history and religion, but his work became one among several factors that caused a crisis for nineteenth-century liberal theology. He paved the way for form criticism and, inadvertently, for kerygmatic neoorthodoxy. His acute observations, terse style, and provocative suggestions still represent a challenge to New Testament scholarship.

During the last part of his career, Julius Wellhausen devoted his major scholarly efforts to the study of the New Testament. His works in this field caused great interest and heated controversies, not only because they were written by the recognized master of Old Testament studies but also because they represented a fresh and provocative approach to the sources and the historical problems. Wellhausen's work on the New Testament never made the impact which his classical studies on Israelite history and literature had done. Only in conjunction with the works of, e.g., W. Wrede, A. Schweitzer, and the pioneers of the history-of-religion school did Wellhausen's contributions mark a period of transition from nineteenth- to twentieth-century New Testament scholarship. Wellhausen, however, had a profile of his own and cannot simply be considered one among several representatives of radical criticism. His studies have retained an interest of their own, even apart from their importance as part of the lifework of a scholarly giant. In recent decades there has been a renewed interest in the pioneering work of German scholars at the turn of the centuries. But, if I am not mistaken, only scant attention has been paid to Wellhausen.

In order to relate Wellhausen's work on the New Testament to his entire scholarly production, biography, and personal religious attitude, one would have to study a variety of sources, including his extensive correspondence. The present essay is only based upon a reading of works which he himself submitted for publication/1/. I have not tried to give a comprehensive, well-balanced presentation but have highlighted points which have been of special interest to myself, hoping that these points will also be of most relevance for a comparison of Wellhausen's *Prolegomena* with his approach to the sources for and the history of Jesus and the origins of Christianity. Even so, I shall not come close to the sovereignty of Wellhausen, who preferred only to deal with those questions on which he had something new and important to say.

I. PRELIMINARY SURVEY AND CHARACTERIZATION

All of Wellhausen's main works on the New Testament appeared during a remarkably short span of time: the commentary—if commentary be the right word—on Mark in 1903, those on Matthew and Luke in 1904, and the Introduction to the three first gospels in 1905. Critical analyses, or notes, on the Fourth Gospel, the Book of Revelation, and Acts followed in 1907, and a book on the Gospel of John in 1908. A revised edition of the Introduction appeared in 1911, and a more comprehensive analysis of Acts not until 1914, although most of the work on this project seems to have been completed earlier (1914:35, n. 1).

Wellhausen did, probably from the outset, assume that the religious history of Israel aimed at Jesus as its fulfiller (Eissfeldt). The work of his teacher in Göttingen, Heinrich Ewald, celebrated by Wellhausen in an eloquent testimonial (1901), had embraced both Testaments. At an early stage of his career, Wellhausen had himself written on the Pharisees and Sadducees (1874). His major work on Israelite and Jewish history (1894) included a chapter on Jesus, entitled "Das Evangelium," which in later editions became the concluding chapter of the book. Having completed this great historical synthesis, Wellhausen turned to more penetrating investigation of problems in the New Testament area, beginning with the Semitic background of the Greek language in the Gospels (1895, 1896, and 1899).

The intensity with which Wellhausen worked on the problems during the first decade of the twentieth century and the immediately preceding years is apparent in the way in which he modified or even changed his position on several problems, e.g., the Aramaic substratum of the Gospels, the "Son of man," and the messiahship of Jesus. The second edition of the *Einleitung* was expanded by a number of appendices (1911: §§ 11-20, pp. 107-76). The chapter on the language of the Gospels (1911:7-32) was completely rewritten, and there were also important changes in those portions which on the whole were left as they were. Wellhausen tended to state his opinions in an apodictic form, but both the shifting points of view and apparent self-contradictions indicate that many of his proposed solutions had the character of experiments. He wanted to provoke, to call attention to neglected areas of study, to point to inconsistencies in the texts that called for explanation, to raise radical historical questions, and to do all of this with the utmost vigor, so that it would not be possible to sweep the problems under the rug again. Once the problems were clearly recognized, the solutions might be modified both by Wellhausen himself and by others.

It is not a matter of chance that most of what Wellhausen wrote on the New Testament had the form of notes and comments on the sources. The results of his Gospel studies were summarized in a double form, a fresh translation of the three first Gospels (except Matthew 1-2 and Luke 1-2) on the one hand and the discussion of textual, linguistic, literary, and historical problems in the Introduction (1905, 1911) on the other. He started with examination of the sources, making fresh observations and raising questions of his own, rather than taking over the problems from others and repeating what had already been repeated. His remarks about scholars to the right and to the left were often ironic or even sarcastic, sometimes nasty and sometimes absolutely devastating. In the second edition of his Introduction Wellhausen omitted many such asides—the point did not have to be repeated once it had been made—but he added some new ones, e.g. about Deissmann, who compared the literary level of the sayings-collection with that of papyri written by illiterate people (1911:162). The second edition, however, pays more serious attention to the history of research and current debate than did the first one (see, e.g., 1911:170-76, on Kirsopp Lake)/2/.

Wellhausen did not care to reproduce the stuff that might be found in standard commentaries. He only adduced a small number of parallels in order to give reasons for his understanding of vocabulary or syntax. In general, he only commented on a passage if he had something of his own to contribute. Without aiming at any systematic order, he offered scattered remarks about text-critical, linguistic, literary or historical questions. Apart from the full translation, the form of his exposition of the first three Gospels did not differ substantially from his critical analysis of Acts, whereas his studies on the Fourth Gospel mainly dealt with the original source and later expansions. This peculiar type of commentary was of little value to a beginning student or to a pastor but fascinating, instructive and provocative to the initiated reader (cf. Jülicher, 1904). The cool, critical attitude of an outside observer did not exclude occasional expressions of unabashed subjectivity, blame for inept redactors, praise for beautiful and moving stories, even reluctance to add comments to the translation of the Gethsemane pericope.

II. ARAMAIC BACKGROUND AND TEXT OF THE GOSPELS

Wellhausen was one of the pioneers for the study of the Aramaic background of the Gospels. He started with the assumption that at least the original form of Mark and the sayings common to Matthew and Luke had been written in Aramaic (1895 and 1896) but gradually modified his claims (compare 1905:35–38, 57, 68 with 1911:26f., 48, 60). He became increasingly skeptical about conjectural mistranslations and translation variants even though he retained some examples which he found convincing (1911:25–28). At the end, he mainly drew attention to syntactical constructions which were common in Aramaic but unusual, if not impossible, in Greek (1911:11–25; see also Black: 1f. et passim).

The question of which Aramaic dialect came closest to the Aramaic spoken in Palestine at the time of Jesus caused a somewhat heated debate between Dalman (1898) and Wellhausen. Dalman objected that Wellhausen was not really familiar with rabbinic Aramaic, while the latter objected that the Aramaic spoken at the time of Jesus must have differed from the Aramaic of Palestinian Targumim and rabbinic texts and that exact retroversion of sayings of Jesus was impossible (1911:28–32). At this point, he seems to have been right, but recent discoveries have provided so many new texts that the debate between the two pioneers has become obsolete.

Wellhausen's interest in textual criticism was related to the study of the Aramaic background of the Gospels. His procedure is very characteristic for the way he worked. He hardly consulted critical editions but worked with editions of the most famous manuscripts, Vaticanus, Sinaiticus, and Cantabrigiensis (D), under comparison with the earliest Syriac witness (Syr. sin.) and, to some extent, Old Latin evidence. What especially drew his interest was the Semitisms of the D text, most of which he considered to go back to the original. Wellhausen was, however, not a onesided advocate of the Western text but practiced text-critical eclecticism on the basis of the manuscripts he had consulted, in general favoring variants which deviated from literary Greek or making his decisions on exegetical grounds (1911:1–7; 1908:127–32). This form of reasoned criticism on the basis of primary evidence still has some value, at least as a stimulus for an exegete not to rely too comfortably upon any standard edition.

III. SOURCE ANALYSIS

For the purpose of this paper, and perhaps for other purposes as well, it is practical to make a terminological distinction between *source criticism* and *source analysis*. Source criticism is a historical discipline whose aim is to discern the value of a text as a source of historical information either about the persons and events about which if purports to report or about the time and the conditions in which it was written. "Source analysis" is used in the sense of German "Quellenscheidung," efforts to distinguish between various discrete sources or between various, original or secondary layers in a literary text. In the tradition of the great German historians of the nineteenth century, Wellhausen used source analysis as one, but by no means the only, tool of source criticism.

Wellhausen accepted the Two Source theory as the basic solution to the synoptic problem. He assumed that the Gospel of Mark had been expanded and altered at some points but refused to use synoptic comparison as a tool for reconstruction of the original form (1905:53–57 = 1911:45–48). The copies used by Matthew and Luke were on the whole identical with the text of Mark transmitted in the manuscripts. In most cases it was impossible to tell whether the secondary elements in Mark had been added in oral or written transmission. Wellhausen assumed that variants in Matthew's and Luke's renderings of sayings of Jesus presupposed that a written collection of sayings ("Q") had already existed in Aramaic, but he never attempted any exact reconstruction of the source and grew increasingly skeptical about the possibility of any such attempt. Matthew and Luke had access to different recensions of the Greek Q which had been subjected to several corrections, some of which were based upon the Aramaic original (1911:59f.). On the whole, internal source analysis of the writings is of little importance for Wellhausen's criticism of the first three Gospels.

By contrast, the questions of sources, alterations, and additions are at the center of Wellhausen's investigations of the Fourth Gospel. He started with observations which indicate that we do not possess the original form but a second, expanded and revised edition of the Gospel. Chapters 15–17 have been inserted between 14:31 and 18:1, the sequence in chapters 5–7 has been rearranged, 8:44 must originally have referred to Cain as the murderer, and there are several other interpolations (1907a). In his comprehensive analysis of the Gospel (1908), Wellhausen revised his position, assuming that a gradual expansion had occurred both before and after the major revision of the original writing (the "*Grundschrift*"). He detected not only seams and discrepancies but also a number of doublets, additions and additions to additions, variations of similar themes and even conflicting points of view.

According to Wellhausen's reconstruction, the original draft contained only one Galilean and one Judean period, John 7:3–4 marking the transition. It was mainly narrative but included some discourse material, including the coming of the Paraclete but not the presence of the risen Lord. The later layers include, i. a., the pilgrimages of Jesus to festivals in Jerusalem, the most typical Johannine sayings, and materials from the earlier Gospels. Some accretions were early, others late (e.g., 5:43, a reference to Bar Kochba), but exact reconstruction of various layers would be a hopeless enterprise.

The details of Wellhausen's analysis have proved to be of less permanent value than his general insight that the present shape of the Fourth Gospel presupposes a long and complicated prehistory which includes written drafts. As most of the additions were made in the circle in which the "*Urschrift*" originated, the Gospel was to be considered a historical unity in spite of its various layers. The Gospel presupposes the break between Judaism and Christianity; the Jews are seen as representatives of the hostile world. The universalism is, however, due to developments within a circle that originated among Christian Jews, as is the christianization and alteration of the history and teaching of Jesus. The Fourth Gospel is inner-Christian, esoteric; even discourses addressed to the Jews are intended for a Christian audience. Preceding forms of Christian faith are corrected, but there is no good reason to assume an influence of non-Jewish, e.g., Greek, ideas. Neither the idea of the Logos nor other concepts demonstrate any real affinity to Philo, and Johannine "gnosis" differs from genuinely gnostic ideas about redemption of the individual soul (1908:119–25). Many of these suggestions have been elaborated and widely accepted in recent years, but modern scholars have hardly been aware of the degree to which Wellhausen had anticipated some of their insights.

It is, by contrast, difficult to find much continuity between Wellhausen's analysis of the Apocalypse of John and present-day research. It was published at a time when source analysis of apocalyptic and other writings flourished and is mainly of interest as an illustration of Wellhausen's special methodology. He was skeptical about overly subtle literary analysis and always tried to find a correlation between sources and historical situations. In this case, he found the key to be that Christian hatred against Rome did not begin before Domitian, if then (1907b:4, 34). For that reason, fragments which bore traces of an earlier origin and yet were anti-Roman had to be of Jewish origin, e.g. Rev 11:1–2 and parts of chapters 12, 13, and 17. The author who incorporated these fragments had also reworked earlier Christian texts, including the letters in chapters 2–3, and there were some secondary additions.

In the critical analysis of Acts, Wellhausen's main concern was to detect which historical information the book might contain. He did not find very much. The speeches were literary compositions, and many of the reports were distorted, the descriptions of the tumult in Ephesus and the sea voyage of Paul (Acts 19 and 27) taken over from non-Christian sources. The author made use of several cycles of traditions, including an itinerary of Paul in Acts 16ff., but Wellhausen made no attempt to separate discrete sources—a remarkable fact. On the basis of Gal 1:23, Wellhausen assumed that Paul had indeed persecuted the churches in Judea. He further conjectured that Paul had been converted before the death of Stephanus, with whose circle Paul had no special connections (1907c:16, 21). In accordance with the chronology of Eduard Schwartz (1907), Wellhausen assumed that Paul's second journey to Jerusalem (Gal 2:1-10) had occurred before the persecution of Herodes Agrippa (44 CE). The report in Acts 12 contained valuable historical information even though it glossed over the fact that not only James but also John the son of Zebedee was martyred at that time (1907c:22f.).

IV. HISTORICAL CRITICISM OF THE GOSPELS

It would be onesided but not really inappropriate to regard Wellhausen's New Testament studies as kind of "prolegomena" to a history of Jesus and early Christianity which Wellhausen never wrote, and to my knowledge never intended to write. Even in his philological and source-analytical investigations one can detect vestiges that show that he was primarily a historian of great stature. A close correlation and mutual interdependence of history and source criticism are characteristics of his New Testament studies as of his *Prolegomena* to the history of Israel.

Wellhausen worked on the principle that the earliest source is the most reliable one and tried to demonstrate that the principle does in fact apply to the Gospels. Not only Matthew and Luke but already their other common source, Q, were secondary sources, dependent upon the earliest Gospel, Mark. Wellhausen did not *a priori* deny the possibility that the later sources may contain early, even genuine traditions, but found only very few examples in which it could be established that this was indeed the case (e.g., 1904a:75, on Herod and Jesus). His skepticism at this point was based upon the assumption that Mark wanted to write down the whole of the tradition (1905:86; 1911:77) and upon other reasons as well.

For Wellhausen, the exile and the restoration in Judea marked a sharp distinction between the ancient religion of Israel and Judaism, the religion under the Law, codified in the Priestly Codex and the Pentateuch. In a somewhat similar way, the crucifixion of Jesus marked the watershed between Judaism and Christianity. Christianity is faith in the Gospel, i.e., in the message about Jesus as the crucified and risen Christ. Jesus, however, was a Jew and not a Christian (1911:82, 99f., 102). The Christian concept of the crucified Messiah is not simply an alteration of the Jewish concept; it runs contrary to it and has only the name in common. The leap from one concept to the other is only to be understood as something that happened after the facts (1911:81f.). This insight is the result of Wellhausen's critical investigation of the sources, but it is also a presupposition for his evaluation of their historical reliability.

Mark wrote his Gospel in order to show that Jesus was the Christ (1911:44). During his public ministry in Galilee (Mark 1:16–6:13), Jesus did not proclaim himself as the Messiah, but to Mark his miracles were primarily evidence of his messianic power and authority. In the section that precedes the passion (Mark 8:27–10:52), the Christian Gospel comes into the foreground in the form of esoteric, proleptic instruction of the disciples about the suffering and the resurrection of the Son of Man and, more indirectly, in the call to follow him on the road to martyrdom. In general, Mark has only collected disconnected stories and sayings which have been arranged as pertaining to three periods, Jesus in Capernaum, walking around, and in Jerusalem (1903:9). Only scattered pieces provide historical information about Jesus; the judgment that the Gospel as a whole lacks the marks of history extends even to the passion (1911:43).

In the later Gospels the story of Jesus has been thoroughly christianized (e.g., 1911:75). Not only John but also Matthew and Luke have projected the themes Christ and the church back into the history of Jesus, each in his own way.

Matthew is a Christian rabbi who represents Jesus as the present Messiah who already in the present lays the foundation for the kingdom of Heaven on earth and as another Moses gives laws and instructions to the church. The animosity against the official representatives of the Law is part of the competition between two communities which both strived for the same goal, fulfillment of the Law in righteousness (1911:61f., 73f.).

Luke had the aspiration to be a historian but did not succeed. He exercised criticism in omitting some Marcan pericopes, e.g., the repetitions in Mark 6:34–8:26, but included many secondary variants, elaborations and embellishments like the scene in Luke 4:16–30, which makes Jesus introduce himself publicly as the Anointed One (1911:54f.). Luke is not familiar with Palestinian geography; he is more openminded, universalistic and individualistic and more literary and sentimental than Matthew. In general Luke represents a later stage of development, but the differences between Luke and Matthew should not be exaggerated. Both of them combine heterogeneous materials, and neither is a theologian. Luke can, e.g., express the most vivid expectation of the parousia but at the same time internalize the gospel (1911:60f., 63f.).

The anonymous author whose work is at the basis of the Fourth Gospel was, according to Wellhausen, a creative personality who handled the tradition with great freedom. The Johannine chronology is correct to the extent that Jesus was crucified before passover and that his ministry in Jerusalem had lasted over some period of time (cf. III above), but otherwise the Christian gospel has not only penetrated the tradition but overpowered it.

Thus, the Fourth Gospel stands apart and does not represent a stage in the development of the common tradition. John presupposes Paul but goes further in emancipating Christianity from its basis in Judaism. He does, however, not reintegrate the historical person into a Pauline type of christology; rather: "The historical Jesus is completely and right from the beginning absorbed by the heavenly" (1908:121). It is not necessary to give further details, but it should be mentioned that Johannine Christianity, as Wellhausen understood it, is church oriented, not individualistic.

Wellhausen's studies in the Gospels led to the conclusion that in the course of transmission the discourse materials had been developed and enlarged to a much higher degree than the stories about Jesus (1911:76). Most contemporaneous and later scholars have reacted against his radical criticism of the logia tradition, but one has to try to understand his reasons.

Wellhausen could point to the creation of new sayings of Jesus in apocryphal Gospels and agrapha and also to the Johannine discourses in the same connection. There are also examples, especially in Matthew, that oblique reports have been turned into direct discourse. Moreover, the special character of, e.g., the parables in Matthew and the paradigmatic stories in Luke indicate that the materials peculiar to the later evangelists do not belong to the ancient tradition (1911:60f.). Aramaisms pervade the whole Gospel tradition and constitute no criterion for authentic sayings of Jesus.

The most controversial part of Wellhausen's radical criticism was his devaluation of the materials common to Matthew and Luke ("Q") as a source for the teachings of Jesus (e.g., Jülicher, 1906; Harnack). Wellhausen had argued that Mark had the primary and Q the secondary version of sayings of Jesus when the two sources overlapped, a theory which presupposed that the Greek Mark was a translation of an Aramaic Gospel (1905:74-78; 1911:65-70). In the controversy with Harnack, Wellhausen did not insist upon this point. In any case, Q presupposed familiarity with the Marcan tradition, including the Galilean miracles and the passion of Jesus (1911: 160). Wellhausen further argued that the isolated apophthegmata in Mark represented the ancient tradition whereas the more coherent discourse compositions in Q belonged to a later stage (1911:75-77, 160-62). Still more important, the teaching in Q is more esoteric, addressed to the disciples and, in fact, aimed at the church for whom Jesus was already the present Messiah (1911:72-75, 163-67).

Both Wellhausen himself and his critics observed the analogy between his Gospel criticism and his chronology for the sources in the Pentateuch. The ancient sources (JE) were predominantly narrative; the discourses and laws in Deuteronomy and the Priestly Codex were later and had been incorporated into the narrative framework by a redactor. In a similar way, Matthew and Luke had incorporated the logia into the narrative of Mark.

In his work with the New as well as with the Old Testament Wellhausen remained a source critic who held to the earliest written form of a text without attempting to reconstruct its hypothetical prehistory in oral tradition. In some respects he anticipated the later "form critics": the Marcan framework is redactional, not historical; the ancient tradition consisted of isolated, small units, handed down, shaped and expanded in popular tradition (1911:45; 1905:53, n. 1). Wellhausen could himself make bold historical conjectures in order to recover the historical events, but he was very skeptical about attempts to save a historical kernel of sayings which in their preserved form presuppose a post-Easter situation like, e.g., the passion predictions in Mark. Thus, he was very critical of Jülicher's attempt to reconstruct authentic "pure parables"; in Wellhausen's opinion, the elimination of "allegorical features" often spoiled the point of the tales (e.g., 1903: 100; 1904a:69, 133; 1904b:86f., 98).

With great consistency, Wellhausen refused to attribute to Jesus simply whatever was original, true, or valuable: "The truth attests only itself and not its author" (1911:77; see also 158f.). Wellhausen could be merciless when he found examples of redactional ineptitude, but I know of no other scholar who has been more generous in his praise of the beauty and splendor of inauthentic sayings and unhistorical tales (e.g., 1903:37, 77; 1904a:77.).

Wellhausen's criticism left only a minimal amount of materials as reliable sources for the teaching of Jesus, mainly some scattered, occasional and polemical sayings, mostly to be found in Mark 1:16–4:12 and 11:15–13:2. Most of the parables were eliminated, as was the Sermon on the Mount, together with the rest of Q and the materials peculiar to Matthew or Luke, not to mention John. What remains is no more than inadequate fragments, barely sufficient to give an impression of the teachings of Jesus (1911:103).

Having reached this conclusion, Wellhausen in a somewhat surprising move reintroduced the secondary materials, not as a direct source for the teaching of Jesus but as evidence for the impact which his person made upon the church which came into being after his death, upon its ethics and way of life as well as upon its theology: "Without this aftereffect in the life of the Christian community we too (i.e., like Paul) would have been unable to visualize the religious personality of Jesus. It appears, however, only in the shape of a reflection, broken through the medium of Christian faith" (1911:104). "The spirit of Jesus lived on in the earliest church, which not only created the gospel about Jesus but also further developed his ethics" (1911:77, cf. 168–70). Such statements are not pious mollifications of Wellhausen's radical criticism. They explain how it was possible for him to think that the Jerusalem church was capable of producing some of the most impressive sayings of Jesus, at the same time as they explain why he himself did not write a history of Jesus but prepared a fresh translation of the Gospels with critical notes, comments, and introduction.

V. FRAGMENTS OF THE HISTORY OF JESUS

At the time of Wellhausen's most important contributions to New Testament studies, the leading scholars in the field no longer tried to write a comprehensive "Life of Jesus"; they were satisfied to write about "Problems of the Life of Jesus" (1911:79). It is an exaggeration to say that Wellhausen himself "sought to furnish proof that the Gospels cannot be used as sources for the history of Jesus, but offer only testimony to the messianic faith of early Christianity" (Kümmel: 282). The scattered fragments of historical information which he found might well, with the help of historical conjectures and imagination, have been synthesized into a sketchy but coherent picture. What we do find is a number of scattered, fragmentary, and often tentative remarks about the history of Jesus. What Wellhausen achieved by this procedure was to cut through the filigree work of conventional historical and pseudohistorical criticism in order to concentrate on the key issues, the crucifixion of Jesus, the emergence of the Christian faith, and the question whether and in what sense Jesus considered himself to be the Messiah.

Wellhausen found it quite unreasonable to doubt that Jesus was indeed crucified as "King of the Jews." He accepted the historicity of the inscription of the charge and of the mockery by the soldiers (1903:136, 139). More important, however, the resurgence of the conviction that Jesus was the Messiah and the transformation of the Jewish concept into the Christian faith in the crucified and resurrected Christ would be incomprehensible unless Jesus had in fact been executed as a Messiah (1911:82; 1914:6, n. 1).

Wellhausen doubted that a Jewish court could have condemned Jesus because he confessed to be the Messiah and considered Mark 14:61–62 a secondary addition to the trial scene. Jesus was, rather, found guilty of blasphemy because he had spoken against the temple. While this provided the legal basis for the sentence passed, it would not suffice as an accusation before the Romans; to Pilate the high priests did therefore denounce Jesus as a messianic pretender (1903:132f., 136, see also 106; 1911:98).

To Wellhausen, as to others, the most important problem in the life of Jesus was whether and in what sense Jesus considered himself to be the Messiah. The fragments which Wellhausen considered authentic sources for the teaching of Jesus aggravated rather than solved this problem.

In his *Israelitische und jüdische Geschichte* Wellhausen had, in the fashion of nineteenth-century liberalism, depicted Jesus as the teacher who planted the seed of the kingdom of God and made it the goal of moral endeavor (1897:380). His historical source criticism made him abandon this view. The notion of the presence of the kingdom was a correlate of the faith in Jesus as the present Messiah who had proclaimed the coming of the kingdom of God and thereby anticipated the Christian Gospel (1911:94f., 98–102). Like most of the materials in Matthew and Luke, even the parables in Mark 4:26–32 are secondary creations. Wellhausen did not deny that Jesus occasionally used the term "the kingdom of God" in its futurist sense, eliminating the political connotations of the Jewish concept, but he denied that the kingdom was the main topic of Jesus' teaching. Calling to repentance, like John the Baptist and the prophets before him, Jesus stressed the threatening doom more than the promise (1911:97).

Jesus did not proclaim a new faith but taught to do the will of God. The teachings preserved by Mark, the primary source, are mostly polemical but include also some occasional utterances, made according to the needs of a general public that was misguided by its leaders (1911:102 and 95, where the term "evident truths," used 1905:106, was dropped). Rejecting the traditions of the scribes and the Pharisees, Jesus did not rebel against the Law, but neither did he feel constrained by it; he evaluated its statutes according to their inner worth, whether they promoted or inhibited the life of human beings. One might say that to Wellhausen the double commandment, to love God and one's neighbor, is the summary of the teachings of Jesus as well as of the Law (1911:102f.; 1903:103f.).

Wellhausen understood the teaching of Jesus within the context of and in contrast to the Judaism of his time. He did not overcome the inherited tendency to depict Pharisaism as the dark foil for Jesus, but he realized that Jesus' free attitude to the Law together with his polemic against the scribes and, especially, his prediction of the destruction of the temple might appear to undermine the foundations of the Jewish religion and the Jewish commonwealth (1911:97f., 103).

Neither the public teaching of Jesus nor the hostility of Jewish leaders provided sufficient explanation for the fact that the teacher from Nazareth was crucified as king of the Jews. In dealing with the key question of the messiahship of Jesus, Wellhausen wavered and modified his position over the years.

During his ministry in Galilee, Jesus spoke and acted with authority, but not with messianic authority. In authentic sayings of Jesus, the term "Son of man" is not a messianic self-designation but is used in the general sense of a human being (1911:83, 123–30; and already 1899). Having abandoned the view that Jesus secretly planted the kingdom of God on earth (see above), Wellhausen found the parable of the Sower to contain the clearest expression of the self-consciousness of Jesus: He was a teacher who scattered his seed at random and reflected over the uncertain success of his words (1905:94; slightly modified 1911:84).

In his first sketch, Wellhausen had found a striking formulation for the attitude of Jesus to the hope of the Jews: "Only in this sense he can have called himself the Messiah: they should not expect anybody else. He was not the one whom they wanted but he was the true Messiah whom they ought to want" (1897:382). This, however, did not provide a satisfactory answer to the historical question.

As the crucifixion of Jesus as a messianic pretender had to have some basis, Wellhausen saw no reason to doubt that already in Galilee Peter confessed Jesus to be the (Jewish) Messiah. On the Mount of Olives a crowd of Galileans hailed Jesus, in the expectation that he would restore the kingdom of David, and the cleansing of the temple may have enhanced their hope (1903:94–97). It is difficult, however, to recognize how Jesus himself reacted (1905:92 = 1911:82).

Wellhausen dismissed the popular theories of a crisis in Galilee that caused Jesus to withdraw in a state of depression or to go up to Jerusalem with militant heroism to challenge the enemy in his den. According to Mark, Jesus was rather at the peak of his popularity when he left Galilee, most likely in order to escape Herod (1911:80f.; see also 40f. and 1904a:75). In the first edition of the *Einleitung*, Wellhausen added that Jesus intended a religious regeneration of his nation; in order to win individuals, he would not have had to go to Jerusalem. As the regenerator, and as the one who was to fulfill the hopes of Israel, Jesus could accept the name of the Jewish restorer—as an act of accommodation (1905:93; cf. 1903:71, 104).

As one might expect, Wellhausen was not in the long run satisfied with the rationalist concept of accommodation. More than earlier, he was in 1911 inclined to think that in Jerusalem Jesus no longer acted merely as a teacher but also acted as an agitator, who at least gave the impression that he claimed the authority of a messianic ruler for himself. He did not, certainly, plan an insurrection against the Romans, but he wanted to free his nation from the yoke of hierocracy and nomocracy. "To a certain degree Reimarus may possibly be right" (1911:83). This somewhat enigmatic statement is left without further comment. I take this to imply that, at the end, Wellhausen found that the historian could perceive reasons for the charge that Jesus pretended to be the Messiah but that the sources did not permit an answer to the question of whether or not Jesus thought of himself as the Messiah.

In accordance with his historical source criticism, Wellhausen found all predictions of the passion and resurrection of the Son of man to be secondary, as were sayings about the parousia of Jesus. Jesus is likely to have expected the end of the world to be near and even to have anticipated his own death. At least in his comments on Mark 14:22–25, Wellhausen even assumed that during the last supper Jesus established a covenantal fellowship with his disciples, whereby the idea of communion by sacrifice was added to that of table fellowship (1903:119–26; see also 1911:134). If any, the saying of Jesus in Mark 14:25 must be authentic, as Jesus here speaks of a reunion in the kingdom of God where he will be one of the guests, without claiming any special role for himself (1903:126; 1911:96).

Wellhausen perceived a similarity between Jesus and the Old Testament prophets from Amos onward, to a degree that may have conditioned his general view from the outset. He did, however, also see important differences. The prophets preceded the written law; Jesus presupposed both the codification of the law and the minutiae of its interpretation in scribal tradition. He was a sage, not a prophet. The prophets made monotheism the foundation of social morality; in a different historical setting, Jesus was more individualistic and internalized the ethos of practical monotheism, by his own way of life as much as by his teaching (1897:377–84; 1903:103; 1911:102f.). At one time, Wellhausen had drawn a direct line from Jesus to the faith in God held by free individuals in an invisible community of the spirits (1897:388, the last page). With the years, his approach became more consistently historical: the teaching and the person of Jesus, as well as his crucifixion, were presuppositions for the origin of Christianity and for the church which was the outcome of his life although he neither founded nor foresaw it.

Opposed to Pharisaic Judaism and contrasted with the church, Jesus appears as a lonely figure, perhaps more so than Wellhausen intended. He was accompanied by disciples who thought of him as the Jewish Messiah. However, we mainly learn that Jesus did not select the group of twelve, that he did not send out apostles, did not call them to follow him in service and suffering. Jesus is not likely to have given them any private instruction about the kingdom of God, or about his own fate, or about how to pray and to organize a common life (e.g., 1911:71f., 77f., 102f.). Yet, Wellhausen asserted, the conversation with Jesus in everyday life made a lasting impression upon the disciples in whom he continued to live after his death, in their hearts more than in their memories (1911:103f., 168f.). This affirmation does not follow from the premises of radical source criticism; it appears to be a postulate conditioned by Wellhausen's conviction that a paradigmatic life and an individual type makes greater impact upon religious history than concepts and rules (1897:384; see also the quotation from Goethe, 1911:168, n. 1). This conviction would even seem to be a presupposition for Wellhausen's treatment of the sources, as it explains why he treats secondary Gospel traditions as indirect evidence for the impact made by the personality of Jesus more than as sources for the history of the early church.

VI. BEGINNINGS OF CHRISTIANITY

Wellhausen never drew a coherent sketch of early Christian history, but it is possible to assess his views by collecting a number of scattered remarks.

The Easter appearances convinced the disciples that the crucified Jesus had been vindicated and was now the heavenly Messiah. The story of the empty tomb is secondary even though the Gospel of Mark from the beginning ended with 16:8 (1911:84f.; 1903:145f.). In his last publications Wellhausen stressed more than before that Christianity was born out of enthusiasm, in a moment of ecstatic vision (1911:85 and, especially, 149f.; 1914:6f.). If the term "myth" is to be applied, Christianity was not at a later stage contaminated by myth but was from the beginning founded upon the myth of the resurrection. What happened was not a gradual idealization but a sudden metamorphosis of the crucified Messiah (1911:149).

As the basis of Christian faith the resurrection of Jesus also became the warrant for the hope of future redemption. Thus, the Jewish concept of the Messiah was applied to Jesus, with the difference that Jesus at his parousia would vindicate his own, the Christians, and punish their enemies, the Jews (1905:96). After some hesitation, however, Wellhausen increasingly emphasized that the expectation of the parousia was secondary. According to the circumstances, it might be actualized or recede into the background, whereas faith in the elevation of Jesus as the heavenly Messiah constituted Christianity from the beginning and remained its foundation (1911:85f., 151f., 170–76). Wellhausen even modified his own view of the "Son of man" sayings: the passion and resurrection predictions of Mark represented an earlier stage of development than the sayings about the coming of the Son of man (1911:128–30, in contrast to 1903:66–69; 1905:96f.).

It deserves to be mentioned that Wellhausen clearly, although only in passing, considered Peter to have played the most important role at the origins of the Christian gospel of the crucified and risen Christ. His experience of an apparition of the risen Christ was contagious, and later both Paul and the Fourth Gospel built upon the foundation laid by Peter (1911:147; 1914:29; 1908:121). This, however, does not imply that Peter in any way stands behind the Gospel of Mark (1911:155). For those who had known Jesus, the message that he who was crucified had been elevated as the heavenly Christ was sufficient. The traditions which were collected and written down in the Gospels are, by and large, not memories of the Apostles but products of the community in Jerusalem for whom Jesus was founder, head, and teacher of the church (1911:148f., 168f.).

The analogy with Paul is one, possibly the major reason for the view that tradition about the earthly Jesus did not constitute the gospel of the first apostles either (1911:147f., cf. 99–101). In spite of the shift of audience and various modifications, Wellhausen did not find that the substance of the gospel of Paul differed from the gospel of Peter (1908:121; 1911:169).

Wellhausen was less interested in diversity and conflicts within early Christianity than in the main lines of development. The Gospel of Mark, the Q tradition, and Matthew represent successive stages in the growth of the the tradition in Jerusalem and vicinity, with the Gospel of Luke a sidebranch of the same tradition, transplanted to a non-Palestinian soil (1911:79f.). The Fourth Gospel had a character and prehistory of its own, but nevertheless it represented the last stage of the development that led from Jewish origins to alienation and separation from Judaism. In spite of a late date of the last redaction, the main content of the Fourth Gospel is still assigned to the first period of Christian history and literature. By contrast, the present form of the Book of Revelation marks the beginning of a second period, characterized by the conflict between the church and the empire (1908:126f.). The first period was one of gradual emancipation of

Christianity from Judaism. Within this period the most important turning point was the persecution under Herodes Agrippa (44 CE) at which, according to Wellhausen, both James and John, the sons of Zebedee, suffered martyrdom. Peter left Jerusalem where James, the brother of the Lord, became the leader, while Paul started out on his great missionary journeys (1908: 119f.; 1911:142, 145f.; 1914:22ff.; cf. above, III).

To the extent that it is permissible to make any generalization on the basis of Wellhausen's remarks about early Christian history, he seems to have understood history as a continuous process in which major events, in this case the crucifixion of Jesus, the persecution under Herodes Agrippa, and the beginning of Roman persecutions, marked the beginning and end of discrete periods. Within this continuum great personalities might well make more impact upon posterity than upon their own generation. I find no traces of a Hegelian pattern of dialectical evolution.

VII. RELATIONSHIP TO NEW TESTAMENT SCHOLARS

In the history of New Testament scholarship, Wellhausen's studies belong to the last phase of a period which came to an end with World War I. They were as controversial as his *Prolegomena* but never gained the same importance. The impact made by Wellhausen was conflated with that of other scholars, with the result that the specific value of his contribution has too often been overlooked.

In retrospect we tend to see Wellhausen as one among several radical German scholars who in the decades before 1914 found that the historical criticism, as practised by persons such as H. J. Holtzmann and Harnack, had resulted in an unhistorical and uncritical modernization of Jesus and early Christianity. A closer look makes it clear that these scholars differed a great deal among themselves and were often highly critical of each other.

Already before Wellhausen, William Wrede had placed Mark at the side of Paul and John as a witness to a "dogmatic" faith in Jesus as the crucified and risen Christ. The two most outstanding representatives of radical Gospel criticism reached similar results along different paths. Wellhausen could express partial agreement (1903:70f.), but he could also brand Wrede's theory a failure which rendered the gospel of the resurrection and thereby the origin of Christianity incomprehensible: "The rabbi from Nazareth could never have become the Messiah by virtue of his death"—unless he had already on earth been considered to be the Messiah and been crucified for that reason (1914:6, n.1).

Albert Schweitzer's consistent eschatology ran contrary to the views of Wellhausen, and their scholarly approach, method, and style differed greatly. Wellhausen's disparaging remarks about "most progressive theologians" and "ignorants" are likely to reflect the way in which the German academic aristocracy looked upon the impertinent young genius (1905:98, 107). After the publication of the latter's major work, whose title ought to have been "From Reimarus to Schweitzer," Wellhausen exchanged his irony for a sharp but fair criticism (1911:151, n.1). In fact, the two of them fought at the same frontiers, against traditional conservatism, against nineteenth-century "Life of Jesus" theology, and against the history-of-religion school. The affinity between Schweitzer's "ethical mysticism" and Wellhausen's "practical monotheism" may have been greater than either of them sensed.

At least in some respects, the "Jewish Jesus" discovered by Wellhausen "closely resembles the one portrayed by the history-of-religions school" (Kümmel: 282). The reasons for the similarity may have been that both he and the members of the school were rooted in the tradition of liberal theology and that their source criticism widened the gap between Jesus and Christianity, to the extent that Jesus appears as a lonely figure, contrasted with the Judaism of his time and separated from Christianity. In contrast to Gunkel and other members of the school, however, Wellhausen found genetic questions about the ultimate origin to be a matter of no consequence for the meaning of the materials used by an author of apocalyptic or other writings (1899:233f.). He did not think that influence from the syncretistic environment was a factor of major importance during the first period of Christian history. Christianity attracted Gentile converts for the simple reason that it was a monotheistic religion that did not require circumcision and observation of purity laws (1914:26). As Wellhausen found that the historical events of the crucifixion and the resurrection appearances explained the origin of Christianity, the prehistory of christological concepts was a matter of secondary importance to him. He was himself a historian of religion—but one whose interest was focused on the origin and history of the three great monotheistic religions, Judaism, Christianity, and Islam. One might say that in Wellhausen's presentation Christianity appears as a mutation of biblical monotheism. Even the Johannine variety is characterized by monotheism which is the motivation of moral life and the source of knowledge (1908:123).

Wellhausen, the historian, drew the conclusion that it is impossible to elevate Jesus to a religious principle and to play him off against Christianity. The concluding paragraph of the "Introduction" is a classical text which would have deserved to be quoted in extenso (1905:114f. = 1911:104). Some excerpts must suffice: "Whence is the belief that Jesus is the religious ideal derived in fact, if not from Christianity?" One can neither comprehend Jesus nor do justice to his significance if one does not also consider the historical outcome: "Even a Jesus without the gospel and without Paul cannot be detached from the Judaism to which he adhered although he had outgrown it. We cannot go back to him even if we would like to." The necessary consequence of making the historical Jesus a religious dogma is to eliminate "time-conditioned" features and, at the end, to exchange history for a rationality about which one can hold highly divergent concepts: "As a foundation of religion, the historical Jesus is a dubious and unsatisfactory substitute for what is lost with the [Christian] gospel. Without his death he would not have become historical at all."

As these excerpts indicate, Wellhausen's New Testament studies led him to the conclusion that the type of theological liberalism for which Harnack was the leading representative was built on shaky foundations. The following controversy between Harnack (1907) and Wellhausen (1911:157–70) centered on the collection of sayings of Jesus preserved by Matthew and Luke, its relation to the Gospel of Mark, and its historical reliability, but both participants realized that more was at stake. The two great masters had still much in common, not merely a distance from the history-of-religion school. Both emphasized the difference between the preaching (Wellhausen would have said the teachings) of Jesus and the apostles' proclamation of Jesus as the Christ, and neither of them accepted the slogan "Back from Paul to Jesus." Wellhausen was even willing to concede that the religious value of the later Gospels might be greater than that of Mark (1911:168f.). Nevertheless, the two masters went separate ways. To Harnack, the essence of Christianity was contained in the gospel which Jesus preached, with the fatherhood of God and the infinite value of the human soul at its center. The apostolic preaching about Jesus was a secondary form of the gospel, historically necessary as the means of communication and preservation of the primary gospel. For Wellhausen there was but one gospel, the gospel about Jesus as the crucified and risen Christ. Without this gospel, which had also been retrojected into the history of Jesus, there was no Christianity. Harnack, the leading liberal theologian, grew increasingly conservative in matters of historical source criticism. Wellhausen, the Semitist, historian, and radical critic, maintained that historical, genuine Christianity was faith in the crucified Jesus Christ, the faith attested by the Gospels as well as by Paul.

Having resigned from the theological faculty at Greifswald in 1882, Wellhausen stood at some distance from the theological controversies in Germany at the turn of the century. He found an appreciative and sympathetic critic in Adolf Jülicher, but even Jülicher (1906; 1931:274, 346f., 366–69) found Wellhausen's criticism of the sayings tradition to be excessive. At the time of his New Testament studies, however, Wellhausen was engaged in a mutually stimulating exchange with Eduard Schwartz, the outstanding classicist and historian of antiquity, including the ancient Church, professor at Göttingen 1902–9 (see Schwartz, 1919). Like Schwartz, Wellhausen stood in the tradition of the great nineteenth-century historians. He did not see it as his task to discuss theological or philosophical issues and was reticent to expose his own religious belief in public writings. He did not share Harnack's interest in mediating between religion and culture and thought that only a religiously motivated morality could remain independent of "the variable idol culture" (1911:102).

VIII. IMPACT AND RELEVANCE

It is not possible to add more than some scattered remarks about the more permanent effects and the lasting value of Wellhausen's work in the New Testament field. Some of Wellhausen's observations and conjectures were picked up, accepted, or at least discussed by other scholars and have passed into the learned tradition reproduced in commentaries and other works.

Wellhausen's critical analysis of the Gospels, especially Mark, and his assumption that sayings of Jesus, as much as stories about him, were products of the creative community called for a closer, less impressionistic study of the history of tradition and redaction. Thus, Wellhausen paved the way for the fresh approach to the study of the Gospels that was inaugurated immediately after World War I. Thereby, the pioneering works of K. L. Schmidt and R. Bultmann built upon the foundations laid by Wellhausen to a higher degree than did Dibelius's version of "Form Criticism." To some extent, however, Wellhausen anticipated the type of critical analysis of Acts that was later carried out by Dibelius and Haenchen.

It had to cause some upheaval that a person with Wellhausen's authority turned against the attempt to make the Jesus of historians a foundation of Christian faith. Wellhausen had in fact done little to prevent conservative theologians from trying "to gather apologetic figs from skeptical thistles." Inadvertently, Wellhausen's studies became one factor among many that contributed to the change of theological climate in Germany after World War I. In spite of opposite points of departure, Wellhausen's conclusions had some genuine similarity to the thesis of Martin Kähler (1892), that the impact upon posterity makes an outstanding person truly "historic" (*geschichtlich*) and that the object of Christian faith is the "biblical historic Christ" and not a reconstructed historical Jesus. A confluence of impulses from Wellhausen and Kähler favored a "kerygmatic" approach to New Testament theology, an approach for which Rudolf Bultmann was not only the most outstanding representative but also the one whose critical attitude was akin to Wellhausen. Bultmann had a remarkable ability to assimilate observations and insights of highly diverse scholars into a synthesis of his own and was hardly more indebted to Wellhausen than to others, e.g. the members of the history-of-religion school, Wrede, Schweitzer, Schlatter, and even Karl Barth. One can, however, in Bultmann's works detect many passages that are reminiscent of Wellhausen's formulations, even where there is no direct quotation.

To the younger generation Wellhausen's New Testament studies are probably mainly known, if at all, as a presupposition for the work of Bultmann and other scholars of his time. Especially in the United States, the work of other German pioneers at the turn of the century, e.g., Wrede, Bousset, and even Kähler, has been rediscovered and translated into English in the last couple of decades. To my knowledge, there has been no comparable new interest in Wellhausen's work on the New Testament. This may, at least to some extent, be due to the lack of any major historical work and the often unsystematic, sometimes aphoristic form of presentation as well as to the extravagance of Wellhausen's radical criticism, in comparison with which even Bultmann may appear to be moderate, e.g., with respect to the parables and the sayings of Jesus about the kingdom of God. Much of what Wellhausen wrote was critical comments, not to say marginal notes, upon the state of New Testament scholarship at his time, and it is therefore dated. Nevertheless, there are elements in Wellhausen's studies which are important today as ever, especially if historical questions, rather than biblical theology and existential interpretation, will once more come into the focus of scholarly interest.

What seems most important to me is Wellhausen's insistence that the crucifixion of Jesus as King of the Jews is a historical fact which provides a main clue to the origin of Christianity as well as to the history of Jesus (see above, V). Wrede thought that the dogmatic theory of the messianic secret explained the contrast between the non-messianic life of Jesus and the evangelists' conviction that Jesus was the Messiah, while Schweitzer found the nature of the Jewish messianic conception to provide the explanation. Later scholars have continued to discuss these theories, with manifold variations. Few realized that Wellhausen had pointed to the possibility of a third explanation, more solidly based upon the historical facts and therefore more plausible. One does not find a reference to this central aspect of Wellhausen's studies even where one might expect it (see, e.g., Schweitzer: 247, n. 2, 375, 590f.; Kümmel: 280–84; Barrett: 36–39). I myself wrote an article on "The Crucified Messiah" without being fully aware of the degree to which Wellhausen had anticipated much of what I had to say (Dahl: especially 21–28).

Few scholars will today sit down and read Wellhausen's New Testament studies in their entirety unless thay have to write an article about them or have a special interest either in Wellhausen or in German biblical scholarship at the turn of the century. The works are in many respects outdated. New Testament scholarship has, after all, made progress during the last seventy years. Yet Wellhausen's works remain mines of observations, suggestions, and critical asides which have not lost their actuality. As a historian, he raised basic questions which still deserve serious reflection and further research, whether one is inclined to agree with his results or not. Depending upon one's mood, one may be irritated or amused at his terse style and dry wit, but one is not bored. Young scholars should not try to imitate him, but they might learn to concentrate on saying what they have to say. In the life of an old professor there are moments in which he is tired of reading books and articles which, if they do not rehearse old stuff, may make fresh proposals about approaches, methods, models, structures, philosophical, sociological or linguistic terminology and much else, while they have little to say about precise exegetical details and important historical events. In such moments it is a refreshing relief to sit down and read Julius Wellhausen.

NOTES

/1/   There are even some published items which I did not have at hand, including the first and some of the other editions of the *Israelitische und judische Geschichte*, the second edition of *Das Evangelium Marci* (see Wellhausen, 1897 and 1903), and a short article on "Strauss' Leben Jesu" (Rahlfs· 367, no. 234). Wellhausen reviewed several editions of Christian Syriac texts and other works of indirect interest for New Testament studies (see Rahlfs: nos. 180, 196, 219, 220, 223 and, e.g., 85, 96, 173)

/2/   Only in the years between the first and the second edition of his *Einleitung* (1905 and 1911) did Wellhausen read the works of D. F. Strauss and F C. Baur with some care.

WORKS CONSULTED

Barrett, Charles Kingsley
    1968   *Jesus and the Gospel Tradition*. Philadelphia: Fortress.

Black, Matthew
    1946   *An Aramaic Approach to the Gospels and Acts*. Oxford· Clarendon.

Bultmann, Rudolf
    1921   *Geschichte der synoptischen Tradition* Gottingen. Vandenhoeck & Ruprecht. (2d ed 1931)

Dahl, Nils Alstrup
    1974   *The Crucified Messiah and Other Essays*. Minneapolis· Augsburg.

Dalman, Gustaf
    1898   *Die Worte Jesu* Leipzig Hinrichs.

Eissfeldt, Otto
    1962   "Julius Wellhausen " *RGG*, 3d ed. 6· 1594–95

Harnack, Adolf
    1907   *Spruche und Reden Jesu*. Beitrage zur Einleitung in das Neue Testament, II. Leipzig· Hinrichs

Julicher, Adolf
    1904   Review of Wellhausen's *Das Evangelium Marci*. *TLZ* 29· 256–61.
    1906   *Neue Linien in der Kritik der evangelischen Ueberlieferung*. Giessen· Topelmann.
    1931   *Einleitung in das Neue Testament* 7th ed , with Erich Fascher. Tubingen. Mohr

Kahler, Martin
    1892   *Der sogenannte historische Jesus und der geschichtliche, biblische Christus* New edition by E Wolff, Munich. Kaiser, 1953.

Kummel, Werner Georg
1972   *The New Testament: The History of the Investigation of its Problems.* Translated by S. McL. Gilmour and H. C. Kee. Nashville/New York: Abingdon.

Rahlfs, Alfred
1914   "Verzeichnis der Schriften Julius Wellhausens." Pp. 351–68 in *Studien zur semitischen Philologie und Religionsgeschichte: Julius Wellhausen zum siebzigsten Geburtstag,* ed. K. Marti. BZAW 27 Giessen: A. Topelmann

Schmidt, Karl Ludwig
1919   *Der Rahmen der Geschichte Jesu.* Berlin. Trowitzsch

Schwartz, Eduard
1907   "Zur Chronologie des Paulus." *NGWG,* 262–99. = Pp. 124–69 in *Gesammelte Schriften,* vol. 5. 2d ed. Berlin: de Gruyter, 1963.
1919   *Julius Wellhausen.* Berlin: Weidmann. = Pp. 326–61 in *Gesammelte Schriften,* vol. 1. 2d ed. Berlin: de Gruyter, 1963.

Schweitzer, Albert
1913   *Geschichte der Leben-Jesu-Forschung.* Tubingen: Mohr. (2d ed. of *Von Reimarus zu Wrede,* 1907)

Wellhausen, Julius
1874   *Die Pharisaer und die Sadducäer.* Greifswald: Bamberg.
1895   "Der syrische Evangelienpalimpsest von Sinai." *NGWG,* 1–12.
1896   Review of A. Meyer's *Die Muttersprache Jesu. GGA:* 265–68
1897   *Israelitische und jüdische Geschichte.* 3d ed. Berlin: Reimer (1st ed. 1894; 8th ed. 1958.)
1899   *Skizzen und Vorarbeiten.* Vol. 6. Berlin: Reimer. (Pp. 187–215: "Des Menschen Sohn"; pp 215–49. "Zur apokalyptischen Literatur".)
1901   "Heinrich Ewald." Pp. 61–88 in *Festschrift zur Feier des 150jahrigen Bestehens der Kgl. Gesellschaft der Wissenschaften zu Gottingen.* Berlin: Weidmann.
1903   *Das Evangelium Marci übersetzt und erklart.* Berlin. Reimer (2d ed 1909)
1904a   *Das Evangelium Matthaei ubersetzt und erklart.* Berlin: Reimer.
1904b   *Das Evangelium Lucae übersetzt und erklart.* Berlin: Reimer.
1905   *Einleitung in die drei ersten Evangelien.* Berlin: Reimer
1907a   *Erweiterungen und Aenderungen im vierten Evangelium.* Berlin. Reimer.
1907b   *Analyse der Offenbarung Johannis* AGWG NF IX/4. Berlin: Weidmann
1907c   "Noten zur Apostelgeschichte." *NGWG,* 1–21
1908   *Das Evangelium Johannis.* Berlin. Reimer
1911   *Einleitung .* (= 1905), 2d ed.
1914   *Kritische Analyse der Apostelgeschichte.* AGWG NF XV/2. Berlin: Weidmann

WELLHAUSEN AS AN ARABIST*

Kurt Rudolph
Karl-Marx-Universität Leipzig

ABSTRACT

Wellhausen's Arabic studies, to which he devoted a major part of his scholarly career, have been of considerable significance. With a sound training from Ewald in both the Arabic as well as Hebrew languages, he shifted in 1882 from the theological faculty to a chair in the philosophy faculty, becoming thereby an Orientalist, a Semitic philologian In his Arabic studies he applied a historical, source-critical, and philological method very similar to the approach he had taken in his Old Testament work, not the least in his *Prolegomena to the History of Israel* Also in both areas he focused above all on the literary documents, not on preliterary traditions or comparative evidences. Wellhausen's own area of interest was the pre-Islamic and early Islamic periods. He published numerous studies dealing with Arabic history, literature, language, and religion, and at many points his contributions have maintained their worth up to the present time

Wellhausen's reputation among theologians is based primarily upon his Old Testament studies, but thereby an important dimension of his work goes unnoticed. Apart from the investigations into the New Testament which he undertook in later years and regarded as the continuation of his research into the Old Testament and Judaism, Wellhausen also made outstanding contributions to Arabic studies. Indeed, one may even conclude that "the genius of individual accomplishment" was greater perhaps in this area, since here there were neither sufficient resources nor very great interest, in comparison with Old Testament scholarship (cf. C. H. Becker: 474f.).

But the distinction which is commonly made between Wellhausen's biblical and Islamic studies is in general false in that it fails to do justice to his intentions. Wellhausen was an Orientalist and a historian. Out of particular interests he devoted himself to both disciplines, which he saw as intimately related. Indeed, in Wellhausen's day they were not yet separate, as they are today, but were often united, personally as well as institutionally, in the character of a single professor (such as Wellhausen's teacher H. Ewald!). Wellhausen began as an Old Testament scholar, but no sooner had he established himself in this field than he turned to Arabic sources. "I have made the transition from the Old Testament to the Arabs," he wrote in

1882 in his first great Arabic work, the German edition of al-Wāqidī's "Book of the Campaigns (of Muhammad)," "with the intention of getting to know the wild vine upon which priests and prophets grafted the Torah of Yahweh. For I have no doubt that some idea of the original characteristics with which the Hebrews entered history may most easily be won by means of a comparison with Arabic antiquity" (1882a:5, preface) /1/. For this reason, throughout his life Wellhausen was engaged in Arabic-Islamic studies, alongside work on the biblical tradition—yet, one must add, in a highly original, epoch-making way. His Arabic-Islamic studies did not merely remain in the service of Old Testament research, despite his account of the conditions of their inception, but from the start clearly attained an importance of their own, which ensures Wellhausen a lasting place in Arabic studies. As we shall see, there was no difference in the method which Wellhausen employed in the two fields of research, except where the material itself drove him to ask new questions. The historical-critical, or literary-critical (source-critical), enterprise dominated his Arabic studies as well, and led to novel insights.

Hence the verdict of Orientalists on Wellhausen is unanimously positive/2/. His accomplishment here was the same as in the Old Testament, namely, to have introduced a strictly historical point of view, based on source criticism, into the study of the early Islamic period. For this reason E. Littmann described him as "one of the greatest pioneers and explorers," with whom a new era in Oriental studies began. He numbered him among the greatest Orientalists of the nineteenth and twentieth centuries, who cleared the primeval forest and fashioned beautiful sculptures from crude blocks of marble (18f.). He is unanimously regarded as one of the most important historians (Littmann: 20; Becker: 474; Eissfeldt: 409f., 424; Schaeder: 416f.). Thus it is essential for an understanding of Wellhausen to include consideration of his Arabic studies in this collection of essays, so as to bring the unity of his work to expression. With this in mind, we shall first comment on his Arabic studies in general (I), then on his method and procedure (II), concluding with a brief presentation and evaluation of each work related to the subject (III).

I. FOUNDATIONS OF WELLHAUSEN'S ARABIC STUDIES

Wellhausen received his education in Oriental studies from Heinrich Ewald (1803–75) in Göttingen. As Wellhausen himself reports in a tribute to his teacher (1901a; see also Schwartz: 49ff.; and Fück: 167), he was fascinated by him, despite his unorthodox teaching methods and his rather difficult character. From him Wellhausen obtained, in any case, a thorough education in Arabic and Hebrew. His interest in both these areas goes back to Ewald, as well as his preference for old Arabic poetry (Ewald had received his degree for a work entitled "De metris carminum arabicorum" in 1875) and his impartial treatment of biblical and Islamic literature (Wellhausen, 1901a:64f.). When

Wellhausen remarked that Ewald knew how to identify the essential and elemental amidst the dense undergrowth, how to bring cosmos out of chaos (1901a:66f.), he described, at the same time, a trait of his own character, which may be understood as the inheritance of his teacher, as well as an expression of his distrust of an exaggerated comparison between them (1901a:70f., with critical remarks). Wellhausen was all too familiar with the weaknesses of his teacher; nevertheless, he continued to profess his admiration for him, as did other notable students of Ewald, such as J. Gildemeister, A. Dillmann, and T. Nöldeke.

In this connection, Wellhausen emphasized—in contrast to his teacher and thus in contrast to centuries of theologically influenced Arabic studies (if, indeed, the studies up to that time are worthy of the name)—that one ought to begin with *Arabic* in order to understand Hebrew. He acknowledged that Arabic was no more a Semitic "*Ursprache*" (a "hypothetical ideal that can only be approximated") than Hebrew, as Ewald also thought, but he believed that it contained more "archaisms" (1901a:71). As Wellhausen remarked in a review of H. Reckendorf, he nearly "always employed grammar as a means to the comprehension of the literature," and he was "suspicious of the attempt to trace out all the imaginary drives, themselves contradictory and irrational, which gave shape to speech" (1896c: 777). But though Wellhausen was not interested in language as such, he often expressed himself on etymological matters in his writings with great expertise and offered his opinion, for example, in the discussion of the relationship between classical Arabic and the modern dialects/3/.

Hermann Cremer, Wellhausen's colleague in Greifswald, described from personal acquaintance his linguistic gifts in a letter as follows: "His command of the Semitic languages is like that of no other in his field, even if it assumes a somewhat unusual form. Languages come alive for him; he comprehends their spirit, not only their grammar. Thus though his writings are full of the most subtle grammatical observations, he never puts himself forward as a grammarian. He refuses to pay homage to the etymological trend in linguistic research, emphasizing, rightly, the gulf between etymological basic meaning and historical linguistic usage"/4/. With these linguistic skills he combined an agreeable style, so that he may be regarded as a congenial translator, or better "Germanizer," as his works on Old Arabic poetry or Muhammad's letters to the princes plainly show/5/.

Worthy of note in this connection is Wellhausen's attempt to develop a practical transcription of Arabic, which he achieved for the first time in his edition of al-Wāqidī (1882a:8ff.) and continued to employ in subsequent works. He was concerned in the first place to develop a simple, clear and consistent transliteration, which would also do justice to the *history* of the language, that is, a transliteration which bore in mind the old Semitic alphabet. He expressly avoided a phonetic reproduction of modern pronunciation; instead he rightly followed the established manner of writing without attempting to make corrections in Arabic orthography. This attempt to develop a linguistic-historical transcription of Arabic, using ordinary Latin letters and a few diacritical marks, was the first reasoned attempt of its kind in German Oriental studies. Wellhausen knew: "it is only by degrees that one attains the goal."

We have already made clear, in the above citation, on what grounds Wellhausen began to occupy himself intensively with Arabic sources for "the pre-Islamic and early Islamic period." Wellhausen believed that there was much to be learned about "Hebrew antiquity" when viewed as a part of the overall Semitic world, without at the same time making Arabic studies subservient to theology. Therefore he used every opportunity which these studies afforded to call attention to parallels and differences alike, whether of a legal/6/ or a religious/7/ nature. What was of concern to Wellhausen was the essence of Semitic antiquity—as it presents itself to a historian on the basis of the sources at his disposal, irrespective of the particular forms it assumed—the foundation upon which Israel and Judaism, on the one hand, and Islam, on the other, arose. Both of these expressions of the Semitic essence exercised an equal fascination on Wellhausen and led to his now famous investigations. Furthermore he early recognized that the cuneiform literature, which had begun to appear in his lifetime, also had to be taken into consideration. He had already dealt rather thoroughly with their decipherment and with the problems of the Babylonian-Assyrian script, as an essay of 1876 shows/8/. "Really concrete material on old Semitic paganism," Wellhausen remarked in a review of W. W. Graf Baudissin's *Studien zur semitischen Religionsgeschichte* (1876 and 1878), "may only be derived with certainty from cuneiform literature; everything else remains mere chaff, which leaves one unsatisfied" (1879:110; see also 1877:191f.)/9/. Perhaps there was still something to be learned from Syriac or Arabic. Wellhausen was later to attend to the latter himself (see below, pp. 125–30).

Like all his works, Wellhausen's Arabic studies are mainly interested in literary sources and their critical analysis, in the comprehension of their tendencies and historical value. Yet Wellhausen was not content to stop there, but only hoped, in this way, to obtain building materials for a reconstruction of the historical process, as it appeared to him from the sources. Nearly all of Wellhausen's studies serve this purpose and are guided by an enduring, fundamental idea: to find out how it really was. This genuinely historical concern made Wellhausen one of the best historians of his day (and of our own). He combined diverse gifts: text-critical and literary-critical skills, exegetical, linguistic and stylistic strengths, a poetic sensibility, and "an ingenious imagination, governed by the the strictest discipline"/10/. All this was guided and given coherence by a critical acumen, an unerring love for truth, and an unfailing eye for what was essential. Wellhausen might have characterized himself in the terse phrase formulated in response to G. Dalman: "It does not only depend on the glasses, but also on the eyes"

(1899a:viii). As we can see, Wellhausen was by no means a typical partner in such dialogues, and his many, always very thorough critical reviews bear witness to the sharpness of his judgment/11/. They often show us a less well-known side of Wellhausen and demonstrate the range of his interests and expertise (for which reason we are referring to them repeatedly). On the other hand, he was always prepared to acknowledge publicly his mistakes committed in "momentary absence of mind," as, for example, in the case of his opinion on the subject of the Aramaic speech of Jesus vis-à-vis G. Dalman, with whom he was often engaged in disputes (1899a:vii).

It is also noteworthy that Wellhausen was thoroughly familiar with his own limitations and candidly admitted them, as over against the works of Ignaz Goldziher, for example. It had been Goldziher's intention to describe the spiritual physiognomy of the Islamic world (in his *Muhammedanische Studien*, 1889/90); Wellhausen made a similar attempt, but it resulted in failure (see 1892:202). As Wellhausen pointed out, Goldziher had devoted less attention to the great historical events (which interested him) than to the inner course of things (Islamic theology). However, in his underestimation of (external) history, Wellhausen saw a darker side of Goldziher and subjected it to the sharpest censure (particularly with respect to the final dissolution of the Arab tribes in the Abbasid period, and the overestimation of theology as the measure for Islam in the Umayyad period). "*Fecit cui prodest* is a critical principle that cuts both ways" (1892:203) /12/. He resisted the one-sided identification of Islam with pietism and saw rather the practical, political aspects of the religion, which had been a part of the movement ever since Medina. The strict antithesis between *murūwwa* and *dīn*, which Goldziher propounded, Wellhausen found inadmissable; he was too much impressed by the survival of the "Arabic" within Islam, and its eventual revival. But he was less interested in this side of Arabic history. He saw Islam, almost from its very beginning, as a part of Arabic history; thus he felt a certain antipathy toward the Abbasid dynasty, in which theocratic tendencies (Wellhausen speaks of "Caesaropapism") again appeared and in which the old Arab kingdom finally abdicated in favor of Persian rule and a "mixture of peoples" (see below, pp. 143–44). His love was for the Arabs, not for their Islamic posterity, just as he made no attempt to disguise his preference for the ancient Hebrews above their Jewish descendants. All this did not exclude the possibility, as one can see from his works, that he was capable of providing an impressive description of these "late eras," at least in the case of Judaism. Likewise, if one but glances at a series of reviews which deal with medieval, and even modern, Islamic history (especially editions of source materials), it is astonishing with what interest Wellhausen followed this literature and with what expertise he was capable of passing judgment in these areas/13/. He clearly had it in him to have extended his historical work over the Abbasid period; he lacked only the time and strength for the task. It would have been necessary first of all to lay a foundation in the

Umayyad period, and this in itself would have constituted a life's work.

Apart from his years as a student and a university docent, Wellhausen obviously laid the foundation for his future Arabic works during his period in Greifswald (1872–82), where he was ordinarius professor of Old Testament. At the end of this period Wellhausen wrote: "As for me—for years I have been occupied exclusively with Arabic antiquities, including the rise of Islam, and in the near future a historical-philological publication related to these studies will appear . . ."/14/, by which his edition of al-Wāqidī was meant (see below, pp. 121–23). It was in Greifswald as well that Wellhausen held his first public lecture on "The Origin and History of Islam" (Winter Semester 1881/82)/15/. As is well known, it was also in Greifswald that Wellhausen openly completed the break with contemporary theology, which his Old Testament investigations had unintentionally begun. This break, however, was effected in a manner that compels respect, and that was wholly in keeping with his sincere, consistent character. We may allow Wellhausen to speak in his own defense in a letter, from which we have already quoted, of 5 April 1882, to the Prussian Minister of Education/16/: "I became a theologian because the scientific treatment of the Bible interested me; only gradually did I come to understand that a professor of theology also has the practical task of preparing the students for service in the Protestant Church, and that I am not adequate to this practical task, but that instead despite all caution on my own part I make my hearers unfit for their office. Since then my professorship in theology has been weighing heavily on my conscience." Wellhausen requested, therefore, to be transferred to a philosophy faculty; yet as he expressly remarks in this connection, he had no desire to cut the tie between Hebraic studies and Semitic philology. He argued that on account of its "exceptional importance" Hebrew "should also be represented here and there on the philosophy faculty." He regarded himself as a Semitist who, on account of his previous publications, was considered a "Hebraist." In 1882, Wellhausen accepted a position as "Ausserordentlicher Professor" on the Faculty of Philosophy of the University of Halle, and thereafter was never again member of a theological faculty. Thus in accordance with his own intentions, he was outwardly a theologian no longer, but an Orientalist, or Semitic philologian. In Halle, Marburg (1885–92), and finally in Göttingen (1892–1913) as the successor of Paul de Lagarde and his own teacher Ewald, Wellhausen published the many Arabic and Islamic works which established his reputation as an Orientalist.

II. METHODOLOGY

Wellhausen was a philologian at heart, and as such also a historian; for in his day philology meant not only the study of languages but immersion in the history and culture associated with the language one studied. All the great philologians of Wellhausen's day were to a greater or lesser extent also historians (a state of affairs which, in my view, still holds true today); or conversely, there is strictly speaking no historian who must not also practice philology, for which reason one speaks of the philological–historical method as *the* method of the nineteenth century. Wellhausen once gave brief expression to this insight: "Philology takes revenge on those who treat it with disdain" (1882a:26, against A. Sprenger)/17/. Yet Wellhausen was never willing to stop there but placed all his philological learning and ability at the service of history; and in this too he showed himself a true historian, a historian indeed of the highest caliber. One senses repeatedly that it was the historical question which was at stake in all his investigations and that it always formed the criterium of judgment in his critical reviews/18/. What was decidedly new about Wellhausen was that he placed source criticism in the center of his reflections and made it the presupposition of his historical presentation. Again Wellhausen himself aptly characterized it thus: "Our historical interest generally does not coincide with that of the sources; precisely for this reason is research necessary" (1889:67). This is the essential point in the historian's treatment of the sources.

Aside from concrete questions which arose in the course of his work, Wellhausen did not express himself further on methodological issues in general. He was reluctant to do so; he preferred to keep to the material, and thereby made his own method more concrete. In contrast to the way in which previous Arabic scholars, such as G. Weil, F. Wüstenfeld, and in his own day A. Müller, had gone about writing history, Wellhausen adopted a rather critical point of view. In his opinion these works did no more than supply material which might, in the future, be made fruitful historically (1881:1477; also 1899b—both on Wüstenfeld). What was missing from these works was the guiding, source-critical perspective. In a review of a book on the Umayyad statesman al-Ḥajjāj b. Yūsuf by J. Périer (Paris, 1904), Wellhausen remarks that the author has not succeeded in moving beyond the raw material to genuine historical reflection, because the following considerations are lacking: critique of the sources, accentuation of essential elements, preference for the earliest reports, information about the authorities that Ṭabarī cites, historical analysis of party struggles, and so forth (1906b:255f.). These are the principles that we encounter in Wellhausen's own historical works. They may be summarized as follows (see also Becker: 476ff.; Eissfeldt: 412ff.):

(1) Written traditions are authoritative for Wellhausen; archaeological remains and monuments can, at best, supplement the evidence of literary sources.
(2) The literary tradition is to be subjected to criticism, or analyzed, according to its contradictions (literary criticism), basic tendencies (*Tendenzkritik*), and authorities (tradition criticism).

(3) Source-critical analysis establishes the (relative) chronology and thus is the presupposition for historical reconstruction as such; that is to say, critical analysis has as its consequence a new synthesis—the creation of a historical image.

Furthermore, the priority of political history is characteristic of Wellhausen's concept of history. It is this which was predominate; everything else was subordinate to it—at least in his Arabic works—even the history of religion/19/. Material and ideal interests closely determine human affairs, such as the Arab–Islamic conquests for example, in which "cunning leaders controlled the instincts of the masses" and exploited them for their own purposes (1899a:51). His axiom was: "It is not for history, in the end, to make known the hearts but to assess the deeds of humans" (1901c:89, regarding the role of al-Mukhtār; see below, p. 139). It is the effects which are historically relevant, not the nature of an individual, or the idea as such.

Wellhausen also saw religion in intimate relation to culture and politics: "The life of ancient religions was by no means restricted to the holy days but permeated all areas of activity and undertaking" (1904a:41)/20/. "Religion changes with culture" (1887:47; 1897b:51). "Just as the Hebrews transferred the cult of the indigenous Canaanite god to Yahweh after they had settled in the land, so did the Arabs under similar circumstances. Neither Urotal nor Dusares was Dionysus in the desert; they were each transformed into Dionysus by culture" (1887:47; 1897b:51). The form of a religion is always determined by cultural factors: "The importance which the camel had for the life of the ancient Arabs, it had for their poetry and religion as well, as did the cow among the Indians and the reindeer among the Lapps" (1887:111; 1897b:114). Wellhausen clearly attached little importance to the influence of religion on the public realm, at least among the ancient Arabs: "The public religion of the cult has little practical influence; superstition is the practical religion of private life." The multitude of that era were governed by superstition—"as we are today," he added sarcastically in 1887 (193, n.1; omitted from the second edition). He sees a process of secularization ("the profane course of progress") at work in different areas, whether in law (1887:104f.; 1897b:107f.; see below, p. 131f.) or in the sacrificial cult (1887:113; 1897b:117, regarding the prohibition against drinking blood), from an early period onward. That which originally belonged to God (in the way of land), in the course of time fell to the sovereign, and finally in Islam to the state, i.e., to Allah. "Enlightenment and emancipation from religious notions" and the spread of "a profane, egoistic way of thinking" demoralized Arabic paganism; Islam only drew the consequences of these developments (1887:104f.; 1897b:108). The following statements are almost reminiscent of Marxist concepts: "Above the real world humans build their own world, and this upper story wins a greater importance for them than the foundation. Nature recedes behind culture. Even the old elemental character of the gods begins to fade; the concept of the divine takes on a new content through its predominant relationship to the human world" (1887:180f.; changed in 1897b:213f.)/21/. Despite the foundation of the old cultic rituals in nature, Wellhausen states: "The worship of God is never the same as the worship of nature; the very idea of God already contains a certain moralization of nature" (1887:172). In every change in the image or idea of divinity "it is the relation to the human community which remains of greatest importance; amidst transformations, the concept of the divine retains its social and historical character" (1897b:214).

What is remarkable about Wellhausen's treatment of religious-historical problems, especially in the *Reste arabischen Heidentums*, is how little he was dependent on contemporary theories in ethnography or the study of religion. He professed neither the totemistic theory advocated by his friend and colleague W. R. Smith (whom Wellhausen criticized on that account; see especially 1887:176f.; also 1900b:1303), nor the animism of E. B. Tylor (more noticeable in the second edition), nor manism (ancestor-cult theory). There are traces of certain nature-myth conceptions in his work (particularly in the first edition), but they are held in check by their relation to history, as we have seen. He decisively rejected the astral-myth interpretation; only secondarily was a greater sidereal character attributed to the old Arab deities (1897b:211f.). To be sure, he speculated about the roots of the cult of demons in the "projection" of a "vague sense of the divine," in itself inexplicable (1887:212, n.1, see also pp. 102f.; 1897b:214), but in the new edition he modified this concept, placing it in the context of the historical transition from nature to culture. We shall return to these problems again in what follows (see below pp. 127-30). Wellhausen recognized that "the scientific study of religion will still have to make much progress." "That which goes by the name 'science of religion' is still limited to the study of the cult and its *origines pudendae*" (1900b:1302f.).

Beyond a doubt, Wellhausen's concentration on the written (literary) tradition determined his method and his image of history. Therein lay his strength—but, as we now know, also his weakness; this applies both to his study of the Old Testament and to his works on Arab-Islamic history. Wellhausen sets to work on a source after he has managed, often by the most ingeneous insights, to establish its existence amidst the tangled mass of traditions and to discern its historical relevance and authenticity. This is the procedure in all his historical works on Arab-Islamic history, as we shall later show. For Wellhausen our first informant is in every case the earliest historical author, who like any historian gathers and compiles his material from sources, guided all the while by a uniform historical conception (1899a:4). For the Arabic sources these authors are seldom anonymous, as they are almost without exception for the Old Testament. Thus Wellhausen's task was easier here; but there was also a greater risk involved in committing oneself to one of the so-called "first authorities" (see also Becker: 477f.;

Eissfeldt: 413f.), without also bringing this informant under close critical scrutiny (e.g., Abū Mikhnaf). Without doubt Wellhausen exhibited great skill in his work on Arabic historians, geographers, and encyclopedists and identified the most essential and valuable sources with astonishing certainty (e.g., in Yāqūt or Ṭabarī), but even in this respect he remained a "master of reduction" (Becker: 479) in that he did not inquire about the prehistory of the literary composition, nor about extraneous sources/22/. For him historiography was built upon historical literature; the study of the history of preliterary traditions and comparative studies, whether in the realm of the history of religion or literature, seemed to him of secondary importance and of no historical consequence.

One can pursue Wellhausen's attitude toward the sources in his critique of H. Gunkel's *Schöpfung und Chaos* (1895), for in this book he encountered a work which originated in the new history-of-religions and traditio-historical school (1899a:225ff., especially pp. 233f.). We may summarize his objections as follows:

(1) *Proton pseudos* dominates the question of origins.
(2) What is methodologically decisive is what the author of a text (in this case the Apocalypse of John) has made out of the material; whence the material comes "is of no consequence methodologically"; everything depends upon the author's meaning.
(3) Gunkel's project of opposing the original understanding of a work to the author's own interpretation "may have antiquarian interest, but is not the task of the theologian and exegete."
(4) Gunkel converts subsidiary points into the main issue, a practice which shows a want of proper method. "For proper method concentrates on the major point at issue, and its only concern is the comprehension of the evidence."
(5) Methods designed to study the history of traditions and methods oriented on the history of a given period belong together and do not exclude one another (in the interpretation of the Johannine Apocalypse).

Without going any further into particulars here, Wellhausen's position may be clearly expressed as follows: investigations of preliterary traditions behind written works are of no importance for him; indeed they fail to comprehend the essence of such works and cannot be regarded as scientific or methodical. Thus source criticism stands opposed to tradition history (which one may designate "tradition criticism" in a wider sense), although, as subsequent research into the Old and New Testament (less frequently in Arabic literature) has shown, they actually belong together. Wellhausen was the culmination, but at the same time the conclusion, of the source-critical method or school. He provided an unsurpassed demonstration of what this method was capable of achieving. Others have built upon his results, even if with different methods and different ways of posing the problem.

III. SURVEY AND CRITIQUE OF WELLHAUSEN'S ARABIC STUDIES

1.   *Muhammad in Medina*

Wellhausen's Arabic studies began, as if with a roll of drums, in 1882 with the "abridged German edition" of the *Kitāb al Maghāzī* (Book of the Campaigns) of al-Wāqidī (died 823). In the choice of this work the future historian of early Islam, for whom the political side of history, the politics of power, was of decisive significance, already shows himself. *Muhammed in Medina* (1882a) provided him entry into the first stages of this development. It was not the Muhammad of Mecca who interested him, but the theocrat and statesman of Medina; for it was from the latter that actions of world-historical significance emanated. This work was, nevertheless, as he explicitly stated in the introductory remarks cited above (pp. 111–12), an attempt to get to know the "wild stock" of the ancient Arabs upon which Israel was later grafted (5). Thus Wellhausen continued to adhere to his intention: to lay bare the old Arabian kernel within the Islamic husk, whether the covering was of a literary or a historical nature.

For his German edition of al-Wāqidī, Wellhausen was obliged to make use of a rather deficient textual tradition. In 1880 he had himself copied those portions of the only complete manuscript, the Prestonianus of the British Museum (Or. 1617), which did not coincide with the fragment published by A. von Kremer in Calcutta in 1856, found today in Vienna (881). Still another part of the manuscript was discovered in the British Museum (Add. Ms. 20737). Wellhausen recognized that all three manuscripts were derived from a single recension of Ibn Khaiyuwaihī (tenth century) (61). As the prototype for his own work Wellhausen named A. P. Caussin de Perceval's three-volume *Essai sur l'histoire des Arabes avant l'Islamisme* (Paris, 1847/48). "I have endeavored," he wrote, "to preserve as many of the essential features of the work as possible and to emphasize that which is most characteristic of Wāqidī. Moreover, I have tried to capture the tone of an Arabic tale without obscuring the original idiom. I have not made use of the abridgment to render harmless a partial understanding of the material by means of the most general expressions. Naturally one cannot change the fact that in a number of situations a great deal is left to the translator's discretion by such a procedure. Yet how seldom the faithful rendering of meaning coincides with literal translation is shown by familiar examples; only too often a want of understanding is concealed behind a translation which slavishly follows the letter of the text" (10). These statements afford an insight into the *modus operandi* of Wellhausen's translations, which one may classify, without hesitation, among the best of their kind.

Wellhausen apologized forthrightly for the fact that he had published a translation ("a lengthy excerpt") before a critical edition of the Arabic text, but the unfortunate condition of the manuscripts and the thought of a protracted search for variants, which he wished to avoid, forced him to it (10f.). He kept open the possibility of a critical edition (20), but it did not come to pass. Only in 1966 did a critical edition of the Arabic text finally make its appearance (see below).

Naturally Wellhausen also expressed his opinion on the historical value of al-Wāqidī (11f.). He decisively rejected W. Muir's and A. Sprenger's overestimation of his work and demonstrated at a number of points that Ibn Isḥāq, despite the fact of his revision by Ibn Hišām (Sīra of the Prophet), was in possession of better and older traditions. Without reference to Ibn Isḥāq it is not always possible to understand al-Wāqidī (12). Without doubt he constituted his source. Whatever else is found in al-Wāqidī is for the most part "legendary accretion," correction or a "progressive denaturing of historical motives," embellishments, ornamentations, and typifications. "The tradition, as represented by al-Wāqidī, has already gone a step beyond Ibn Isḥāq; it has evolved from what was held to be true to what was accounted beautiful. Miracles have increased, angels and devils have a greater role to play, the entire tone has grown more spiritual. The lines of the picture have been retraced, the colors applied more heavily" (14). Wāqidī is also onesided and tendentious in his chronology (15f.). The dating of a whole series of events must be placed in doubt. Nothing beyond a few dates of principal importance may be regarded as certain (17). The introduction of a strict lunar calendar by Muhammad in the year 10 of the Hegira (632 CE), in place of the "crude solar calendar" of the ancient Arabs, is to blame for the confusion (17). Wellhausen offers a number of important observations which demonstrate "on what unstable ground we tread in the period before the year 10." Nevertheless, Wāqidī's data are "useful in most cases," when carefully weighed (20).

Finally, Wellhausen discussed A. Sprenger, whose work set the tone for Arabic scholarship in his day (20–25). His use of sources and his philological data are subject to doubt, but he had an invigorating effect upon Arabic scholarship in Germany, in any event, "because of his wholesome, lively feeling *for the material*, and his genuine, unmediated interest in the *content* of the tradition, which had nothing pedantic about it" (24). Despite his uncritical procedure, "he had a grasp of the real, living problems of history" (24). But he had no sense of the importance of particulars, of the understanding of individual sources. Thus Wellhausen judged that his work is "a rich storehouse of material and ideas ... for the experienced Arabist, but is not to be recommended as an introduction to the subject for the larger reading public, although it appears to have been written with such a popular audience in mind" (26). He recommended instead Caussin de Perceval's

Essai, the Koran (which G. Weil had first used as a primary source for the life of Muhammad), Nöldeke's little book on the life of Muhammad (1863), and his own edition of al-Wāqidī (20, 25). If he had really hoped thus to supplant Sprenger's book on Muhammad among laity, he was mistaken. It came to be used even more among scholars in place of the original text, access to which remained difficult (Fück: 224).

Wellhausen's edition was not only clearly organized but was also furnished with a synopsis of the 71 campaigns of Muhammad and his lieutenants (1882a:29–31) and a comprehensive register of the names of persons and places (438–72). In this way Wellhausen created a tool for research into the life of Muhammad which remains irreplaceable to this day; the work merits even more admiration when one recalls that it was written in Greifswald without sufficient resources for Arabic studies/23/.

The first critical edition of the text of al-Wāqidī was published 84 years later by the English scholar Marsden Jones (with an Arabic introduction and comprehensive indexes). It was likewise based largely upon the London manuscript (B.M. Or. 1617) used by Wellhausen, supplemented by the two fragments (Add. 20737; A. von Kremer) which he had also employed, excerpts from a Cairo manuscript of Ibn Ḥajar al-'Asqalānī, and citations of Wāqidī in other authors (as Wellhausen had aspired to do). This edition is now regarded as authoritative and as the most reliable, and finally makes von Kremer's text unnecessary. "Nevertheless, Wellhausen's abridged German edition will continue to be used alongside the others, above all in the German-speaking countries. Despite many shortcomings in particulars, which can only be identified and corrected by consulting the original text, the work continues to testify to the sovereignty with which the translator carried out his task" (Paret: 134).

2. *The Hudhail Songs*

Following the presentation of an initial summary of his source-critical investigations in an article entitled "Mohammed and the First Caliphs" for the ninth edition of the *Encyclopædia Britannica* in 1883, Wellhausen increasingly devoted his attention to the ancient Arabian period, attempting to identify its sources in Islamic literature. The first product of this undertaking was the edition of Hudhail songs which he translated for the first volume of his *Skizzen und Vorarbeiten* (1884a:103–75), which, as is well known, also contained the German version of his article "Israel" from the *Encyclopædia Britannica* (Vol. XIII) of 1881. His interest in this Bedouin poetry, which went back to his days as a student under Ewald and which stayed with him to the end of his life, was not expressly poetic, as he himself acknowledged, but philological and historical. Like the Greek and Roman inscriptions, they provided him with "artifacts in the broadest sense"; it is in this that their significance for Arabic antiquity lies (105). He declared the matter of their authenticity to be of secondary importance; they accurately reflect for him the life, customs, and thought of the pagan Arabs (105). The poems stand higher linguistically than the Koran, with its "wholly un-Arabic Arabic." They are the most important source for a lexicon of old Arabic. The only song cycle of the Arab tribes which has been fully preserved is that of Banū Hudhail from the Hijāz. Only the final part of the collection (songs nos. 139–280) stood at Wellhausen's disposal in a Leiden (Cod. 549 Warnerianus) and a Paris manuscript (Suppl. arab. 1427; songs nos. 175–280). He chose to translate only those songs, nos. 139–241, which he considered most important, since his translation was not intended for a large audience but as a preliminary study for Arabic scholars (107). A year later he published a list of textual emendations, along with additional manuscript variants, revisions in the translation (for the most part suggested by Nöldeke), and the scholia so important for the understanding of the text (1885a; 1885b)/24/. Wellhausen's preoccupation with this formidable body of literature (which belongs in my experience to the most difficult of Arabic texts) is reflected not only in the notes to his own works (especially to the *Reste arabischen Heidentums*) but also in related critical reviews. Here, too, Wellhausen showed himself the master of the genre; for while he occasionally pronounced rather harsh judgments, he always provided ideas and material which served to supplement the works of others and to further the discussion/25/. He greeted the publication of T. Nöldeke's and A. Müller's chrestomathy of old Arabic poets (*Delectus veterum carminum arabicorum*) in 1890 enthusiastically and remarked, moreover, that while the student was formerly obliged to purchase a copy of the *Hamaṣa* of Abū Tammām and a lexicon for some 100–150 marks, now, thanks to the new edition, one was able to manage with only seven marks (1891d). The journals of travelers to the Near East, such as C. M. Doughty and A. Musil, also seemed useful to him. He regarded these reports as highly informative introductions to the world of the ancient Arabs (1891b; 1907b). He was so impressed by Doughty's *Travels in Arabia Deserta* that he remarked in his lengthy review of the work (one of the longest he ever wrote): "I have seldom read a book from which I have learned so much," and recommended its reading to all students of the Old Testament (1891b:179f.). "The book will never go out of date." One can trace its influence on him in the notes to the *Reste arabischen Heidentums* (see below p. 126) and elsewhere.

Wellhausen was also the author of a less well-known, but beautifully written introduction to the world of old Arabic poetry, which did not appear until 1896. In this work one gets the impression that the aesthetic dimension of the poems was not after all a matter of indifference. To be sure, he emphasizes here as well that his interest remains predominantly philological and historical. "Aesthetic appreciation takes second place, but is not wholly lacking" (1896a: 600). He points to the concrete nature of the poetry (598), created out of the harsh realities of bedouin life. It is "camel-poetry" in which "sensuous metaphors" take the place of abstractions; yet these metaphors "are always of a qualitative, not a quantitative sort" (598). "No contemplative, sentimental spirit" speaks here, "but a man of deeds and passion" (599). The poems are topical in nature and seek to have an effect upon public opinion (600). In this way they contributed to the "creation of a common intellectual heritage of the Arab tribes, and a common language raised above the competing dialects" (600). For Wellhausen the true nature of Arab civilization was revealed in these poems, an intellectual and moral culture which had been wrested from the desert by constant struggle and which evolved "out of the system of inter-human relations." "It was precisely because the soil was so barren and nature so hostile that the invisible superstructure created by humans through their mutual society attained such overwhelming importance. Since there were no institutions which functioned by themselves in Arab society apart from the actions of individuals, and since mutual relationships, rights, and duties were not under the supervision and protection of a central authority, they were not of such an automatic and indifferent nature as they are today, but personal and passionate, and thus poetic" (602). The religion of this poetry is fatalism/26/. "It is the source of reckless energy: there is no use in seeking to avoid death—so forward!" (603). The fruits of this attitude were liberality and nobility, occasionally marked by despair and the presentiment of death (603f.). Wellhausen refers in this connection to Imru' al-Qais, son of the last king of the Kinda. Wellhausen recognized that the real attraction of this literature was "the insight which it afforded into the development of a sophisticated intellectual life out of nothing, as it were, without the support of a political and technical culture" (604). "The contrast between the primitive, external conditions of the Arabs' life and their remarkable intellectual culture is a very attractive, even elevating, phenomenon. There is scarcely another barbarian folk which has left behind such literary remains in such a language; scarcely another was able in so short a time as the Arabs to assimilate culture, or to be assimilated by it" (604). It is in this context that we may come to understand Wellhausen's liking for this people, their early history and literature. His scholarly work was guided, or rather motivated, by this hidden, personal relation; it is this which finally explains his astonishing life's work.

3. *Vestiges of Arab Paganism*

The study of old Arabic poetry enabled Wellhausen to explore an important dimension of Arab civilization, but he still lacked access to ancient Arab religion as such (about which poetry provided only very imperfect and disconnected ideas of a cult-religion already in decay; cf. n. 26). He found his way into this sphere through an exemplary source-critical study which succeeded in recovering early reports from later Islamic authors, especially from the encyclopedist Yāqūt (ca. 1179–1229 CE); this led eventually to the reconstruction of the "Book of the Idols" (*Kitāb al-Aṣnām*) of Ibn al-Kalbī (died 819/820 CE), a work which was presumed lost until 1924. The result of these efforts was the publication of the *Reste arabischen Heidentumes* in 1887 as the third volume of his *Skizzen und Vorarbeiten*. A revised second edition appeared in 1897, which included above all the corrections and additions of T. Nöldeke (to whom the edition was dedicated)/27/. Apart from these emendations, the second edition also included changes in the final sections of the work (1887:171ff.; 1897b:208ff.). We can do no more than take brief notice of these alterations in what follows, devoting our attention to the first edition (which contains an index, at least, in contrast to the second!). With this work Wellhausen succeeded in creating a phenomenology of ancient, pre-Islamic Arab religion which remains unsurpassed to this day. "The subject is inexhaustible," he wrote. "I am satisfied to have laid the foundation and erected the framework. I feel that my work is most indebted to that of Doughty" (1897b:243). His book not only utilized the Nabataean inscriptions at his disposal in the nineteenth century, but was also based on literary sources, principally the *Kitāb al-Aṣnām* of Ibn al-Kalbī (1887:8–11; 1897b:10–13), derived largely from excerpts and citations in the "Geographical Dictionary" (*Muʿjam al-Buldān*) of Yāqūt (ed. F. Wüstenfeld, 1866–73). To be sure, Ibn al-Kalbī is not particularly reliable, "but he satisfies all the demands which one is entitled to make of him, in view of the nature of the subject and the times, and generally agrees with the best Arabic historian, Ibn Ishaq, in the information he provides on religious history. His scholarly interest transcends the horizon of Islam" (1897b:12f. n.2; 1887:10 n.2). In this respect, all other authorities stand upon his shoulders; only the older source, Ibn Isḥāq, is independent (1887:11; 1897b:13). This judgment has stood the test of subsequent scholarship and remains valid today. Furthermore, the composition of the work which Wellhausen uncovered and commented on in the first part of his book (1887:11–60; 1897b:13–64) has essentially been confirmed. In 1924 the Egyptian scholar Aḥmad Zakī Pacha published the only manuscript hitherto discovered of Ibn al-Kalbī in Cairo/28/. This unique text goes back to a manuscript of Ibn al-Jawālīqī (before 529 AH/1134 CE); thus it derives from a period in which Yāqūt was the last to have been acquainted with it. R. Klinke-Rosenberger, a student of August Fischer, edited, commented on and translated the text into German, and thus created an easily accessible edition/29/. Understandably she was able to identify a number of readings which were superior to those which Wellhausen possessed, but in the main he had already done what was correct: above all, from among the mass of traditions he had made the right choice.

In addition to a discussion of the Arab gods, including theophoric proper names and divine names attested only on inscriptions (1887:60ff.; 1897b:64ff.), Wellhausen provided an account of the religious life of Mecca in the pagan era (1887:64–98; 1897b:68–101) and a phenomenology of the cult (1887:98–135; 1897b:101–47). Naturally all reports from the Islamic period are "colored" by the later state of affairs (1887:69; 1897b:73); nevertheless, Wellhausen was able to "filter out" the pre-Islamic situation, as for the Ḥajj for example 1887:71; 1897b:76), so that a truly living image of the diversity of the religious life, which Islam centralized, unified, or wholly abolished, appears. In the process much light is cast on the role of Mecca: its importance was "less religious than political in nature; the city was distinguished less for its sanctity than for the power and prestige of its inhabitants. The influence of the Quraysh extended further and went deeper than the attraction of the Ka'ba. So it was before Islam, and so it remained under Islam, as long as the kingdom was an Arab kingdom" (1887:89; 1897b:94). With respect to the whole area of the cult, Wellhausen clearly gives prominence to aspects which stand in contrast to those of the Islamic period. In the matter of ritual sacrifice in particular (1887:114ff.; 1897b:117ff.), he sees secularizing tendencies at work even before the coming of Islam (1887:104f.; 1897b:108f.) and calls attention to the "unmistakable family resemblance to the Hebraic cult" (1887:164ff.; 1897b:141ff.). He regards "lordship" as the essential content of the Semitic concept of God, to which corresponds, on the human side, the state of servitude (1887:169; 1897b:145). In this connection he is led (especially forcefully in the first edition!) to attack false oppositions and conclusions:

> A growing scholarly anti-Semitism now seeks to profit from the hopelessly abstract antithesis between the Semitic and the Indogermanic races in order to demonstrate the servile attitude of the Semites toward the divine. But servility was less a matter of general attitude than of the offices and liturgies of public worship Of the Arabs, at least it may be said that they showed rather too much than too little recalcitrance and independence of mind in relation to their gods Moreover, the Semitic notion of servitude was quite different from the Roman institution of slavery. Furthermore, the Arabs seem to have called themselves sons as well as servants of God, at least in their tribal names It is a sheer waste of time to have to refute such childish nonsense. Is the German worship service or the pride Germans feel in loyal service to the monarch also servility? (1887 169, revised somewhat in 1897a:145, but unchanged in intention)

Wellhausen also dealt with "popular paganism" (1887:135-64; 1897b:147-207), including necromancy, belief in ghosts, and magic, in addition to burial customs and divination, etc. The second edition is not only revised in this respect but is also enlarged through the addition of a separate chapter on Fiṭra (1897b:167-77), or religious customs designed to bring about ritual purity, and a section on "Sacral Law, its Forms and Agencies" (1897b: 186-95), a subject of increasing interest to Wellhausen. "The most powerful influence which religion had on human affairs it exercised through oaths" (1897b:186). Even Islam was unable to abolish superstition; its forms "are somehow peculiarly cosmopolitan" (1897b:147). Wellhausen regarded a monistic explanation (by which animism is meant) in this area as "completely unnecessary and even dangerous" (1897b:157). He concedes that the "analogy of the human soul" has a certain significance, but even this has no general validity. The "animation of nature by the intellect is not something which proceeds consistently or systematically, but capriciously and irrationally"

(1897b:157). Thus Wellhausen guards himself against a simple adoption of the animistic theory (which, naturally, he could not dispense with entirely)/30/.

Of special interest are the concluding sections to both editions, in the first entitled "The Overall Character of Arab Paganism" (1887:171–212), in the second, "Religio-Historical Considerations" (1897b:208–42). Here Wellhausen gave expression to problems which are still of immediate interest today. On the subject of "the nature of the Arab gods" (1887:171ff.; 1897b:208ff.), he had already spoken out against Smith's totemistic theory in the first edition (1887:176ff.); at the same time he rejected Sprenger's thesis of the belief in spirits as the center of old Arab religion (1887:178; 1897b:211ff.), and accepted the idea of the origin of the gods in the cult of the dead (manism) at most in individual instances (1887:178f.). With the growth of the "enormous abstraction" of a transcendental subject, which is what the gods signify in contrast to the simple veneration of natural objects, the worship of God is no longer the worship of nature but acquires a moral character (1887:172). This section has been revised in the second edition, which is characterized by its rejection of the hypothesis of the primitive astral character of the Arab gods (1897b:209ff.). The gods were originally terrestrial, not celestial, in nature (1897b:211); only the loss of contact with nature made room for their association with heavenly phenomena (1897b:214). Nevertheless, a tendency toward the veneration of light may already be observed at an early period (1897b:210f.; 1887:173–75). A theocracy existed at the very beginning, not merely at the end (1897b:212). Wellhausen sees development in a number of areas: in the "dissolution of the polytheistic cult," in the relaxation of the ties to the religious life, and above all in the tendency toward the unification of the gods (1887:182ff.; 1897b:215ff.). He sees the basis for these developments first of all in the rise of a syncretism which is able to accommodate supraregional tendencies and which promotes the growing unity of the Arab tribes (in contrast to Israel, as Wellhausen observes: 1887:183; 1897b:215). "A community of spiritual interests emerges which embraces the whole of Arabia: a body of literature, though yet unwritten, a common language, which transcends the dialects, a certain education and viewpoint common to all" (1897b:216; 1887:183f.). Wellhausen does not regard syncretism as the essence of polytheism, but rather as its gradual dissolution (1897b:217). Out of the ruin of polytheism, monotheism arises in the guise of Allah. Wellhausen sees this process at work above all in the language: "It was the language more than anything else which created Allah; what I have in mind is, of course, not merely the word but the god himself" (1887:185; 1897b:218). Allah, "the God," evolved imperceptibly from an originally appellative attribute of a particular (tribal) god (1887:185) to a common supraregional idea of God. "As is so often the case, language prepared the way for thought by offering a general term, or notion, which only needed to be animated" (1887:186; 1897b:219: "which was then personified"). It was no plural, but a generic term in the singular which was elevated to the level of an idea, or hypothesis (1887:186; 1897b:219). At the same time the cult, which in the beginning constituted religion, also fell into ruin. This becomes especially clear in the process of conversion to Islam (1887:186ff.; 1897b:219ff.). "It was with the decline of the cult that religion, as we understand it, in contrast to the cult, actually arose—and this in connection with Allah" (1887:188; 1897b:221). The domain of Allah lay outside the traditional cult and was generally associated in Arabia with the sphere of law (1887:190f.; 1897b:223f.). Wellhausen sees the latter tendency strengthened by the penetration of Judaism and Christianity into Arabia (1887:197ff.; 1897b:230ff.); it is to Christianity above all (thanks to Aramaic culture) that he ascribes a dominant role. "If Islam had not intervened, the whole of northern Arabia, from the Red Sea to the Persian Gulf, would have become Christian in a short time" (1887:199; 1897b:231). Christianity had a great part in the intellectual development of the Arabs, as Christians were the first to make use of Arabic as a written language. Thus, according to Wellhausen, the ground for Islam was prepared (1887:203; 1897b:234). For him Jewish and Christian influences on Islam were plainly visible (1887:204-12; 1897b:234-42). It is certain, for example, that the earliest followers of Muhammad were known as "Sabaeans," because they practiced uncommon ablutions (1887:205ff.; 1897b:230ff. with additional evidence). The "Ḥunafā'" or "Seekers," individuals who had been touched by Christianity without having formed communities, constituted a further bridge to Islam (1887:207f.; 1897b:238f.); it was from them that Muhammad received the first impulses (1887:209; 1897b:240). His earliest sermons, which deal with judgment and the end-time, point in this direction. The very soul of Islam is derived from Christianity (1887:210; 1897b:241). Wellhausen sees an ascetic trend dominating early Islam. In anticipation of the well-known view of Tor Andrae, Wellhausen writes in conclusion: "Thus it was Christian ascetics who disseminated the spiritual seed of Islam; its oldest means of community formation, the forms of its worship, Islam probably owes to the Sabaeans. The leaven may not have come from the Jews, but the flour that was later mixed in was for the most part of Jewish origin." According to Wellhausen, this was also the outcome of the religio-historical development to Islam. "The Allah of Muhammad only helped the Allah of the ancient Arabs to attain the full consequence of his own being" (1887:212; 1897b:242). The picture of the prehistory and development of Islam which Wellhausen thus drew has remained unchanged in its essential features until today; his thesis regarding the part played by Christianity in this development has never been seriously challenged. The notion that the rise of the inter-tribal god "Allah" was due in large measure, even if not so exclusively as Wellhausen thought, to the influence of the language is likewise undisputed. The epigraphical evidence for the diffusion of the god in pre-Islamic Arabia has since increased considerably/31/.

4.   *Marriage among the Arabs*
    In the course of his work on the conditions of life in ancient Arabia before the rise of Islam, Wellhausen dealt with various themes, in part as a

result of his own research and in part as a consequence of articles he was asked to write. Thus he produced a substantial account of "Die Ehe bei den Arabern" for the *NGWG* in 1893, which he regarded as "gleanings" from earlier works, above all from that of W. R. Smith (*Kinship and Marriage in Early Arabia*, 1885), but in which he also put forward important modifications in the prevailing view. Here as well he makes use of early Arabic literature and modern reports (Doughty, Snouck-Hurgronje). The "statistical arrangement" of the work, in the sense of an "uncontroversial schema," makes the study even today a source of information on all areas concerned with relations between the sexes in the time of Muhammad and earlier. Of special importance are the undogmatic portrayal, embracing all deviations from "the dominant type of marriage" (460ff.), and the reserved treatment of what Wellhausen prefers to call "metrarchy" (474–81). That the latter constituted the older system in comparison with patriarchy "may be assumed on general grounds, but cannot be definitely proven" (479). Both marital structures go back among Semitic peoples to the earliest times, a fact which Wellhausen illustrates with a series of noteworthy examples (479ff.), which might be supplemented today with further evidence, particularly from Mesopotamia and Syria.

5.   *A Commonwealth without a Government*

Less well known is the address which Wellhausen delivered in Göttingen on 27 January 1900, on the occasion of the birthday celebration of the Kaiser, under the title "Ein Gemeinwesen ohne Obrigkeit." Here Wellhausen was concerned to show, in relation to modern society, how a functional polity, complete with a system of laws, could have been attained in the Arab domain (by which the Arabian Peninsula is meant) apart from the existence of a governmental apparatus, an "official government." This masterly address remains to this day one of the best introductions to the nature of tribal society among the ancient Arabs (without the ballast of modern sociological terminology). With a few brief strokes he depicts the public life of this gentile system based upon "the principle of blood," or kinship, in which public spirit takes the place of "political order" (5) and the departments of government consist in an aristocracy based on personal merits and abilities (7). Law is bound to the morality of the tribe or clan and possesses no executive power or "criminal justice administration" of any kind (9). Blood-revenge is "a sacred, primeval law" (10), which is not even broken by the *lex talionis* (11f.). Wellhausen sees a process of secularization at work in the tribal law of the ancient Arabs (14f.). Only with Muhammad, who founded a "sovereign community" in Medina, did religion once again become the basis for law rather than blood; it was then, too, that the blood-feud was abolished in favor of the *lex talionis*, but only after the fall of the Umayyad dynasty did this really take effect (12f.). By comparison the development of the Hebrews, who had already devised a system of criminal law based on religion over a millennium and a half earlier, proceeded differently (13f.). "The law of the ancient Arabs is remarkably profane, prosaic and informal. It is through and through a law of commerce and contracts; even criminal law operates exclusively by means of reparation and payment" (15). In conclusion Wellhausen carries out a comparison with the modern state which does not attempt to gloss over the defects of Arab society but points out weaknesses and strengths on both sides (15f.). He sees clearly that an established system of law is an achievement which must not be lost. One must constantly remind oneself of the difficult beginnings which gave birth to law, for it is not something given by nature (16). No truly enlightened culture could arise in the desert; the "weak foundation was not capable of supporting a towering superstructure." Intellectual freedom "generally thrives only in the state, which, like Noah's ark, harbors all sorts of creatures and gives them full play" (15).

6. *Arab–Israelite Penal Law*

In an article written in response to an inquiry by Theodor Mommsen, Wellhausen deals with "Arabisch-israelitisches Strafrecht"; the article was completed in 1902 but was not published until 1903, and then appeared in a second edition in 1905/32/. Here he describes the legal situation in its "primitive condition" (1905:91) among the Arabs of the pre-Islamic period, in comparison with ancient Israelite law (especially 93ff.). The early Arabs possessed a common law without an executive, as was also found in prehistoric times among the ancient Hebrews (93). But while the latter developed a "religious criminal-law" by means of a "reforming renewal" (95), ancient Arab law, as he had already pointed out in the address delivered on the Kaiser's birthday, is characterized by a "prosaic secularity" (99). This was not the original state of affairs, but it arose "in connection with the notion that the tribe as a *religious community* was no longer viable, and that religion insofar as it existed at all existed as a superstition and a petrified cult but was of little significance in the practical affairs of life" (99). But this negative image may be the fault of the sources at our disposal/33/. It is only through Muhammad in Medina that religion again becomes the foundation of the community and the law (92f., cf. 102f. [Goldziher]). Islamic law, as Wellhausen explains elsewhere, is religious in nature and more firmly anchored historically, but old Arab law is often sanctioned in the Koran (1898). "The spirit of Islam, which is in truth humane and objective and not inclined to quibble over words," is not opposed to the modernization of the law, for which there are points of contact in Islam itself. It is in keeping with this spirit that the emancipation of law from religion is of ancient origin with the Arabs and that the judge should preside not in the mosque but in the market place.

7. *Medina*

If Wellhausen had provided a basis for understanding developments after Muhammad with his studies on the pre-Islamic world of the

Arabs, he was also clearly preoccupied with the work of Muhammad himself and the consequences which it produced. It was the beginning of the Muslim community in Medina which interested him above all, and which provided the foundation for the world dominion of the Arabs. In 1889, in the fourth number of the *Skizzen und Vorarbeiten*, Wellhausen brought together three works which dealt with Medina in the time of Muhammad and before. In the first article he describes *Medina vor dem Islam* (1889:3–64), on the basis of relevant Arabic and non-Arabic (Greek and Latin) reports. Geography, social structure, economy, and history are dealt with in equal measure, and a picture is drawn which has kept its validity to this day. Wellhausen depicts both the roots of this synoecious "commonwealth without a government" (21) and the consequences of the disruption of its life by old feuds among the Arab tribes and their descendants. His picture is based not only on historical sources but also on poems and genealogies. With regard to the latter, Wellhausen remarked: "Genealogy is no less history than statistics; it takes account just as much of conditions which once existed as of those which now exist" (27). The unstable relations in Medina were rooted in the quarrels which naturally arose in a settled oasis economy with a nomadic heritage, above all between neighbors (21f.). As for the three Jewish tribes, Wellhausen sees in them nothing Arab (13f.), as was the case, for example, with the Christian tribes in the vicinity (15). Precisely because they were Arab, the latter, in contrast to the Jews, were "carried away . . . by Arab national consciousness, as soon as it had been awakened by Islam" (15). But both groups helped to acquaint the inhabitants of Medina, the later Anṣār, with "monotheistic religion and thus prepared the way for Islam" (15). This is the explanation of Muhammad's success and of his position in history; he put an end to the dissolution of the community, even though the old quarrels between particular groups continued to be felt for a long time afterwards. Several appendices provide translations of Arabic sources on the history of tribal feuds among the inhabitants of Medina (36–64).

The second article included by Wellhausen in this volume was *Muhammeds Gemeindeordnung von Medina* (1889:65–83), as contained in Ibn Isḥāq, or Ibn Hišām. Alongside the Koran, it is the most important document on the internal relations of the new Muslim community in Medina. Other representatives of the tradition (such as Wāqidī) are primarily interested in foreign military campaigns. Wellhausen added to the German translation, with its paragraph divisions, a number of notes and a summary on the significance of the document, which has likewise retained its value to this day. He places the work at the beginning of the Medina period, when Muhammad's position was not yet firmly established (80f.). It is more indebted linguistically to the old legal terminology than to the new Muslim parlance. Unsettled relations can be observed in other areas as well. Thus, the pagans still belong to the *Umma*, and the relation to the Jewish tribes is placed above that to the Anṣār (82f.). "It is a simple decree of Muhammad in which he codifies the order of the community as it had evolved in practice since his arrival in Medina." It is no law, "but only a public statement of the main articles of the communal law in force within the Umma" (83). The new characteristics of this new polity are already strongly apparent: it is based on a religious, and no longer a tribal foundation. It is "an association for the defense of Allah," in which the inner rule of feuds is transcended in an outward direction for the benefit of the community as a whole. War and peace are now the concern of the entire community (78). Islam was the new cement which made the old, ruined community in Medina into a community which was again capable of taking action (76). Muhammad's ability as a statesman shows itself in the balanced relations between old laws and new obligations which he was able to bring about.

The third study is also devoted to the Medinan period, and in particular to Muhammad's relations with the Arab tribes. For this purpose Wellhausen makes use of the *Schreiben Muhammeds und die Gesandtschaften an ihn* (1889:87–194), found in the unpublished Sīra of *Muhammad Ibn Saʻd* (died 845 CE). A number of gaps in this work may be filled in with information from Ibn Isḥāq (Ibn Hišām)/34/. Thus Wellhausen deftly uncovered one of the most important sources for the "conversion of the Arabs," the value of which A. Sprenger had already recognized (88). The genuineness of the work is not, by and large, in doubt, although, as Wellhausen admits, one should not expect "diplomatic accuracy" (90). Ibn Saʻd copied his texts as a rule from other sources (al-Wāqidī, Ibn al-Kalbī and al-Madāʼinī), occasionally shortening and revising them (88f.). Several fictitious passages may be clearly identified (90f.). In his diplomatic writings Muhammad shows himself to be an opportunistic politician, not a rigorist as later authors portrayed him (91). Most of the writings are "decrees" sent by him from the period after the consolidation of Islam (92). "Not the religious but the political transition to an Islamic theocracy is of principle concern" (93). The terminology (*baiʻa*, "homage") which he uses and the demands which he makes, even of the leaders themselves, show this very clearly (94f.). Muhammad confirmed the old authorities, as a rule, and allowed the aristocratic ancestral constitution to remain in force. "The most important advantage which membership in the Islamic community brings with it is the guarantee of peace and security, both without and within" (95). Wellhausen clearly recognizes that Islam initiated a feudal development through frequent grants of land and confirmations of property rights (95). Thus with the triumph of Medina everything in the Arab realm received a "new seal of legality" (96). The texts were edited and translated by Wellhausen himself. He does not provide information on the manuscripts which he employed (one from Gotha and one from London). Matters such as these had ceased to interest him; the content of the work was more important to him. During his lifetime the relevant volume of the great edition of Ibn Saʻd (published by E. Sachau *et al.*) made its appearance; it contained the two chapters with which he had also dealt (1889:65–83).

It is appropriate at this point to emphasize the fact that Wellhausen expressed himself rather positively on Muhammad and spoke out clearly against "too excessively stressing his human commonness," characteristic of A. Sprenger's approach (Wellhausen, 1891f:307). "He achieved great things for his time; the mistake was only that he intended that it remain valid for all time. That is the shortcoming of a *theocracy*; it overlooks the fact that the organization of a human community cannot be something divine and eternal but has to satisfy changing human needs" (1900c). Otherwise one can detect a noticeable reserve in Wellhausen on the subject of the religious substance of Muhammad's message. On the origin of that message, however, he expressed his opinion clearly/35/.

8. *Prolegomena to the Earliest History of Islam*

For Wellhausen the work on Muhammad in Medina constituted the point of departure for subsequent investigations into early Arab–Islamic history. As early as 1887, as he himself writes, he had already begun an intensive study of M. J. de Goeje's large edition of the "Annals" of aṭ-Ṭabarī, then in the process of publication. The first fruit of these readings was the *Prolegomena zur ältesten Geschichte des Islams* of 1899. Naturally it had no more than the title in common with his *Prolegomena zur Geschichte Israels* of 1883; in content they are very different, apart from the use of the source-critical method as such, which Wellhausen employs here. Taking Ṭabarī as his basis, he attempts to describe, in accordance with scientific and historical criteria, the period of the first caliphs, the "rightly guided ones" (*rāšidūn*). As a result, source criticism goes hand in hand with the description of events as reflected in the sources. Insofar as the work is concerned with the elaboration, characterization, and comparison of the "various traditions of the compiler" (i.e., of Ṭabarī), it represents for Wellhausen a series of "preliminary observations" toward a future monograph or historical description. His caution led Wellhausen into understatement with regard to the title ("Prolegomena"); what he offers is, in fact, much more. It is not only analysis but also synthesis. His method and form of presentation do not differ from that employed in the later work, with which he concluded his investigations in this area, *Das arabische Reich und sein Sturz* (1902a), which he also intended originally to publish under the title "Prolegomena" (see below p. 142). As in the *Prolegomena zur Geschichte Israels*, which had already been published in 1878 as the first volume of his *Geschichte Israels*, we have before us in this instance the same close combination of historical criticism with positive reconstruction (for Israel, the consequence of his Hexateuch studies!). Wellhausen did not choose to express himself further on the title; evidently he found it in the course of his Ṭabarī-investigations to be the most suitable one in that it presupposes the historical account still to be written. Had he already surmised that the literary investigation of the sources would only be one of the building-blocks of a future monograph (by means of the inclusion of evidence from monuments, coins, etc.)? We do not know. The nature of the later works, as we have already said, leaves the matter in doubt. What was of decisive importance to Wellhausen was the fact, as he himself says in conclusion, "that without such prolegomena history remains suspended in the air" (1899a:146). This statement undoubtedly makes reference to earlier presentations of Arab-Islamic history, which hardly pursued source-critical methods and which compiled more than they differentiated (cf. August Müller). Such was the pioneering achievement which Wellhausen made in this area with his Prolegomena. There can be no subsequent return to earlier approaches.

Unlike the Old Testament situation, in the Arabic sources Wellhausen was dealing with tradents known by name and with proper historians. The latter were, however, as in the case of Ṭabarī, no more than compilers. This makes it necessary to distinguish between the different accounts, to assess their value, and to identify the best tradition. Wellhausen carries out this agenda in brief fashion in the first section of his work, entitled "Saif ben Umar" (3–7). He establishes the priority of Ṭabarī over against Ibn al-Athīr, Balādhurī, and Ibn Saʿd and then evaluates the isnād, "that is, the chain of transmission as it comes down from its point of origin," as found among all Arab tradents. Of real importance is Wellhausen's realization that the compilers of historical material are themselves "the representatives of a uniform point of view" which determines the way in which they use this material (4). Thus one need set no great store by the "colorful isnāds of individual traditions" but must hold to the authoritative bearers of the tradition, who are at the same time the first historical authors, such as Abū Mikhnaf, Ibn Isḥāq, Abū Maʿšar, al-Wāqidī, etc. They must be regarded as the final authorities. The value of a particular isnād is dependent upon the worth of the historian to whom it appears trustworthy: "in bad historians even good isnāds cannot be trusted, and good historians merit our confidence even when they provide no isnād but only remark: 'I have it from one to whom I give credence.' This represents a real simplification of the task of critical analysis" (4).

As his principal authority for the period of the first four caliphs Ṭabarī cites Saif b. ʿUmar (died 796 CE), who in turn traces his report back to the original source, giving a precise statement of the isnāds. "He presents himself throughout as an independent, primary gatherer and redactor of the material, on a par with Ibn Isḥāq, Abū Maʿšar, and others" (5). But the information which he provides stands in "constant contradiction" to that found in all other authorities. For Wellhausen this situation gave rise to a fundamental question: "For or against Saif?" (5). Judging from external appearances, there is much which seems at first to speak for him. He represents an Iraqi recension as over against the older versions of Medina. But as a *tertium*, or criterium, for deciding the matter, Wellhausen draws upon two independent and contemporary Christian sources which prove that Saif's chronological data (on the battle of Yarmūk and the conquest of

Egypt) are unreliable. "With the collapse of his chronology, Saif's pragmatic approach as a whole collapses" (6). Thus for Wellhausen the matter was settled: Saif's account (and that of Ṭabarī as well, insofar as he reproduces Saif) is to be mistrusted from the very beginning, and the Hijāzī tradition is to be given preference (6). Wellhausen now regarded it as his primary task to corroborate this verdict by means of specific information on the period from the overthrow of the Ridda (632/633 CE) to the so-called Battle of the Camel (656 CE), and "to pursue the forces at work in the degeneration of the tradition" (7). We cannot follow this attempt in detail but may illustrate Wellhausen's method by means of several examples.

The conquest of the Euphrates region by Khālid in 633 CE commenced at Ḥīra according to Ibn Isḥāq, al-Wāqidī, and Ibn al-Kalbī, but according to others, such as Madā'inī, Balādhurī, and Saif, at Basra. Saif is most imaginative in his attempt to combine the two traditions and as a result comes into conflict with his own date, a fact which "even the dim-witted Ṭabarī could not overlook" (44). The following points speak for the historical authenticity of the first version of the tradition (43f.): (1) according to the representatives of the second version, the conquest of Ḥīra in Rabi' I 12 (May/June 633 CE) did not occur from the southeast, thus from the direction of Basra, but from the northwest, without a crossing of the Euphrates; (2) since the preceding battles at Ullais took place in Ṣafar 12 (April/May 633 CE), the later conflicts at Madhār and Valaga cannot also be placed in this time period, as Saif above all tries to do; (3) the province of Basra was first conquered in the year 14 AH (635 CE) by 'Utba b. Jazwān. What gave occasion to the whole displacement of events was, in Wellhausen's opinion, the report of raids that had been made in the vicinity of Basra and Kaškar before the fall of Ḥīra (44). In addition, Wellhausen always endeavored to capture the scenic, topographical color of a region. Thus he refers to relevant studies which make the historical processes understandable (cf., for example, 40ff.). Of value to him were also the short verses preserved in the sources, for they frequently constituted authentic witnesses (e.g., for the battle "at the confluence of the canals," that is, at Ullais = Vologesias, 40). Moreover the conquest of the Persian kingdom was not, according to Wellhausen, a conscious goal but "was, in the beginning, only the wholly unintentional result of gradual but steady success" (39).

In the manner we have described, Wellhausen examines the reports step by step—a laborious procedure, but one which is certainly profitable for the study of history. In this way he is repeatedly able to detect the more or less hidden tendencies in the account of Saif b. 'Umar: Blame is squarely placed upon Abdallāh b. Sabā', and thus upon the Jews, for events which led up to the split in the community, on the occasion of the revolt against the third caliph 'Uthmān (124f.). Thus he seeks to exonerate those who were mainly at fault, namely those involved in the struggle between the "old pagan nobility" (Quraysh) and the "theocratic aristocracy which was rooted entirely in Islam" (that is, the old companions of the Prophet) (132f.). The same observation may be made with respect to his treatment of the so-called Battle of the Camel (135ff.): here the Sabā'īya are to blame (141). "The entire account of their political behavior is a monumental, apologetically motivated falsification of the authentic tradition, an argument for the truth of the old saying: the pious never lie so completely as in their sacred history" (141f.; the original reference was to a Ḥadīth that establishes a Sunna).

9. *The Religio-Political Factions in Early Islam*
Wellhausen published further fruit of his studies of Ṭabarī in AGWG in 1901: *Die religiös-politischen Oppositionsparteien im alten Islam* (1901c). The origin of the party conflicts had already in the *Prolegomena* received source-critical treatment as an important part of early Islamic history. Now this was made the theme of a separate work, and he began to clear the forest of tradition in accordance with the principle of historical truth. In the course of this study, Abū Mikhnaf (died 775 CE), often mentioned by Ṭabarī as his authority for these events, proved to be the oldest and the most reliable source in the entire "Arab Kingdom." Later informants, or historians, offer nothing more than conjectures with no certainty (6). The essay consists of two parts: "The Khawārij" (1–55) and "The Shī'a" (55–99).

In the first part, Wellhausen undertakes, first of all, a critique of previous opinions on the *Khārijites* (5ff.). He finds himself in dispute above all with R. Brunnow (8ff.), as was the case in an earlier review/36/. The Khawārij, the "Nonconformists" or "Separatists" (4 n.2; 16), were not bedouins but "a militant group in the employ of the government," like other Muslims. They were obviously composed of Koran-reciters, a group which should not be conceived as a self-contained class (9f.). They had no connection with Judaism; that was the idea of the Arabic authors (11f.). Wellhausen strongly emphasizes their religious roots; they were a truly Islamic growth which arose in Ṣiffīn (12). "They put the idea of a theocracy into practice and did not introduce anything foreign or strange into the concept" (12). At first they did not constitute a sect but publically recruited new members in various places from representatives of radical Islamic principles. In contrast to the other parties, they were in absolute earnest about these principles and thus came to be called *murrāq*, "those who ram their heads through the wall" (1884b:839). "That shows how deeply they were grounded in the nature of Islam and its theocracy" (1901c:12). They were an extremely pious revolutionary party, which did not derive from Arab paganism but from Islam. Thus "they were formally related to the virtuosi of Islamic piety, the so-called Reciters, almost as the Jewish Zealots were related to the Pharisees," except that the Zealots fought for their country whereas the Khawārij fought for God alone (13). Their piety was politically oriented, as is typical for a theocracy (13). As an uncompromisingly Muslim party, they represent the antipole, within the same religion, to the "catholicity" of the *jamā'a* (16). Their goal was the creation of that kind of community which is desired by

God. For this reason they were hostile to culture and fiercely individualistic: *fiat iustitia, pereat mundus* (16). Despite their high regard for praxis, the group gave rise to "theoretical heresy—that is to say, theology" (17). For "they were the first to raise religious questions which went above and beyond the tradition, and the first to discuss them with their opponents. . . . There can be no doubt that they provided a stimulus for the earliest theologians of Islam" (17). Wellhausen's final verdict on the old Khārijites of Kūfa, for whom Ibn al-Athīr and 'Abdallāh b. 'Uqba b. Janawī in Abū Mikhnaf provide valuable eyewitness testimony (17, 19, 21), was one of secret sympathy: "They were an earnest and a believing people, who were far more noble than the Jewish Zealots and thus were no worse than Christian heretics and saints; for they were persons of the deed, who found martyrdom not on the scaffold but on the battlefield. One who judges them from the profane standpoint of modern culture does not do them justice" (24). Wellhausen then pursues their fate in Basra, drawing upon Ibn Athīr where Ṭabarī's account proves too brief (24ff.). He often gives priority to Kāmil (over against Abū Mikhnaf) (38). For the end he follows Abdūlwahhāb (Abū Hāšim) in Ṭabarī (50f.). He is critical of the unhistorical description (in Abū Mikhnaf) of the divisions which arose among the Khārijites. They had their origin in the extremism of Ibn Azraq (28). There was a considerable growth in this movement toward the close of the Umayyad dynasty (49ff.). The Ibādīs of Basra managed to survive in a more moderate form in sourthern Arabia (52ff.).

In the same manner Wellhausen devoted himself to the origins of the *Shī'a*, giving priority to Abū Mikhnaf (56, 68, 87). All other reports are found to be strongly tendentious (60, 67, 70, 87). That is true in particular of the Shiite accounts, insofar as they are really of such antiquity (67f.). Thus he sketches the following picture (68): "Abū Mikhnaf checks parallel traditions by comparing them with each other. In this way, matters of secondary importance, which appear only once, are allowed to recede, and matters of essential importance, which recur throughout the tradition, gradually come to stand out. Those accounts which are not parallel he arranges in fitting sequence, so that a continuum arises which cannot be broken without making certain choices and adjustments. Variants and uncertainties do appear, but there are no real contradictions on important points. On the whole the picture is firm and uniform, not only with respect to the facts but also with reference to the characters."

The Shī'a likewise did not begin as a sect but as an expression of political sentiment in Iraq (56, 89). 'Alī is its representative and embodies its claim to the kingdom. In the *Prolegomena* Wellhausen had already written: "The Shī'at Ali was originally a political party, just as the Shī'at Mu'awiya, and not a religious sect" (1899a:125). The veneration of 'Alī and of his family grew out of these political ambitions, and indeed only after his death. "Yet within the womb of an obscure sect, a proper cult was developed around him quite early" (1901c:56). A turning point which led to this development was the event of Kerbela 680 CE, with which a new epoch begins for the Shīʻa (71). An organization of "penitents" or "confessors" formed the germ-cell of a growing opposition to the Umayyad regime, with which they would tolerate no compromise (71ff.). Mukhtār became the soul of this movement (74ff., 94f.). Wellhausen was convinced that a generally accurate image of him was provided by Ṭabarī (88f.). The picture of his character may waver, but his accomplishments are of greater historical importance (89, see the above citation p. 118). With him the Shīʻa were transformed into an enthusiastic, religious sect (89). Moreover, the movement abandoned the "the Arab national soil" by its connection with the "oppressed classes," the Mawālī (89f.). A new form of Islam provided the ideological cement: that which was stamped by the Sabāʼīya (89f.). What Wellhausen had in mind was not a religious importation from Iran (he was expressly critical of Dozy, among others, on this point: 90), even if, as is no doubt the case, Shiite ideas happen to agree with those held by the Iranians. Rather, this new form of Islam was the result of a Jewish import, for Abdallāh b. Sabāʼ may have been a Jew (91). Wellhausen grounds this notion, moreover, in the dogmatics of the Shiite faith (91ff. with material from Ṭabarī). Behind the image of ʻAlī not only as the heir of the Prophet (the first stage of development) but also as a prophet himself (second stage) is the Jewish "idea of the monarchical prophet as the sovereign representative of the kingdom of God on earth" (92). This idea had passed over from Judaism into Islam and after the death of the Prophet left "a palpable void": "Shiite dogma began here" (92). Its fundamental principle was that "prophecy, that is, the living, personal representation of divine authority, necessarily belongs to a theocracy and continues to live on in it" (92). The view that every prophet brings his own successor along with him (cf. Deuteronomy 18) is Jewish; and the doctrine of the rebirth (*rajʻa*) of the prophet was nourished in heretical Jewish circles (93, with reference to the "returning prophets" of the Pseudo-Clementine literature). The latter notion was once an article of faith in the prophet's family but was later reinterpreted antithetically as the "periodic eclipse (*Ghaiba*) of the true Imām" (93f.). Thus the reverence of the Shiites for God became reverence for humans, "and this resulted in a kind of Caesaropapism" (94). "They protested against the Imamate of the prevailing authority, but the legitimate Imamate of the prophet's own blood was no better. It led to contempt for the law. The Imām was above the letter of the law and knew hidden things. Whoever followed and obeyed him was relieved of responsibility for himself" (94). What Wellhausen sees as of world-historical significance in the entire affair was the transmission of an extreme Shiite faith to the Mawālī by al-Mukhtār (94f.). He recognized the signs of the time, the untenability of the situation: the fact that "not Islam but Arabic descent assured one of full civic rights in the theocracy. Had al-Mukhtār achieved the goal he set for himself in the beginning, he might have been the savior of the Arab kingdom" (95). Things turned out differently, and only later, under his successor Abū Muslim, did the seed sprout which he had sown. It led eventually to the overthrow of the Umayyad dynasty. "He is at bottom a tragic figure toward whom we need not show the same antipathy as his contemporaries did" (95). With respect to the many kinds of Shiism, Wellhausen sees in them the survival of old connections with various kinds of "free-thinking" (99).

Both Wellhausen's studies of the history of early Islamic sects have retained their importance to the present day because they not only investigated the sources critically for the first time but also succeeded in demonstrating the close connection between politics and religion in these events. Without exception later works are built upon Wellhausen's studies. New sources, especially the Kitāb firaq aš-Šī'a of the Imamite scholar an-Naubakhtī (ninth century), edited and published in 1931 by H. Ritter/37/, supplement and correct Wellhausen's picture in many details. His emphasis on Judaism as the formative factor in the religious development of the Shī'a was certainly one-sided. Gnostic-Iranian ideas, which only came to light in the Ismā'īlīya, played a greater role/38/.

10. *Conflicts between the Arabs and the Romans in the Umayyad Period*

At the same time that Wellhausen completed his investigation of the religio-political opposition parties in early Islam, he also published an essay entitled "Die Kämpfe der Araber mit den Romäern in der Zeit der Umaijiden" (1901b). Here we are likewise confronted with a pioneering study of the sources. This genuinely historical undertaking is an attempt to bring the Byzantine (Greek) data on the chronology of the Umayyad raids into harmony with the information supplied by the Arabs (using the Seleucid era as a point of reference) (416). No one before Wellhausen had attempted to carry out this work so thoroughly. He draws upon Theophanes and Elias Nisibenos on the Christian side, Balādhurī and Wāqidī (who relies, once again, on Ma'šar as his principal authority, 415) on the Islamic. Among Arab historians these battles generally do not occupy the foreground of the discussion; rather, they concentrate more on events in Iraq or Iran. Although the fight against the Byzantine empire was also carried on as an ideological battle, "as a kind of compulsory religious service," on the part of the Umayyads (414), they had no real designs for conquest, according to Wellhausen. The Arab conquest was merely the consequence of repeated raids, in the course of which a "desolate no-man's land" (*aḍ-ḍawāhī*) was created as a buffer-zone to the Byzantine empire (415). Wellhausen deals with the time period from 639–743 CE. In an appendix he makes a number of remarks on the transcription of Arabic names in Theophanes (445ff.).

11. *The Arab Kingdom and Its Fall*

The period of Wellhausen's research into Arab–Islamic history which began in 1884 reached its conclusion with the publication of the great work *Das arabische Reich und sein Sturz* in 1902. Even today this work remains a milestone in this area/39/. In the foreword Wellhausen provides an evaluation of the state of the sources which continues his earlier observations. For him Abū Mikhnaf (died 775 CE) is not only the earliest and the best Arabic prose writer but also the principal guarantor and collector *ex vivo ore*. "With him the isnād, the chain of traditional authorities, remains truth and is not simply a literary form" (ix). As proof of his reliability Wellhausen points to the freshness and vivacity of the narrative; "all is dialogue and scene" (x). In his description of Abū Mikhnaf's way of writing history, one is reminded of Wellhausen's own methods: his emphasis on essentials, the art of his portrayal, his way of citing songs and poems in attestation (x). "On the whole, the picture is firm and unified, not only with reference to the facts but also with reference to the characters. The author's plan and overarching conception control the seemingly chaotic material in spite of everything" (x; cf. the above description, pp. 138f.). What is lacking is a thorough chronology; he relates events individually, without establishing their relation to one another, "in the greatest breadth, without any conciseness" (x). He is a representative of the Kūfic tradition; his sympathies lie with Iraq, the land in which he lived. He is against the Syrian Umayyads and for 'Alī. But he lacks the tendentiousness of purpose which might have led him to falsify the facts (xi). Occasionally he conceals something which does not suit him. He is a principal source for Khārijite and Shiite revolts, but not, unfortunately, for the "history of the Arab kingdom," where the Medina tradition is better and richer than that of Kūfa (xi). Nevertheless, the bearers of the Medina tradition, such as Ibn Isḥāq, Abū Ma'šar, and al-Wāqidī, are more recent than Abū Mikhnaf. With these writers (especially with Ibn Isḥāq) the "annalistic form of history" begins to make its appearance. From this point on, those who are writing history are no longer merely collectors but historians who attempt to place their material in an established chronological frame and to offer "a consecutive historical account." Medina was the intellectual center of the Arab kingdom until Bagdad took its place under the Abbasids (xii). The Syrian tradition is lost; traces may be found in Balādhurī and perhaps in the Kalbi author 'Awāna (who is frequently cited by Ṭabarī for Syria). The spirit of the Syrian tradition is most likely to be found in the Christian chronicles, above all in the *Continuatio* of Isidor of Hispalis (xii). Here the Umayyads appear in a much more favorable light than in the Arab authors, where "their enemies have the last word, doing real damage to their history" (xiii). Al-Madā'inī (died 840 CE) occupies a middle position between Abū Mikhnaf and the historians of Medina. As a learned historian, he is a specialist on Basra and Khurāsān. He is cited by Ṭabarī with reference to these localities. His work is already written from the Abbasid standpoint and provides a corresponding description of the fall of the Umayyads.

It was Wellhausen's intention originally to publish this work as well under the title "Prolegomena to the Earliest History of Islam" and with a similar form of presentation. But the fact that Saif b. 'Umar's account leaves off at the Battle of the Camel means that the thread which might have given continuity to a source-critical analysis slips away—namely the proof of the tendentiousness of Saif b. 'Umar's revision of the events, in contrast to the other tradents cited by Ṭabarī. Thus Wellhausen was obliged, as he himself writes, "to judge on the basis of the evidence from case to case, to plunge into the *merita causae*, and to adopt a rather eclectic, or even harmonizing, approach" (xiii). In this manner the investigation becomes "more intricate, less daring." Where the state of the sources is such that an analysis based on these distinctions is not possible, "positive description" takes its place. It is this which strongly predominates in the present book. He is obliged to accept the "mixture of styles" which results. Thus many of the relevant questions are posed by his predecessors (such as A. von Kremer, A. Müller, F. Wüstenfeld, G. Weil, Dozy, among others) rather than by the sources themselves, and he must find different answers from those which have already been given (xiii). From his previous works we are already familiar with this method of analysis and criticism of the sources followed by a positive synthesis. It remains Wellhausen's own way of writing history.

It is not possible here to pursue the content of the book further. But several matters should be mentioned. Once again Wellhausen begins with the religio-political groundwork of Islam, as it took shape in Mecca and then, above all, in Medina in the form of the *Ummat Allāh*, or the protective community of Allah (4–15). This was also the starting-point for the conflict between the theocratic model of the state and that of the pagan "monarchy," or *Mulk*, as it was established in practice by the Umayyad dynasty, in opposition to the theocratic concept of the state held by the more pious Muslims (38ff., 45f., 192ff.). From the very beginning Wellhausen was preoccupied with the social problems which came along with the conquests and which confronted Islam with the question of whether it was merely an Arabic or truly a universal religion (18ff., 45f.). "Common notions of Orientalism are thoroughly in need of correction and must be left out of consideration as long as the Arabs were the dominant folk. Politics, and not the products of culture, occupy the foreground throughout and absorb the interest of the people. Politics is not regarded as fate in the form of absolute despotism but as the sacred concern of all Muslims, in which they take part with body and soul, though without any real appreciation of the nature and limitations of the human community. It is dominated by general tendencies of a religious, national and social nature" (46). These lines are written with reference to the variety of political phenomena which make their appearance in this period and which often have a bewildering effect upon the observer. It was not his intention to present an exhaustive history of early Islam, as he expressly emphasizes; rather he was concerned with "the conflict between the government which represented Arab domination and the opposing forces which brought about its final defeat by means of a permanent revolution which had been underway since the end of the Caliphate of Medina" (47). Thus the actual account begins with the "first civil war" under 'Alī (47–71), resorting to material published earlier, and continues with a description of the "second civil war" under the Sufyānids (71–125). Then he deals with the earlier and later Marwānids, in which "Umar II and the Mawālī" (166–94) and "Marwān II and the Third Civil War" (231–47) receive their own chapter. To be emphasized in this connection is the accurate treatment of administrative and financial reform under Umar II, which shows this ruler in a better light than in the earlier histories (especially 190ff.).

Two detailed chapters on "The Arab Tribes in Khurâsan" (247–306) and "The Fall of the Arab Kingdom" (306–52), for which the previous sections had paved the way, make up the conclusion of the work. In these final sections Wellhausen described repeatedly, by means of striking formulations, the ideological conflict by which the Arab kingdom went to ruin. "Conservative Islam placed Jamā'a (catholicity) above everything and preached solidarity with and obedience to the government. Revolutionary Islam set up the idea of a theocracy in opposition to the existing governmental organization and called Muslims to a struggle for God and against the Umayyads and their officials—a struggle for right and righteousness, and against injustice and force" (310). This opposition is given a new character by the Abbasids and constitutes the background for the end of Arab rule, a situation which gives Wellhausen occasion for a number of pointed observations (347ff.). Wellhausen understands this change of government as a total change, both within and without: Syrians and Arabs disappear from the government; the Mawālī are emancipated and acquire the upper hand; Arabia completely loses its importance, and with it the Arab tribes. The Arab way of life was transformed into an international culture in which all Muslims took part (348). "The state dwindled to the court" (349). "A hierarchy of court officials took the place of the aristocracy . . ." (350). The people were indiscriminately transformed into a mass of subjects as over against the caliphs (in Bagdad), whose practices were shaped by those of the old absolutistic government of Iran (350). The break is clearest in relation to religion (350f.). Islam now served the ruling class in much greater measure than before. Thus the wind was taken out of the sails of the pious opposition. "Theocracy was realized, and it was no longer possible for it to be the principle of revolution against the ruling power" (351). The extremists, such as the Shiites, were shoved aside and again driven underground. The majority went over to a catholicity, Jamā'a, which served to preserve the state in that it was practiced more strongly than before against insubordinate subjects. "As heirs of the Prophet, they made more use of it than ever, now that they not only had to head the secular government but also the religious order, the Imamate" (351f.). They were no longer based upon a given nationality (the Arab) but "on their guards and on their religion. Their caliphate may be characterized as a kind of Caesaropapism" (352). Thus Wellhausen gave expression once more to his dislike for the Abbasid dynasty and his liking for the Umayyads. His verdict as a historian is certainly not free in this instance from exaggeration and personal preferences, but he no doubt hit upon the heart of the matter here as well.

As it happened, the book was hardly reviewed, as Wellhausen acknowledged in disappointment to C. H. Becker (475), but it had a great effect. It is without reservation his most important work of Arabic scholarship. Becker himself calls it "a Bible of sorts for the historian of Islam" (475), and J. Fück speaks of the "deep and lasting impression" which it made upon the younger generation (225)/40/. As R. Hartmann says in the introduction to the new edition of 1960 (vii), it is "a work of art, of one piece, fashioned by a rare historical, prophetic gift. There is not a single reader who will be able to escape the impression of the superiority of the author's judgments. . . . The work belongs to those few classical books which do not go out of date in the usual sense, in which any alteration would be tasteless; indeed in the final analysis it would mean a reduction of the work's value and overall effect." By reading this work, which is as always with Wellhausen a pleasure from the point of view of literary style, one is given an unforgettable insight into the nature of the historical process. It is able "to school" our eyes "for the knowledge of historical reality" (Hartmann, in Wellhausen, 1902a:vii). Many of his formulations are so pregnant that one is continually reminded of them/41/.

Since the appearance of the book, scholarship has made progress in a number of areas, whether by means of new methods or new material, especially of an archaeological, numismatic, and documentary nature. Wellhausen himself found occasion to comment on a number of these later works. Thus he welcomed the publication of Arabic papyrus documents from Egypt by C. H. Becker, since his *Arab Kingdom* was thus enriched by additional material. He wrote: "I have reason to be glad that my *Arab Kingdom* has not remained merely 'a blow struck in the water'" (1907a). Furthermore, the discovery of the Umayyad "desert palaces" with their fascinating mosaics and murals, such as the Quṣair 'Amra investigated by A. Musil, reinforced him in his judgment on the character of this dynasty: it took over the pre-Islamic art of Syria and did not seek to eradicate it (1907b:724)/42/. He dealt with L. Caetani's thesis of the drying up of Arabia as the cause of Arab expansion (1912, with the following quotations from p. 256). He raises the following objections to it: (1) historical consequences are drawn from geological possibilities; (2) too much credit is given to the influence of the ingenious Assyrians and Sabaeans; (3) a one-sided emphasis on "natural history and matters of survival eclipses everything else"; (4) his approach is pessimistic. Beyond this Wellhausen extols the fact that an aristocrat such as Caetani should devote time to such scholarly work: "in this respect he has no equal among German aristocrats." Finally, he expresses his opinion (1913b) on H. Lammens, one of the greatest French authorities of his day on the early Islamic period. His *Tendenz* critique, however, is carried too far and leads to absurdity. Moreover, he is not wholly impartial as a historian of Islam; rather, he is "a hostile opponent." This poisons his investigation.

Since Wellhausen's historical studies had their origin above all in his critical reading of aṭ-Ṭabarī and since he ascribes (following F. Wüstenfeld) great importance to Abū Mikhnaf (689–775), it is appropriate to refer to a recent study by U. Sezgin which deals with this early Islamic historian in the greatest detail/43/. She pursues questions which go beyond those raised by Wellhausen and attempts to recover the material which lay at Abū Mikhnaf's disposal and to characterize it properly. She not only employs a new, positive way of considering the isnād (the chain of tradents) in historiography, which had been inaugurated by F. Sezgin, but also takes into consideration the new insights into the literary culture of the early Islamic period (eighth century) which had been won by N. Abbott's work on the Arabic papyri. As a result of this thorough investigation, Wellhausen's verdict on the value of Abū Mikhnaf must be qualified in the following respect: he was neither the first Arab historian nor the best Arabic prose stylist, but his enormous body of writing (39 monographs are attested for him) draws upon a long scholarly tradition which is everywhere apparent in the excerpts that have been preserved (even with respect to style). Thus we have to do with a smaller number of proper historians and a larger number of diverse collectors of historical reports (U. Sezgin: chapter 2, especially pp. 84ff. and 89ff.). Nevertheless, this does not call in question his trustworthiness and objectivity in a relative sense; here U. Sezgin (65, 93f., 126ff., on the Kitāb Ṣiffīn) explicitly confirms Wellhausen's judgment/44/. Through the reconstruction of several of the writings of Abū Mikhnaf and his predecessors and later editors, the picture of the sources becomes more colorful and loses somewhat in simplicity and historical clarity in comparison with the account found in Wellhausen. But Wellhausen's reconstruction is not fundamentally shaken, only deepened and refined.

Apart from the last mentioned reviews of works on Arabic history and a few brief remarks on passages in the Koran/45/, Wellhausen had nothing more to say on Arabic questions in his last years (which were marked by severe suffering). He concentrated his energies on the New Testament (the Gospels, Acts, and the Apocalypse), where his work nevertheless met with little response since his views ran directly counter to New Testament scholarship of the period (cf. the discussions by Schwartz: 64–69; and the above chapter by N. A. Dahl). For Oriental studies he was and remains the great master of historical source criticism, from whom much can still be learned today. His basic principle will always retain its validity: "To recognize problems, to be able to raise real and important questions—that is the beginning of all things which turn out well; the solutions come almost by themselves, through collaboration with others" (in Becker: 475). As an Orientalist, he was bound by the material to the Orient, but for the way in which he addressed historical problems he was indebted to the Occident. Or as H. H. Schaeder has said: "One who wishes to be a historian of the Orient must be a philologian—in itself no mean achievement—and at the same time must have been through the school of the historians of the West" (411). In respect to both requirements Wellhausen is a model.

APPENDIX

Autograph Works of Wellhausen
in the Library of the University of Leipzig/46/

Most of the documents are cards which relate to invitations for Wellhausen to write critical reviews (for the *Deutsche Literaturzeitung*, addressed to Zarncke) or other correspondence. Their substance is of little value; they merely serve to indicate the connections which Wellhausen had with other scholars.

> To Zarncke—from Greifswald on 25 November 1878 (a card); 26 November 1878 (a card, canceling a review on account of "a death which concerned [Wellhausen] very closely"); 3 December 1878 (a letter, agreeing to a review).
> —from Halle on 18 June 1884 (a card, declining to review L. Krehl's *Leben und Lehre Mohammeds*); 14 October 1884 (a card, concerning a review which Kautzsch had requested of him).
> —from Marburg on 8 October 1889 (a card, declining a review with the remark: "it is hard for me to read books from which one can learn nothing"; he fears following Ewald in that respect).
> To Zimmern—from Marburg on 5 November 1890 (a card, with thanks for having sent him an article).
> —from Göttingen on 20 May 1914 (a letter, with brief thanks for "undeserved kindness"; probably with regard to his seventieth birthday and the *Festschrift* for Wellhausen on this occasion).
> To Schwally—from Göttingen on 17 August 1897 (a card); 27 May 1898 (a card, with remarks on two etymological questions).

NOTES

Translated by Laurence L Welborn.

/1/ On this work see below, pp. 121-23. Wellhausen's biographers, E. Schwartz and C. H. Becker, bear witness to the dissatisfaction he felt at working only on the Old Testament.

/2/ See C. H. Becker. 474-80, H H Schaeder: especially 416-20; J. Fück. 223-26; E. Littmann. Cf. also O. Eissfeldt; and E. Schwartz

/3/ Wellhausen, 1902c. Alongside of classical (written) Arabic there were dialects, the local "speech of everyday life"; the latter is the mother of living dialects, "although the modern dialects of the provinces do not stand in direct relation to the old tribal dialects" (270). Wellhausen welcomed works on modern Arabic dialects (270f.).

/4/ Letter of 8 February 1892 to Prussian Minister of Education Althoff regarding Wellhausen's anticipated call to Gottingen. Published in Jepsen: 265f.

/5/ Wellhausen, 1884a.107–75; 1886a (a translation of the second Hudhail hymn in comparison with the unsatisfactory edition of this collection by R Abicht of 1879), 1889:87–194; 1896b· 175f. (a sample translation from the Diwan of Abū Firās in contrast to the unsatisfactory edition of R Dvořak). On al-Wāqidī see below, pp. 121ff The same judgment naturally applies also to his Old Testament and New Testament translations, cf Eissfeldt· 411f., and Schwartz· 68.

/6/ See Wellhausen, 1904a 40f. (on Ruth 3·9, Ezekiel 16.8); 1905.93ff. (see below, pp. 131f); 1900a 13f. (see below, pp. 130f), 1893 431ff passim (see below, p 130)

/7/ Especially in 1887 and 1897b; and see below, pp 125ff

/8/ This essay of 1876 is missing from the bibliography of Wellhausen's works assembled by A Rahlfs in the Wellhausen-FS. edited by K Marti

/9/ Wellhausen rejected attempts (such as that by J Curtiss; cf Wellhausen, 1904c) to explain contemporary Oriental folk-religion as "ursemitisch " On the other hand, he held C. M. Doughty's report of his travels to be of great significance for old Arab custom (1891b; and see below, p. 124)

/10/ Thus H. Cremer in the above-mentioned letter of 8 February 1892 (see n. 4)

/11/ Once more we cite from Cremer's letter of 1892 (see n. 4)· "In his judgment of others he frequently behaves with a sovereign disregard which causes him to forget the solid work of others because of their failed results. But this is seldom with malicious intent. It is more the joy of discovering a striking expression than the desire to inflict injury." Schwartz (70) reaches the same conclusion.

/12/ Cf also Wellhausen's comments (1899c.252, in a review of D. S. Margoliouth's *The Letters of Abū'l-Alā of Ma'arra*, 1898) on the exaggerated use of the words "free thinking" in the Umayyad period

/13/ Cf Wellhausen, 1881 (on F. Wustenfeld, *Geschichte der Fatimiden-Chalifen*, 1881), with already here a clear pronouncement on the fall of the Umayyad kingdom (see below, pp. 141ff); 1882b (on an edition of *Abdo-'l-Wáhid al-Marrékoshí, The History of the Almohades*, by R. Dozy, 2d ed , 1881), with pertinent observations on the value of the sources of the work; 1883c (on L M Devic, *Le pays des Zendjs*, 1883); 1884c (on F. Wustenfeld, *Die Ṣufiten in Sudarabien*, 1883), 1886b (on H. Derenbourg, *Ousāma ibn Mounkidh*, II, 1886); 1891c (on an edition of the Egyptian chronicle of al-Jabartī by C. Mansour Bey, 1889); 1911 (on an edition of the Annals of Ibn Taghrībirdī by W Popper, 1909–10), where Wellhausen sees the value of both Taghrībirdī's authorities and of Taghrībirdī himself.

/14/ A letter of 5 April 1882 to the Prussian Minister of Education regarding his request to be transferred to the philosophy faculty, published in Jepsen· 264.

/15/ Jepsen. 256 U. von Wilamowitz-Moellendorff reports (186–89) on his acquaintance and friendship with Wellhausen in Greifswald and mentions that he heard a course of lectures by him on Muhammad (188, n 1) Cf also Schwartz: 60.

/16/ In Jepsen: 256; on Wellhausen's withdrawal from the theological faculty, cf. Jepsen: 261ff.; and the chapter by R. Smend above, p. 6.

/17/ On the philological-historical method, see the discussion in Rudolph, 1981a, with contemporary citations taken from A. Dieterich and H. Usener. Schwartz (55) wrote in connection with Wellhausen. "Scholarship never profits when historians do not wish to be philologians; but by the same token, it is fatal for historical knowledge when they remain caught in literary problems."

/18/ Cf. above, p. 115, in relation to Goldziher; further Wellhausen, 1903, where A. de Vlieger is reproached for writing "like an Oriental" without historical reflection; also 1904b: 940f., where the "historical abstinence" of Brünnow and Domaszewski in their documentation of *Die Provinz Arabia*, vol. 1, is harshly reproved. On F. Wustenfeld and J. Perier, see comments in the text.

/19/ This was rightly emphasized by Becker (478f.). Eissfeldt's criticism (423f.) is unjustified in relation to Wellhausen's presentation of Arab-Islamic history. That he actually believed in "primitive religious forces" as the movers of history is more than improbable, and to my knowledge cannot be demonstrated. Cf. below, pp. 118f.

/20/ For Wellhausen ancient Arab religion is "the quintessence of the collective intellectual life" connected with the common possession of language, poetry, forms of commerce, of law, of habits and customs, of ideas of what is holy, what is allowed and what is forbidden (1893:438). This corresponds to statements which Wellhausen makes elsewhere in relation to the Khārijites. "As is well known, religion and theology are not identical, religious conviction expresses itself in politics and law much earlier than in dogmatics" (1884b:839).

/21/ In his discussion of old Arabic poetry (1896a) Wellhausen also speaks of the "invisible superstructure which humans create through their mutual society" (602, cf. also 604). These are sociological insights which Wellhausen won from his research into the life of the ancient Arabs.

/22/ He defended himself against unwarranted criticism by E. Meyer with regard to his "exclusivity" (cf. Shaeder: 417). One is reminded here, moreover, of his interest in the cuneiform literature (see above, p. 114).

/23/ Wellhausen, 1882a:27f.: "It is easier to determine the proper pronunciation of unfamiliar names in Leiden than in Greifswald... In want of real linguistic resources I have occasionally had recourse to etymology...."

/24/ An edition in keeping with current scholarly standards was published by J. Hell in 1933.

/25/ Wellhausen, 1886a, with a devastating critique of Abicht (see above, n. 5); 1891a; 1891e; 1896b, with the comment on Dvořak: "The author must still wait a while before he ventures further on the translation of Arabic poets"; 1902b; 1906a.

/26/ Wellhausen rejects the treatment of old Arabic poetry as religious or magical in nature (1897c.250f , contra Goldziher). He sees in this view too much that is doubtful, too many indirect lines, too one-sided a point of view.

/27/ Cf. Nöldeke's review of the book in 1887. Noldeke also placed his own annotated copy of the first edition at Wellhausen's disposal for preparation of the revision (see Wellhausen, 1897b.243). The title given to the second edition was *Reste arabischen Heidentums gesammelt und erlautert*. In this second edition Wellhausen followed a more antiquated orthography than in the first edition. An unrevised reprint of the second edition appeared in 1961.

Rudolph: Wellhausen as an Arabist   149

/28/   This is the second edition; the first is unknown to me.

/29/   Further works of importance on this subject have been provided by M. S. Marmadji and H. S. Nyberg W. Atallah has also published an edition and translation which was not available to me.

/30/   Compare 1897b.106 with 1887·102 where nature-mythology and animism are clearly separated

/31/   Cf. especially the state of affairs as represented by M Hofner (especially 354ff) Among older works that of C. Brockelmann is still of importance, on his discussion with Wellhausen, cf especially 103ff

/32/   In this same volume T. Noldeke also dealt with the affairs of the ancient Arabs (Mommsen. 87–89), and I. Goldziher provided an overview of the Islamic situation (Mommsen: 101–12).

/33/   Goldziher placed a higher value on the religious aspect (Mommsen 101f.), see also Goldziher, 1899·29–38. Noldeke's position is closer to that of Wellhausen (Mommsen. 89)

/34/   The chapters of Ibn Sa'd edited by Wellhausen are to be found in E. Sachau's edition of the Kitāb al-Ṭabaqāt (Sachau. 15–86, Arabic text).

/35/   This in response to the not wholly accurate remark of Schaeder (419) Cf also Wellhausen's description of Muhammad in the introduction to his *Das arabische Reich und sein Sturz* (1902a·1ff) On this subject Schwartz (61) writes. "It is characteristic of his manner of thinking and research that he did not trouble himself about Muhammad's personal revelations or waste his time on guesses about the prophet and the Koran, as if there were some secret which could be discovered, given enough patience and intelligence He was content to uncover the foundation from which Islam arose and to grasp as clearly as possible the opposition between the naive, conventional cult, i e., paganism, and that which was specifically religious, precisely the very opposition which had such a different outcome in the development of Israelite religion "

/36/   Wellhausen, 1884b Here Wellhausen already rejects the purely political view and emphasizes the religious roots of the sect

/37/   On the state of the sources in Naubakhti and his younger contemporary Sa'd b.Abdallāh al-Qummī, whose *Kitāb al-maqālāt wa'l-firaq* was first edited by M J. Maškūr (Mashkour) in Teheran in 1963, cf W Madelung

/38/   Cf most recently H Halm, and my review, 1981b On the state of research on the Shi'a, see the summary in W M Watt, 1973·38–62, 271–78; on the Khārijites, see Watt, 1973 9–37, and 1961·215–31.

/39/   In the following I am making use of the second, unchanged edition, Berlin, 1960, with an introduction by Richard Hartmann (v–vii), followed by Wellhausen's preface (ix–xiii). Translations have been published in English 1927 (second edition, 1973), Arabic 1956, and Turkish 1963.

/40/   On the other hand, Schwartz (62) speaks of what little influence the book had in its day There is still no investigation of its concrete effect The translations belong to the history of its influence, although they commence at a rather late date.

/41/ Becker (480) accurately characterizes Wellhausen's style as "splendid" ("grossartig") and "lapidary," with both the artist and the scientist united in him. Already during the Greifswald period, H. Cremer (in a letter dated 8 February 1892, cited in Jepsen. 265) writes. "He handles the language with an ease which, unfortunately, often causes him to be mistaken for an author of light literature " Cf. also Schwartz (70) who emphasizes the picturesque quality, simplicity, and "Schnack" (a humorous, low-German way of speaking) of his expressions.

/42/ Here Wellhausen expresses his warmest thanks to Musil. See above, p. 124.

/43/ Sezgın's first chapter (7–38) contains a critique of previous scholarship since Wüstenfeld.

/44/ That a certain break in the tradition begins indeed with Abū Mikhnaf is shown, among other things, in that with him the ısnād functions in a real sense as a chain of tradition, and not merely as a reference to sources (see Sezgin: 77ff). Whether the historiographical isnād really came into existence apart from the influence of the juristic Hadīth (thus Sezgin: 78) is a problem that cannot be discussed further here.

/45/ On the Koran· Wellhausen, 1913a. We have elected above not to consıder more closely his study of *Der arabische Josippus* (1897a), which is preserved only in fragments (found in Paris and Gottingen) According to Wellhausen it adds nothing to our knowledge of the Hebrew text of the Books of the Maccabees or the history of the period (1897a.42, 47). The translator was a Jew, the copyist a Copt (42f.). The heart of the fragments consists of a history of the Hasmonaeans which was attributed to Josephus when it was added to the *Bellum Judaicum*. Through the confusion of Flavius Josephus with Josef ben Gorion he was made the author (47) Wellhausen edited only a few samples of the text (4f.) and otherwise provided only a table of contents

/46/ I thank my assistant, Herr H. Mürmel, for bringing these documents to my attention.

WORKS CONSULTED

Aḥmad Zaki Pacha
   1924   *Kitāb al-aṣnām l'ibn al-Kalbi (Le livre des idols)*. 2d ed. Cairo (1343 AH).

Atallah, W
   1969   *Ibn al-Kalbî, Idoles. Texte établi et traduit*. Paris· C Klincksieck

Becker, C H
   1932   *Vom Werden und Wesen der islamischen Welt. Islamstudien*, vol 2 Leipzig Quelle and Meyer. Pp. 474–80 originally in *Der Islam* 9 (1918)· 95–99

Brockelmann, C.
   1922   "Allah und die Götzen " *ARW* 21· 99–121.

Caussin de Perceval, Armand Pierre
   1847–48   *Essai sur l'histoire des Arabes avant l'Islamisme*. 3 vols. Paris: Didot. Reprinted, Graz: Akademische Druck- und Verlagsanstalt, 1967

Eissfeldt, Otto
  1969 "Julius Wellhausen" (1920). Pp. 409–29 in *Kleine Schriften zum Alten Testament*. Ed. K.-M. Beyse and H.-J. Zobel. Berlin. = Pp. 56–71 in *Kleine Schriften*, vol 1. Ed R Sellheim and F Maass Tubingen. J C. B Mohr (Paul Siebeck).

Fuck, J.
  1955 *Die arabischen Studien in Europa bis in den Anfang des 20. Jh.s.* Leipzig O. Harrassowitz

Goeje, M J de, cum aliis, ed.
  1879–98 *Annales quod scripsit Abu Djafar Mohammed ibn Djarir at-Tabari* Leiden E J Brill Reprinted, with 3 supplemental volumes, 1964–65

Goldziher, Ignaz
  1889–90 *Muhammedanische Studien*. Halle a S · M Niemeyer.
  1899 *Abhandlungen zur arabischen Philologie*, I Leiden· E. J. Brill

Gunkel, Hermann
  1895 *Schopfung und Chaos in Urzeit und Endzeit: Eine religionsgeschichtliche Untersuchung uber Gen 1 und Ap Joh 12*. Gottingen. Vandenhoeck & Ruprecht.

Halm, Heinz
  1978 *Kosmologie und Heilslehre der fruhen Ismāʿīliya* Abh. f d Kunde des Morgenlandes, 44/1. Wiesbaden: Steiner.

Hell, J
  1933 *Die Diwane der Hu$\underline{d}$ailiten*. Leipzig. O Harrassowitz.

Hofner, M.
  1970 "Die vorislamischen Religionen Arabiens." Pp. 234–388 in *Die Religionen Altsyriens, Altarabiens und der Mandaer*, by H. Gese, M. Hofner, and K. Rudolph. Die Religionen der Menschheit, 10/2 Stuttgart· W Kohlhammer

Jepsen, A
  1978 "Wellhausen in Greifswald" (1956) Pp. 254–70 in *Der Herr ist Gott*. Berlin Evangelische Verlagsanstalt.

Jones, Marsden, ed.
  1966 *Al-Wāqidī, The Kitāb al-Maghāzī*. 3 vols. London. Oxford University.

Klinke-Rosenberger, R.
  1941 *Das Götzenbuch. Kitāb al-Aṣnām des Ibn al-Kalbī* Sammlung Orientalischer Arbeiten, 8 Leipzig.

Kremer, Alfred von, ed.
  1856 *History of Muhammad's Campaigns, by Aboo ʿAbdollah Mohammad bin ʿOmar alWakidy*. Calcutta

Littmann, E.
  1956 "Erinnerungen an Wellhausen." *ZDMG* 106· 18–22 (Reproduction of the funeral address for Wellhausen in 1918· cf "Trauerfeier auf dem Friedhof zu Gottingen am 10 1.1918," privately published)

Madelung, W.
  1967 "Bemerkungen zur imamitischen Firaq-Literatur." *Der Islam* 43. 37–52.

Marmadjı, M S
1926 "Les dieux du paganisme Arabe d'après Ibn al-Kalbî." *RB* 35. 397–420.

Mommsen, Theodor, et al.
1905 *Zum altesten Strafrecht der Kulturvolkern: Fragen zur Rechtsvergleichung.* Leipzig. Duncker & Humblot

Noldeke, Theodor
1863 *Das Leben Muhammeds, nach den Quellen populàr dargestellt* Hannover. C. Rumpler.
1887 Review of J Wellhausen's *Reste arabischen Heidentums*, 1887. *ZDMG* 41· 701–26

Nyberg, H. S.
1939 "Bemerkungen zum Buch der Gotzenbilder." *Le Monde orientale* 346–66.

Paret, Rudı
1969 Review of al-Wāqidī's *The Kitāb al-Maghāzī*, ed Marsden Jones, 1966. *Der Islam* 45. 134–35.

Rahlfs, Alfred
1914 "Verzeichnis der Schriften Julius Wellhausens " Pp 351–68 in *Studien zur semitischen Philologie und Religionsgeschichte· Julius Wellhausen zum siebzigsten Geburtstag*, ed. K. Marti. BZAW 27 Giessen· A. Topelmann.

Ritter, Hellmut, ed.
1931 *Die Sekten der Schī'a von al-Ḥasan Ibn Mūsā an-Naubaḫtī* Bibliotheca Islamica, 4. Leipzig/Istanbul. French translation by M. J Mashkour (Maškūr)· "An-Nawbaḫti: Les sectes šī'ites." *RHR* 153 (1957)· 68–78, 176–214, 154 (1958)· 67–95, 146–72; 155 (1959)· 63–78. Russian translation by S. M. Prozorova. *an-Naubaḫtī, Šiitskıe sekty* Akad nauk SSSR Otd.istorii. Inst. vostok. Pamjatniki piśmennosti Vostoka, 43 Moscow 1973

Rudolph, Kurt
1981a "Basic Positions of Religionswissenschaft." *Religion* 11: 97–107.
1981b "Das Problem der 'islamischen Gnosis'." *BO* 38: 551–57.

Sachau, Eduard
1917 *Bıographıen Muhammeds, seiner Gefährten und der spateren Trager des Islams*, vol 1,2 Leiden· E. J. Brill.

Schaeder, H. H
1960 "Die Orientforschung und das abendländische Geschichtsbild" (1936). Pp 397–423 in *Der Mensch in Orient und Okzident*, ed G Schaeder. Munich. R. Piper.

Schwartz, Eduard
1918 "Julius Wellhausen " *NGWG Geschaftliche Mıtteilungen aus dem Jahr 1918* 43–72. = Pp. 326–61 in *Gesammelte Schriften*, vol. 1. 2d ed Berlin· de Gruyter, 1963.

Sezgin, Ursula
1971 *Abū Miḫnaf: Ein Beitrag zur Historıographie der umaiyadischen Zeıt* Leıden: E. J. Brill.

Smıth, W Robertson
1885 *Kinship and Marriage in Early Arabia*. Cambridge: Unıversity Press.

Watt, W. Montgomery
- 1961 "Khārijite Thought in the Umayyad Period." *Der Islam* 36 215–31
- 1973 *The Formative Period of Islamic Thought.* Edinburgh University Press

Wellhausen, Julius
- 1876 "Ueber den bisherigen Gang und gegenwartigen Stand der Keilentzifferung " *Rheinisches Museum für Philologie* 31. 153–75.
- 1877 Review of W W. Graf Baudissin's *Studien zur semitischen Religionsgeschichte*, vol. 1, 1876. *GGA* 1. 185–92.
- 1879 Review of W W Graf Baudissin's *Studien zur semitischen Religionsgeschichte*, vol 2, 1878. *GGA* 1: 106–11
- 1881 Review of F Wustenfeld's *Geschichte der Fatimiden-Chalifen*, 1881. *DLZ* 2. 1476–78.
- 1882a *Muhammed in Medina. Das ist Vakidi's Kitab alMaghazi in verkurzter deutscher Wiedergabe herausgegeben.* Berlin: Reimer Reprinted, Berlin· de Gruyter, 1970.
- 1882b Review of R Dozy's *History of the Almohades*, 2d ed., 1881 *DLZ* 3 1245–47
- 1883a "Mohammedanism Part I Mohammed and the First Four Caliphs " *EB* 16. 545–65
- 1883b *Prolegomena zur Geschichte Israels.* 2d ed. of *Geschichte Israels*, vol. 1 (1878). Berlin. Reimer
- 1883c Review of L M Devic's *Le pays des Zendjs*, 1883. *DLZ* 4· 1816f.
- 1884a *Skizzen und Vorarbeiten*, vol. 1· 1, *Abriss der Geschichte Israels und Juda's*, 2, *Lieder der Hudhailiten, arabisch und deutsch* Berlin· Reimer.
- 1884b Review of R. Brunnow's *Die Charidschiten unter den ersten Omayyaden*, 1884. *DLZ* 5: 838f
- 1884c Review of F. Wustenfeld's *Die Çufiten in Südarabien*, 1883. *DLZ* 5. 396
- 1885a "Zu den Hudailitenliedern " *ZDMG* 39· 104–6
- 1885b "Scholien zum Diwan Hudail No. 139–280 " *ZDMG* 39. 411–80
- 1886a Review of R. Abicht's *Die Lieder der Dichter vom Stamme Hudail aus dem Arabischen ubersetzt*, 1879. *DLZ* 7. 1372f
- 1886b Review of H. Derenbourg's *Ousāma ibn Mounkidh*, vol 2, 1886 *DLZ* 7· 1608–10
- 1887 *Skizzen und Vorarbeiten*, vol 3: *Reste arabischen Heidentumes.* Berlin: Reimer.
- 1889 *Skizzen und Vorarbeiten*, vol. 4: *1, Medina vor dem Islam* (pp 3–64); *2, Muhammeds Gemeindeordnung von Medina* (pp. 65–83); *3, Seine Schreiben, und die Gesandtschaften an ihn* (pp 87–194). Berlin. Reimer.
- 1891a Review of L. Abel's *Die sieben Muʻallaḳāt*, 1891. *DLZ* 12 1269f.
- 1891b Review of C. M. Doughty's *Travels in Arabia Deserta*, 2 vols , 1888. *ZDMG* 45· 172–80.
- 1891c Review of C. Mansour Bey's *Merveilles biographiques et historiques ou Chroniques du Cheikh Abd-el-Rahman el Djabarti trad* , 1889 *DLZ* 12 308f.
- 1891d Review of T. Noldeke and A Muller's *Delectus veterum carminum arabicorum, 1890. DLZ* 12· 53f 3
- 1891e Review of A Salhani's *Diwān al-Aḫtal*, fasc 1, 1891 *DLZ* 12· 1638f

1891f	Review of A Sprenger's *Mohammed und der Koran*, 1889. *Historische Zeitschrift* 66: 306f.
1892	Review of I. Goldziher's *Muhammedanische Studien*, 1889/90. *TLZ* 17. 201–4.
1893	"Die Ehe bei den Arabern." *NGWG* 11: 431–81.
1896a	"Die alte arabische Poesie." *Cosmopolis* 1· 592–604.
1896b	Review of R. Dvořak's *Abû Firâs, ein arabischer Dichter und Held*, 1895. *GGA* 151/1: 173–76.
1896c	Review of H. Reckendorf's *Die syntaktischen Verhaltnisse des Arabischen*, vol. 1, 1895 *GGA* 158/2: 773–78.
1897a	*Der arabische Josippus*. AGWG Phil.-hist. Kl. N.F. I, 4. Berlin: Weidmann. Reprinted, Nendeln: Kraus Reprint, 1970.
1897b	*Reste arabischen Heidentums gesammelt und erläutert*. 2d ed. Berlin: Reimer. Reprinted, Berlin: de Gruyter, 1961.
1897c	Review of I. Goldziher's *Abhandlungen zur Arabischen Philologie*, part 1, 1896 *GGA* 159/1: 250–52.
1898	Review of E. Sachau's *Muhammedanisches Recht nach Schafiitischer Lehre*, 1897. *GGA* 160/2. 899–902.
1899a	*Skizzen und Vorarbeiten*, vol. 6. 1, *Prolegomena zur ältesten Geschichte des Islams*. Berlin· Reimer. Reprint forthcoming, Berlin: de Gruyter. Turkish translation· İslâmın en eski tarihine giriş. İstanbul Univ. Edebiyat Fak. Yayinlari, 844. İstanbul 1960.
1899b	"Ferdinand Wüstenfeld." *NGWG* Geschaftliche Mitteilungen. 79f.
1899c	Review of D. S Margoliouth's *The Letters of Abū'l-Alā of Ma'arra*, 1898. *GGA* 161/1: 251–54.
1900a	"Ein Gemeinwesen ohne Obrigkeit " Rede zur Feier des Geburtstages Seiner Majestät des Kaisers und Konigs am 27. Januar 1900 im Namen der Georg-August-Universitat gehalten von J. Wellhausen. Gottingen.
1900b	Review of C. Gruneisen's *Der Ahnenkultus und die Urreligion Israels*, 1900. *DLZ* 21. 1301–3.
1900c	Review of O Procksch's *Uber die Blutrache bei den vorislamischen Arabern und Mohammeds Stellung zu ihr*, 1899. *TLZ* 25: 385
1901a	"Heinrich Ewald." Pp. 61–88 in *Festschrift zur Feier des 150jahrigen Bestehens der Kgl. Gesellschaft der Wissenschaften zu Göttingen*. Beitrage zur Gelehrtengeschichte Göttingens. Berlin· Weidmann. = 1965:120–38.
1901b	"Die Kämpfe der Araber mit den Romäern in der Zeit der Umaijiden " *NGWG* Philol.-hist. Kl.: 414–47
1901c	*Die religios-politischen Oppositionsparteien im alten Islam*. AGWG Phil.-hist Kl. N F. V,2. Berlin: Weidmann Reprinted, Nendeln: Kraus Reprint, 1970 English translation: *The Religio-Political Factions in Early Islam*. North-Holland Medieval Translations, 3 Amsterdam North-Holland Publishing Company, 1975. Arabic translation. *Aḥzab al-muʿāraḍa al-siyāsīya al-dīnīya ṣadr al-islām*. Cairo 1968.
1902a	*Das arabische Reich und sein Sturz*. Berlin: Reimer 2d, unchanged ed., with a preface by Richard Hartmann, Berlin 1960. English translation· *The Arab Kingdom and Its Fall*. Calcutta: University of Calcutta, 1927; 2d ed , 1973; Beirut 1963 Arabic translation· *Ad-daula al-'arabīya wa-suqūṭiha* Damascus 1376 AH / 1956 CE *Tarīḫ ad-daula al-'arabīya min ẓuhūr al-islām ilā nihāyat ad-daula al-umawīya*. Cairo 1963 Turkish translation: *Arap devleti ve sukutu*. Ankara 1963.

1902b	Review of J. Barth's *Diwan des 'Umeir b. Schujeim al-Qutāmi*, 1902. GGA 164/2: 595–601.
1902c	Review of G Dalman's *Palästinischer Diwan,* 1901. GGA 164/1: 270–73
1903	Review of A de Vlieger's *Kitāb al Qadr,* 1903. GGA 165/2· 687f.
1904a	"Zwei Rechtsriten bei den Hebraern " *ARW* 7. 33–41
1904b	Review of R Brunnow and A v. Domaszewski's *Die Provincia Arabia,* vol 1, 1904 GGA 166/2. 940–43
1904c	Review of J Curtiss' *Ursemitische Religion im Volksleben des heutigen Orients,* 1903. GGA 166/1 351f.
1905	"Arabisch-israelitisch" Pp 91–99 in *Zum ältesten Strafrecht der Kulturvolker: Fragen zur Rechtsvergleichung* Ed. T Mommsen Leipzig Duncker & Humblot
1906a	Review of A A. Bevan's *The Naḳāid of Jarīr and al-Farazdak,* vol 1, part 1, 1905. GGA 168/2: 574–79.
1906b	Review of J Périer's *Vie d'alHadjdjādj ibn Yousof, d'après les sources arabes,* 1904 GGA 168/1 254–56
1907a	Review of C H Becker's *Papyri Schott-Reinhardt I,* 1906 GGA 169/1. 168–70
1907b	Review of A. Musil's *Ḳuṣejr 'Amra,* 1907. GGA 169/2· 721–27
1911	Review of W. Popper's *Abu lMahāsin Ibn Taghri Birdi's Annals,* 1909, 1910 GGA 173/2. 469–71.
1912	Review of L. Caetani's *Studi di storia orientale,* vol. 1, 1911 GGA 174/1· 251–56.
1913a	"Zum Ḳoran " *ZDMG* 67· 630–34
1913b	Review of H Lammens' *Fātima et les filles de Mahomet,* 1912. GGA 175 311–15.
1965	*Grundrisse zum Alten Testament* Ed R. Smend. TBu 27 Munich. Chr Kaiser

Wilamowitz-Moellendorff, U von
    1928   *Erinnerungen 1848–1914.* Leipzig· K F. Koehler.

Wustenfeld, F., ed
    1866–73   *Jacut's Geographisches Worterbuch aus den Handschriften zu Berlin, St. Petersburg, Paris, London und Oxford.* Leipzig. F. A Brockhaus

scholars press

Sin and Judgment in the Prophets: A Stylistic and Theological Analysis
Patrick D. Miller

A study of the theme and characterization of judgment in the Prophetic literature with particular attention to the ways in which judgment is placed in correlation with sin. Primary attention is given to literary and stylistic matters as well as to the implications of this study for theology of judgment in the Old Testament.

Code: 06 00 27 Price: Cloth $19.50 (16.00)°; paper $16.00 (12.00)

A History of Biblical Studies in Canada: A Sense of Proportion
John S. Moir

This study traces the development of biblical studies as a university discipline against the historic background of Canadian church-state relations and the unique relationship of religion and higher education. It examines the roots of higher criticism in Canada, their international connections and the popular reaction against "modernism." The growth of the Canadian Society of Biblical Studies and the diversification and complexity of biblical studies in the years since World War II are outlined.

Code: 06 11 07 Price: Paper $17.95 (11.95)

Searching the Scriptures: A History of the Society of Biblical Literature, 1880–1980
Ernest W. Saunders

Traces the history of the Society of Biblical Literature by historical periods, situating it within the cultural setting of the time. It also details the major turning points in the discipline of biblical studies and in the Society. This volume will appeal to those interested in the phenomenon of religion in American culture and in the interrelationship of biblical studies with the social, cultural and historical realms.

Code: 06 11 08 Price: Cloth $15.00 (10.00)

°( ) denotes member price

Payment must accompany all orders. MasterCard and Visa accepted. California residents add 6% sales tax. Postage and Handling: $1.00 for first item and $.50 for each thereafter; $4.00 maximum. Outside U.S.: $2.00 surcharge.

**SCHOLARS PRESS CUSTOMER SERVICES
P.O. BOX 4869, HAMPDEN STATION
BALTIMORE, MD 21211**

www.ingramcontent.com/pod-product-compliance
Lightning Source LLC
Chambersburg PA
CBHW031315150426
43191CB00005B/236